BLUECOAT, LIVERPOOL
The UK's first arts centre

First published 2020 by
Liverpool University Press
4 Cambridge Street
Liverpool
L69 7ZU

British Library Cataloguing-in-Publication data
A British Library CIP record is available

ISBN 978-1-78962-163-1

Typeset by Carnegie Book Production, Lancaster
Printed and bound by Gomer Press, Llandysul, Wales

Bluecoat is funded by:

This book has been financially supported by
The Duchy of Lancaster Benevolent Fund

and individual donations.

Cover image: *POP-UP Duets (Fragments of Love)* by Janis Claxton Dance, performed by Valerio Di Giovanni and Albert Garcia at Bluecoat for LightNight 2018. Photo: Brian Roberts.

BLUECOAT, LIVERPOOL

The UK's first arts centre

edited by
Bryan Biggs & John Belchem

LIVERPOOL UNIVERSITY PRESS
and
BLUECOAT

C. Neville Bertram, *Bluecoat Courtyard,*
wood engraving, 1945
Image courtesy of Liverpool Hope University Carter Preston
Foundation; with thanks to Juniper Press.

Bertram trained under Bluecoat sculptor Herbert Tyson
Smith, becoming an accomplished stone carver and teacher,
and was a member of the Sandon Studios Society. Drawn
from Tyson Smith's studio, the composition shows the
overgrown Bluecoat yard (the present garden) and main
block damaged during the War.

Contents

Bluecoat has always represented the forward thinking of the people of Liverpool.
Yoko Ono

Bluecoat gave me, and I'm sure many other artists, a big break early in our careers –
long may the arts centre reign!
Jeremy Deller

It's fairly unusual, as an artist, to have an ongoing dialogue with an arts organisation.
This speaks volumes about the ethos of Bluecoat: of 'becoming family'. I first
encountered the team over thirty years ago during the exhibition *Black Skin/
Bluecoat*. Since then, we've continued to work together whenever possible on
exhibitions and symposia. Most recently, Bluecoat welcomed a group of residents
engaged in one of my art projects about the Royal Docks in East London, to draw
connections between Liverpool and its dockside developments, the legacies of
empire, and the importance of the arts.
Sonia Boyce

Bluecoat is a vital cultural oasis, a fertile environment for visiting and local artists,
audiences, and staff to engage with each other and with the liveliness which
emerges. When Siobhan Davies Dance (SDD) performed *material / rearranged / to
/ be* in 2017 we were delighted to meet the knowledgeable enthusiasm of everyone
working at Bluecoat. It meant we began our performances feeling fully grounded in
a welcoming environment. Audiences also felt relaxed, curious and able to engage
and question us, regardless of how experienced they were with what we were doing.
It takes long-term commitment, forward thinking and hard work to create the ease
of such generous surroundings. We at SDD have benefited from this generosity and it
remains an unforgettable experience.
Siobhan Davies Dance

At their best, arts centres should be like Bluecoat: a cultural, social, political, ethical
and educational hub around which the community revolves. Bluecoat is a place
where new thinking can happen, where new work can be experienced, and where, in
these shabby times, glittering risks can be taken. Let us all try to be like a Bluecoat.
Ian McMillan

Bluecoat is one of the institutions that makes the cultural life of Liverpool so unique.
A special creative atmosphere housed within a truly historical building. It was a
place I discovered as a student and have continued to adore.
David Olusoga

Daniel Defoe loved Liverpool. In 1724 he called it 'one of the wonders of Britain' and noted that 'no town in England, London excepted … can equal Liverpoole for the fineness of the streets, and the beauty of the buildings'. The Blue Coat school, completed in 1718, must have been one of the buildings that so impressed Defoe. Indeed, it is still one of the city's most rewarding – and enigmatic – works of architecture. Although created as a humble charity school and probably designed by local architect Thomas Steers with mason Edward Litherland, the school possesses metropolitan grandeur and supreme authority. It was conceived in the Baroque classical style then fashionable throughout Europe, embodying, in its forms and details, sophisticated and refined references to a number of seminal buildings, architects and ideas. Like all great buildings, the Bluecoat not only satisfies the eye but also, with its rich vocabulary of details and layers of meaning, feeds the imagination, assuring that the contemplation of this world-class building is always a fresh pleasure.

Dan Cruickshank

Foreword

It is fascinating to discover through this book how an empty school building in the heart of Liverpool's city centre was repurposed in 1927 to become an arts centre which very quickly came to be cherished as an intrinsic part of the community.

As charted in this book, there is much to celebrate throughout Bluecoat's development into the arts centre we know today. From the comments of the artists who have contributed here, to the creative tenants Bluecoat has helped nurture – such as FACT, Liverpool Arab Arts Festival and DaDaFest – we can see the huge difference Bluecoat has made and the extent of its impact.

At the Arts Council, we have been proud supporters of Bluecoat from the immediate post-war period, when we awarded funds to help mend its bomb-damaged fabric, right up to the present day, which sees our investment alongside that of the local authority enable the arts centre to deliver wide-ranging exhibition, performance and participation programmes and reach new audiences as well as improve their environmental sustainability.

The importance of arts, culture and creativity to the building's tercentenary celebrations in 2017 is outlined in the final chapter of this book. What however distinguishes Bluecoat from other similar arts venues is the rich history it is able to draw on as Liverpool's oldest city centre building, and which was interrogated in imaginative ways by artists, participants and communities during that year.

This book comes just as we launch the Arts Council's strategy for the next 10 years, where we set out a richer, wider, deeper role for creativity to play across the whole of the country over the next decade. At the heart of this vision is a belief that creative activities and cultural experiences improve lives, challenge perceptions, broaden horizons, form and transform communities, and enable us to flourish in previously unimagined ways.

Everyone should be able to explore their creative potential, both individually and collectively, and this should be valued alongside high-quality cultural experiences. The vibrant cultural offer we see today in Liverpool, and increasingly in its City Region, is testament to the faith shown over a long period in this power of the arts to transform, not just lives, but the whole way a place feels about itself, celebrates its uniqueness, and engages its citizens.

Arts centres can open minds and Bluecoat, in many respects, was a pioneer here. I, for one, am looking forward to the next chapter in this arts centre's rich and illustrious history.

Dr Darren Henley OBE   **Chief Executive, Arts Council England**

Acknowledgements

We would like to express our thanks to the many people who have contributed to making this book possible. It has been a long time in the making, and the stimulus for it was Bluecoat's tercentenary year, of which it was initially seen as an integral part. However, 2017 proved to be such a full celebration that the book had to be put on hold. It was through conversations with former Bluecoat chief executive Alastair Upton that the concept of the building as a symbol of the birth of 'modern Liverpool', built the same time the town began its growth as a major port, started to emerge as ideas for the anniversary took shape. And the current chief executive, Mary Cloake, has continued to give her full support to the project and this book, providing a sounding board as the chapters developed.

Bluecoat's chairs and boards of directors too have always recognised the significance of the arts centre's relationship to the city as part of their custodianship of the building, and its importance as a heritage asset for Merseyside. This century they have overseen dramatic changes, as Bluecoat underwent a major refurbishment, expansion and business remodelling, and Bryan Biggs would like to acknowledge the vision of its board, led in this period by Simon Ryder, Sue Harrison and current chair, Peter Mearns, and its many dedicated members. Some of their forebears, who faced equally challenging periods, are mentioned in this book, and special thanks must go to former chair Alan Swerdlow, who has contributed much information and wonderful anecdotes from his long association with Bluecoat, which began with membership of the Sandon Studios Society and a Bluecoat artist's travel bursary early in his career; and to Peter Urquhart, who had a similarly long and rich engagement with Bluecoat and who sadly passed away in 2018.

Several other individuals were generous with their time, being interviewed or sending valuable information, in particular Gerry Donaldson, Jean Grant, Wendy Harpe, Chris Kennedy (who took some of the gallery installation photos in this book), Samantha Rhodes, Robin Riley, Paul Roots and Phil Saunders. Some of these are former employees of the arts centre and, while other staff are mentioned in the book, it has been impossible to namecheck the many who have contributed to Bluecoat's richly varied work over the years, including present staff. Chris Kerr, Alison Edis and Paul Kelly were at the helm during periods of transition when the arts centre we know today was taking shape. Much research that fed into the book was made possible by the My Bluecoat project, funded by the Heritage Lottery Fund, and the groundwork here, particularly on the school's early years, was carried out by a small team, Gavin Davenport and Samantha Wilson, working with our partners, the current Liverpool Blue Coat school and Liverpool Record Office, and a team of volunteers.

We would like to thank those who have generously contributed funds to the book: the Duchy of Lancaster Benevolent Fund, Alan Swerdlow and Jeremy Greenwood, and Francis Ryan and Peter Woods; and Bluecoat's revenue funders Arts Council England and Liverpool City Council, whose support over many years has made possible much of the activity discussed in the following pages. It was appropriate therefore that the current chief executive of the Arts Council, Darren Henley, kindly agreed to write the foreword for this book, which is greatly appreciated. We are also grateful to the organisations and individuals who have given permission for images they own to be reproduced, and to Seán Street for his poem 'Morning Raga at the Bluecoat'. We owe a very special thanks to Robin Bloxsidge for his copy-editing and indexing, and to the team at Liverpool University Press, with whom Bluecoat first worked on a publication in 1956! To all the writers, we would like to give a special thanks for producing such insightful and engaging chapters, which we very much hope you will enjoy reading.

Bryan Biggs and John Belchem, 2020

Contributors

John Belchem is Emeritus Professor of History at the University of Liverpool. An aspiring honorary scouser, his publications on Liverpool include *Merseypride: Essays in Liverpool Exceptionalism* (2000, 2nd edn 2006); *Irish, Catholic and Scouse: The History of the Liverpool-Irish 1800–1939* (2007); and *Before the Windrush: Race Relations in 20th Century Liverpool* (2014). He edited the history to mark Liverpool's 800th anniversary in 2007, *Liverpool 800: Culture, Character and History*; and to commemorate the centenary of the remarkable events of 1911, *Liverpool: City of Radicals* (2011), co-edited with Bryan Biggs.

Bryan Biggs is Artistic Director of Bluecoat, where he was previously Gallery Director and overall Director, overseeing capital and other developments over many years and curating exhibitions and other visual art and performance work. He also writes about art and popular culture, and has edited and co-edited several books, including *Art in a City Revisited* (2009) with Julie Sheldon, *Liverpool: City of Radicals* (2011) with John Belchem, and *Malcolm Lowry: From the Mersey to the World* (2009) and *Malcolm Lowry: Remaking the Voyage* (2020), both with Helen Tookey. A fine art graduate of Liverpool Polytechnic, he continues to make art and does a drawing a day.

Anjalie Dalal-Clayton is an art historian specialising in the art and exhibition histories of British artists of African and Asian descent. Her research has encompassed developments in the curation of work by black artists (Liverpool John Moores University), the first national audit of work by black artists in UK public collections (Arts and Humanities Research Council-funded Black Artists and Modernism research project at University of the Arts London), the work of black alumni at University of the Arts London in relation to issues of institutional bias and amnesia, and Bluecoat's history of working with black artists.

Gavin Davenport is a writer, musician, project manager and artist, presently chair of Merseyside Civic Society. He has been a visiting teacher at the University of Liverpool, Sheffield Hallam University and Falmouth University. He holds a master's degree with distinction in Oral Culture and Literature from the University of Sheffield and has written on a number of heritage subjects including traditional music, architecture and vernacular culture. He was project manager for Bluecoat's heritage project, My Bluecoat.

Roger Hill is a writer, broadcaster, performer, educationalist and long-time resident of Liverpool. He has travelled widely, including two round-the-world journeys, and recently crossed Central Asia to create artworks, which were premièred at Edge Hill University. His work for the BBC involves producing the longest-running alternative music programme on UK radio. He has contributed work to the Bluecoat over four decades and is currently involved in running its Baby Book Club and participating in a project, *Where The Arts Belong*, based in some of the north-west's 'dementia villages'. He contributed a chapter to *Liverpool: City of Radicals*, edited by John Belchem and Bryan Biggs (2011).

Paul Jones is a Senior Lecturer in Sociology at the University of Liverpool. His research and teaching interests centre on urban change in general, often with a particular focus on architecture and the built environment. Much of this work to date has focused on the political distinction between public and private space in the city. In 2017 he was Bluecoat's sociologist-in-residence.

Julie Sheldon is Professor of Art History and Dean of the Doctoral Academy at Liverpool John Moores University. She has written and co-authored a number of monographs, including *Modern Art: A Critical Introduction* (2000 and 2004), *Making American Art* (2008), *The Letters of Lady Eastlake* (2009) and *Art for the Nation* (2011), alongside edited collections, including *Art in a City Revisited* (2009) with Bryan Biggs and *The Della Robbia Pottery, From Renaissance to Regent Street* (2015).

Panayiota Vassilopoulou is Senior Lecturer in Philosophy at the University of Liverpool. In addition to researching and publishing on aesthetics and neoplatonic philosophy, she has been particularly interested in developing models for interconnecting philosophical research with contemporary philosophical practice, particularly social and reflective practices in non-academic institutions (galleries, museums, the cultural industries and the health sector). She has led research projects supported by the Arts and Humanities Research Council, the European Union, the British Society of Aesthetics and the Wellcome Trust, and has held formal residencies at Bluecoat (2013–15), Bury Art Museum (2017) and the NHS (2018–19).

Introduction

Bryan Biggs and John Belchem

The idea of this book was prompted by the 300th anniversary in 2017 of Bluecoat's dedication as a charity school in 1717. That institution moved to the leafy suburbs of Wavertree in 1906, and a year later a group of forward-thinking artists, the Sandon Studios Society, occupied rooms in the building, eventually establishing the School Lane premises as the UK's first arts centre in 1927, run by a new organisation, Bluecoat Society of Arts. The building's present custodian, now simply called Bluecoat, whose lineage stretches back to the Society, is a limited company with charitable status whose primary function is to maintain Liverpool's oldest city centre building while keeping art at its core.

There are written accounts of the Blue Coat school and both the Bluecoat Society and the Sandon,[1] yet these do not go beyond the 1960s, and while several other publications include aspects of the period since then and much archival material is now accessible both at Liverpool Record Office and on the My Bluecoat website,[2] the tercentenary and the research that it opened up provided an opportune time to look afresh at this history. It was also timely given that, a decade on from its year as European Capital of Culture in 2008, Liverpool was reflecting on what had been achieved in rebranding itself through culture, the city council using it as a key driver for economic regeneration, as it sought to develop new strategies in an increasingly competitive environment for tourism and inward investment. Bluecoat's story of using art to repurpose a historic building and become a cultural beacon for Liverpool is considerably older, and indeed a study it commissioned, *Art in a City*, by John Willett, challenged the council over fifty years ago with an ambitious and visionary blueprint for harnessing art to improve the city's fortunes.[3] This new volume was also being shaped a decade on from the building's reopening in 2008 following a major capital development, designed by Biq Architecten from

Figure 1. New arts wing designed by Biq Architecten, prior to Bluecoat's reopening in 2008.
Photo: Stefan Müller.

Rotterdam, which represented a moment of reinvention for the arts centre. At a
time when history is being questioned from the perspective of an uncertain future,
a reflection on the trajectories that brought Bluecoat to where it is today, and what
sustained it, will hopefully provide a better understanding of its survival and growth

as well as lessons that will help it continue, in difficult times, as a pivotal building at the heart of Liverpool and with an impact beyond.

Notwithstanding Bluecoat's national reputation as a leading centre for the contemporary arts, its popularity as a social hub right in the centre of Liverpool, and the significance of its iconic architecture – both its historic Queen Anne features and its contemporary extension – the building remains somewhat in the shadow of more recent cultural arrivals such as Tate Liverpool. Understandably so, given the international profile of the Albert Dock venue; yet the arts centre's reputation as being the best-kept local secret is belied by the prominence of many of the artists it has hosted, the organisations such as FACT (Foundation for Art and Creative Technology) and LAAF (Liverpool Arab Arts Festival) it has incubated, and the innovation of its arts programmes for over a century. This book is therefore an attempt to present the most rounded picture of Bluecoat to date, bringing its story into the present and considering it in the wider context both of Liverpool's development and of the arts in the twentieth century. In doing so, we hope that the narratives that we and the six other contributing writers present over nine chapters will reveal a much richer history, identifying continuities across 300 years, as well as ruptures, not least the change from school to arts centre. Yet even here, connections across time can be discerned, such as children being housed and taught as part of the building's original function finding echoes in Bluecoat's work today with 'looked after' children. If we accept Michel de Certeau's view that historical time is not linear, 'that past and present can be wrapped and folded together',[4] it is evident that episodes under discussion from Bluecoat's story in the eighteenth century resonate with the present, and can be reframed and brought into dialogue with contemporary realities. Several examples are given where history has proved a valuable resource for developing and enriching the arts experienced in the building.

In formulating the book, the editors were aware (especially given the fact that one of us is an employee of Bluecoat) of the danger of subjectivity and partiality in making claims for the arts centre's heritage significance. As historian and geographer David Lowenthal has said, 'Heritage is not history: heritage is what people make of their history to make themselves feel good.'[5] Certainly our account of Bluecoat is not uncritical, and neither does it pretend to provide a comprehensive chronology of the building's three centuries. As reflected in its title, the emphasis is on the building's life as an arts centre, little over a third of its history, with just one chapter looking at the school. Of necessity we have been selective, either where records are patchy (the interwar years, for instance) or are too voluminous (such as the arts programmes from the 1980s onwards). The book's principal timeframe concentrates on the century from when the school was vacated up to Bluecoat's closure in 2005 for its major capital development, but some more recent activities, including residencies and key exhibitions, are included where they relate to earlier strands, while 2017, the tercentenary year, is the focus of the final chapter.

Three specific aspects of the Bluecoat story are addressed: its foundational years as a charity school; how the arts developed within the building; and its place within Liverpool culture. In Chapter 1, Gavin Davenport traces Bluecoat's eighteenth-century origins, when the rector of St Peter's church, together with master mariner Bryan Blundell, established the school, the latter dedicating the rest of his life and substantial funds to it, 'a tenth part of what it pleased God to bless him with'.[6] Davenport describes how Bluecoat, in 'a kind of serendipity' echoed throughout its history, developed close links with the burgeoning port and the fortunes of its maritime merchants, enabled in large part by Liverpool's Old Dock. This, the world's first commercial wet dock, was built, it transpires, by the same partnership, Thomas Steers and Edward Litherland, that shortly after created the charity school. Peter de Figueiredo, describing this period as the start of modern Liverpool, its 'first speculative boom', has said that

> Despite alterations, extensions and reconstructions, the Bluecoat is remarkable for retaining its early 18th century appearance. It is one of the best buildings in Liverpool to provide testimony to the city's cultural traditions during its growth as an international seaport, demonstrating investments in architectural expression, education, philanthropy and culture.[7]

Bluecoat's connections with Liverpool's religious life and its global trade, mercantile philanthropy and economic, political and social growth constitute a continuing thread in our story and are crucial to an understanding of Bluecoat's symbiotic relationship to the port and the affection with which it has always been regarded. Local people continued to support it as a school: by 1852, for instance, there were 1,733 subscribers donating £2,063, the second largest charitable giving recorded in Liverpool, only behind the Royal Infirmary, which had fewer subscribers.[8]

While this book barely touches on the nineteenth century, the echoes of the school, which relocated to the suburbs in 1906, still resonate. Its motto, *Non Sibi Sed Omnibus* ('Not for Oneself but for All'), seems appropriate for what the vacant building would become. The arrival in 1907 of the Sandon Studios Society, a breakaway group of students from the department of Applied Art at University College Liverpool's School of Architecture, is charted by John Belchem in Chapter 2. Their vision – together with that of Charles Reilly, who brought his architecture department from the university to take up residence at Bluecoat – was to create, under one roof, a place for creativity, with working studios and exhibiting spaces, and for art lovers. Additionally, by inviting in the public to experience a range of visual art, music, drama and other cultural activities, they ensured that Bluecoat had a profound impact on art in the city. The Sandon was also a social hub, whose dining room and parties attracted not just locals but visiting professionals from across the cultural spectrum, including Stravinsky, George Bernard Shaw and members of the Ballets Russes. The Sandon laid the foundations for Bluecoat Society of Arts, formed in 1927 following a successful campaign to buy the building and secure its future as the UK's first arts centre. Against all the odds, the enterprise succeeded in the face of continual financial struggles, compounded by wartime bomb damage to the building. In subsequent decades, as Liverpool descended into the shock city of post-colonial, post-industrial Britain, Bluecoat, undaunted in aspiration and mission, continued to survive and adjust. Belchem concludes by reflecting on Bluecoat in the context of Liverpool's cultural and regeneration environment in the new millennium, in which a refurbished arts centre sits as the oldest building in the UNESCO World Heritage Site, and how it shows 'the value of regeneration through conservation and creative activity … [and] … that redevelopment and conservation should not be polarised in debate'.

Part of the argument for saving Bluecoat when under threat in the 1920s was an appeal to its relative antiquity: 'In the heart of Liverpool, which is become a rather aggressively modern city, there has been preserved for us this well-favoured example of an architectural style that embodies the past almost in its most charming form.'[9] Bluecoat's future, however, would take it far beyond such nostalgic framing. As the first such centre for the arts anywhere in the country, it pioneered the idea of combining different art forms, together with working studios for artists, in a single venue. Predating the UK's post-war explosion in arts centres, Bluecoat's development was quite different, and in Chapter 3 Bryan Biggs explores this in relation to Liverpool and the wider arts environment as he considers the significance of both the building as a cultural hub and the artists who took up studios there, and some of the arts programmes, including seminal exhibitions by the Post-Impressionists, featuring work by Picasso and Cézanne, that helped define Bluecoat. He continues this analysis in Chapter 4, tracing the experimentation that followed post-war reconstruction, as the arts centre reflected the democratisation of culture driven by national government policy, and as the Arts Council gained greater funding and influence. Bluecoat also joined in Liverpool's new-found, if short-lived, optimism that flowed from the success of The Beatles and Merseyside's pop culture. In this period, when a new generation of arts centres was emerging, many funded by local authorities amid debates about widening access and the participation of local communities, Bluecoat modelled itself as a sort of 'village hall meets the avant-garde', where amateur and high art mixed and the multi-art-form and interdisciplinary developments involving dance, performance, live art and literature that would become increasingly prominent from the 1980s onwards took root. Like the Everyman Theatre and alternative music club Eric's in Mathew Street in the late 1970s, Bluecoat tapped into and gave voice to a distinctly Liverpool creative culture whose impact was felt beyond the city.

The distinctive strands that Bluecoat has developed in visual art and in music are explored in Chapters 5 and 6 respectively. Anjalie Dalal-Clayton and Julie Sheldon chart the encouragement of a 'dissident view' in the gallery's programming, as they select exhibitions from which to highlight particular trends, including the development of collaborative curating, looking far beyond an 'art world' nexus, and giving support for artists early in their career. They also point to Bluecoat's encouragement of a generation of diverse British artists exploring issues of race and identity who emerged in the 1980s and 1990s. Roger Hill, meanwhile, takes a longitudinal view of music in the building across a century, told through the stories of several musicians and programmers closely associated with the arts centre. In histories of music in Liverpool, particularly post-war, Bluecoat as a venue has tended to be somewhat overlooked, yet Hill describes the eclectic breadth of its programmes as 'experimental, a bridge between old and new, classical and fanciful and between art forms, playful individualism intersecting with social engagement, gatherings both private and public, haphazard and focused, timeless but contemporary, harmonious and discordant, eccentric and sometimes wilfully esoteric, inclusive and exclusive, retrospective and futuristic'.

Bluecoat has long provided a networking focus for Liverpool's artists, a 'pre-internet hub' in the days before digital communication.[10] For many others, Bluecoat is not just a centre for the arts, and we felt it important to give a sense of the other histories that have shaped the venue. Chapter 7 therefore takes a look at what we describe as a 'creative community' – the artists, organisations, retailers and other tenants that have rented spaces, a process that started in 1907, as well as external hirers of rooms, partners that the arts centre has worked with, festivals, workshops, parties and other activities – some of them perhaps unexpected – that are part of the narrative of the inclusive arts centre. Much of this is unseen and hitherto undocumented. In addition, the arts centre's long-established participation work is referenced in several chapters and, with an innovative approach particularly in the area of learning disability, Bluecoat's work here, notably its Blue Room project, is worthy of a further study as it grows and is enriched by recent developments, including four of the group's members establishing their own independent practices in visual art and dance.

Chapter 8 comprises the perspectives of two recent residents of the arts centre from the University of Liverpool, a philosopher, Panayiota Vassilopoulou, and a sociologist, Paul Jones. Their respective accounts describe how they brought academic disciplines into dialogue both with the venue and its arts programmes, and with the public, in very interactive and accessible ways through workshops, symposia and other events. In bringing the university 'down the hill', as Charles Reilly had done in 1909 by relocating his department of architecture to Bluecoat, academia was brought into direct contact with the cultural life of the city, a process that sought to demystify academic discourse through public and accessible contexts while bringing to the arts centre's thinking new lines of enquiry. The two residents found common points of interest with Bluecoat's own ambition to connect its arts activities in a more engaged way with audiences and the city, intersections that helped inform Vassilopoulou's and Jones's own research and teaching.

The final chapter reflects on Bluecoat's tercentenary year, 2017, and the threads that were woven through that programme, connecting the building's foundational narratives to the present, and seeking contemporary resonances through a series of commissions, performances, exhibitions, symposia and other events. The unfolding legacies of transatlantic slavery, in which Liverpool played a prominent role, overtaking Bristol by the mid-eighteenth century as Britain's busiest slave-trading port, is examined in relation to the charity school's origins and maintenance, and the ways in which the arts centre has worked with artists over the past thirty-five years to explore this and the wider impact of colonialism. While the old gallery space hosted many such projects, notably *Trophies of Empire*, when the new arts wing opened in 2008, Hew Locke was commissioned to create a large wall drawing (Fig. 2) – a deconstruction of the Liverpool coat of arms with its imperial references – that dominated the upstairs gallery, continuing this ongoing interrogation of histories with which Bluecoat's own is intertwined. The tercentenary was an even more pertinent anniversary in which to further explore these legacies – in a symposium with the International Slavery Museum, in an exhibition, *In the Peaceful Dome*, and in a performance, *Sweet Tooth* by Elaine Mitchener. This aspect of the 2017 programme has since stimulated more debate at Bluecoat, including a talk by the eminent historian and broadcaster David Olusoga the following year on the contemporary ramifications of the slave trade.

Liverpool is the backdrop to the Bluecoat story and also what feeds many of the creative energies that have flowed through the building – mercantile philanthropy, international perspectives and connections, architectural distinctiveness and ambition, support for the new, amateur enthusiasms, the importance of a dynamic social scene. There is a correlation – which this book seeks to identify – between Bluecoat's development and some of the shifts that have taken place in Liverpool, for instance in terms of the expansion of the arts over the last two to three decades and its use in urban regeneration, and the city's reinvention as a cultural destination.

Figure 2. Hew Locke, *Sin Eater*, 2008, wall drawing of beads and cord, commissioned for *Now Then*, the first exhibition in the gallery in the new arts wing.

For audiences to the arts centre, now larger and more diverse than ever, with some 650,000 visits recorded annually, an account of the role Bluecoat has played in this growth of the city's arts infrastructure is now more readily available. It is hoped that this book will contribute to and enhance this understanding. The venue also occupies a significant and resilient position in relation to the UK's contemporary arts landscape, and several chapters provide evidence of Bluecoat's national contribution, particularly in relation to the development of arts centres. There is a dearth of research into how these centres evolved in the twentieth century,[11] and hopefully this book will add to the discourse and make an argument for why the idea of the arts centre is today more pertinent than ever. The following chapters were completed before the devastating global impact of the 2020 pandemic. Bluecoat was one among many arts organisations compelled to temporarily close, its resilience severely put to the test. The situation reminds us of what we miss, and what we value most, in times of crisis – and to think about what role cultural venues like Bluecoat can play in people's lives as the future is re-envisaged.

Finally, as outlined in Chapter 7, the building has been referred to by several names over its long history. Our writers, and those quoted in their chapters, are not consistent in their use of either 'the Bluecoat' or 'Bluecoat', and are adamant about their choice; consequently, we have permitted both.

Notes

1   W. S. MacCunn, *Bluecoat Chambers: The Origins and Development of an Art Centre*, Liverpool: Liverpool University Press, 1956; R. F. Bisson, *The Sandon Studios Society and the Arts*, Liverpool: Parry Books, published on behalf of the Sandon Studios Society, 1965.

2   Relevant publications are listed in 'Further Reading' at the end of this book. Liverpool Record Office holds archival material on Blue Coat school, the Sandon and the arts centre. The Bluecoat archive website is mybluecoat.org.uk

3   John Willett, *Art in a City*, London: Methuen, 1967, republished Liverpool: Liverpool University Press, 2007, with an introduction by Bryan Biggs.

4   Frances Spalding, review of Lynda Nead, *The Tiger in the Smoke: Art and Culture in Post-War Britain*, New Haven, CT: Yale University Press, 2018, in *The Guardian*, 6 January 2018, p. 8.

5   Quoted in 'David Lowenthal gives first Annual Lecture of UCL Centre for Critical Heritage Studies', https://www.geog.ucl.ac.uk/news-events/news/news-archive/2017/october-2017/ heritage-is-not-history, accessed 8 July 2019.

6   Referenced in John R. Hughes, 'A sketch of the Origin and Early History of the Liverpool Blue Coat Hospital', lecture delivered 5 May 1859, *Transcriptions of the Historic Society of Lancashire and Cheshire*, XI (1858–59), 1859, p. 185.

7   Peter de Figueiredo, *Liverpool World Heritage City*, Liverpool: Bluecoat Press, 2014, p. 93.

8   *Transcriptions of the Historic Society of Lancashire and Cheshire*, 7 (1854–55), 1855, pp. 22–26. Blue Coat Hospital subscribers also made up three-fifths of giving to other charities.

9   'Old Blue Coat School. Liverpool's oldest building', *Daily Post*, 27 July 1926.

10   Alan Dunn, in Alan Dunn and Brigitte Jurak, *The Ballad of RAY + JULIE*, Liverpool: erbracce-press, 2019, p. 19.

11   See Robert Hutchison, *Three Arts Centres: A Study of South Hill Park, the Gardner Centre and Chapter*, London: Arts Council of Great Britain, 1977; and John Lane, *Arts Centres: Every Town Should Have One*, London: Paul Elek, 1978.

Chapter 1

The Bluecoat Building: Origins and Continuity

Gavin Davenport

Bluecoat has been described as 'not just a pretty façade'. And yet, architecturally, this Grade I listed building is on many levels just that: a static mask behind which the whole structure, purpose and life of the space, for which that façade serves as shorthand in the long collective memory of Liverpool, has changed, flexed and metamorphosed over time. That memory is itself multifaceted and myth-laced – for example, the popular belief that the institution was a boys-only school, an orphanage built entirely on slavery – all layerings of conjecture and frequent inaccuracy (the first claim is untrue, and in relation to the second, recent research has revealed the extent of funding from slavery, which is discussed below), placed on the shoulders of an indifferent building that has steadfastly got on with the job of being the space that Liverpool didn't quite know it needed for the past three centuries. Behind the enduring frontage, the extant building bears little relation to the historic structure or purpose of the early days, yet the meta-functions and social networks that the act of delineating the space created in the first place echo throughout the 300-year history. Indeed, the founding of the arts centre in the early twentieth century has resonances that can be discerned in the early genesis of the building itself when – in similar fashion – philanthropy, the drive of key individuals connected to a wider group of influential local people, and an expression of Liverpool independence together characterised the establishment of a new institution.

When a building is created, it not only establishes physical space, but suggests a kind of social dialogue between wider questions of internal and external, inclusion

and exclusion. In this, Bluecoat is no exception. The story of how it came to be, how it was built, how it evolved and changed from educational institution to a centre for the arts can be viewed through the lens of who knew who, and through what mechanism. Bluecoat's charity school beginnings – brainchild of the seafaring Bryan Blundell and the land-bound rector of Liverpool, Robert Styth – are set against the background of pressing social need, specifically in Liverpool, but also in the country as a whole: the decline in the efficacy of the Poor Law and the rise of pauperism in the late seventeenth century. Many of the key developments in what is characterised as 'modern Liverpool' arose from the swirling and unsettled social and political echoes of the English Civil War, the overturning of centuries-old social hierarchies, particularly the disenfranchisement of previously powerful Catholic landowners, and a national freedom for the middle classes to pursue wealth.

The origins of Bluecoat spring from this critical moment in English history, a collision of social and political currents which, beyond the many epithets with which the eighteenth century has been saddled (suggesting the dawn of industrialism or the kindling of modernity), generated a cultural drive towards public benevolence, particularly among the emergent middle classes. This has led some commentators to describe it as the 'age of philanthropy'. Viewed against the backdrop of the religious persecution and marginalisation of Catholics following the English Civil War, and the iniquities of the trade in enslaved Africans, this seems ironic or disingenuous when viewed through the filter of our contemporary cynicism. And yet the concerns of those capable of philanthropy were deeply held, diverse and far reaching – from domestic and foreign missionary activity to the inexorable pull towards the abolition of slavery that would take almost a century to bear fruit, and the plight of child labourers and the poor of several strata – albeit under the mantle of the kind of conformist Anglicanism with which Bluecoat itself is inscribed.

An Act of Parliament in 1699 created a new, separate parish of Liverpool, distinct from the older Walton-on-the-Hill, which had previously taken administrative primacy over the growing town. In doing so, the Act also called for the erection of the new church of St Peter's (said to be the first new parish church built in England since the Reformation) to cater for a growing population not adequately served by the older chapel of Our Lady and St Nicholas overlooking the river Mersey. The two churches in effect served as a single Liverpool parish church, with rectors serving each side of the 'Pool' – the tidal creek, following roughly the path of modern-day Paradise Street and Steers Way to the Mersey, from which the city takes, in part, its name. On the eastern side on the Town Commons, at St Peter's, the aforementioned Robert Styth found himself in place as rector and was instrumental in establishing the early school. St Peter's itself would become one of the defining institutions of the new town, bringing English Baroque architectural trends and many other metropolitan ideas with it over the ensuing century. It was here that Liverpool's first music festival, first oratorio, first lending library and key book sales of the eighteenth century took place. The church, designated as Liverpool's pro-cathedral in 1880, remained on Church Street until its demolition in 1922, by which time it was at the centre of a busy metropolis, unrecognisable from when the church was consecrated, when there were few other buildings on this side of the creek, the majority of the congregation having to cross via a bridge at what is now the Whitechapel/Lord Street intersection.

The first gleamings of industrialisation were drawing ever greater numbers of people to concentrated population centres in towns across England, including Liverpool, and they brought with them all the attendant issues, as poverty and disease sprang up alongside wealth and opportunity. Which side of the balance one might find oneself on was not viewed in this period as mere luck, but as a result of God's beneficence – be more holy and reap the benefits – and if one was already wealthy, it was because God had smiled on you, and you could therefore afford to invest a little in improving the lot of others, not only bodily by feeding and clothing them, but by intervention in their moral and spiritual development. It was thus that the boom in privately funded Christian charity schools, of which Bluecoat is Liverpool's finest example, came about. The School Lane building's purpose was enshrined in a Latin inscription still visible above its entrance – *CHRISTIANAE CHARITATI PROMOVENDAE INOPIQUE PUERITIAE ECCLESIAE ANGLICANAE PRINCIPIIS IMBUENDAE SACRUM. ANNO SALUTIS MDCCXVII*: 'Dedicated to the promotion of Christian charity and the training of poor children in the principles of the Anglican Church. Founded in the year of salvation 1717.'

Blue Coat Hospital was established as a day school in the boom of Liverpool's early modern growth, when the first two decades of the eighteenth century witnessed a doubling of the population from almost 6,000 in 1700 to over 10,000 by 1720.[1] The transformation of the former fishing town was in part due to an influx in the second half of the seventeenth century of people from London, following the city's devastation by plague and fire, when 'several ingenious men settled in Liverpool, which encouraged them to trade with Plantations and other places; which occasioned sundry other tradesmen to come and settle here'.[2] Blundell, recognised as the *de facto* founder of the school and principal funder, had himself been left fatherless at an early age, though he was not at the mercy of the privations that Blue Coat Hospital's later wards would suffer. Benefiting from substantial family wealth and connections, the young Blundell went to sea at around 13 years of age, and his own journal suggests that at this point he had a solid education in reading, writing and the geometric facility required for maritime navigation. In a few short years, he progressed through a combination of time served and personal wealth to become owner and master of a vessel. His journal recounts many of the voyages – to the West Indies, Virginia and Europe – via ports all around Britain, that not only enabled him to fund the Blue Coat but provided access to the social networks that would attract funders and board members to the fledgling institution.

In 1708 the school existed as an idea, if not in a physical form, and in order to realise their vision, Styth and Blundell had to invite collaboration. In a similar manner to the emerging joint stock companies of the period, subscribers were gathered who would commit the necessary annual finance required to build, staff and later feed and clothe pupils at the new school. The rolls of subscribers point

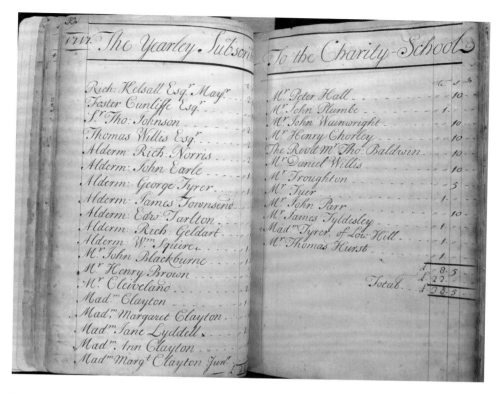

Figure 4. Blue Coat school accounts book 1709–55, showing subscriptions for 1717. Liverpool Record Office, 377.72 ACC.

to two existing and pre-eminent social networks in Liverpool: the Corporation of Liverpool and the Anglican Church. The Corporation linked in body politic the affluent mercantile middle classes to the established regional aristocracy, as represented by the house of Stanley, and the critical social hub of the Church. In central Liverpool, the Church had seen a significant upgrade in status – the creation of the new parish of Liverpool and the subsequent building of St Peter's – and records show the populace vying for possession of spaces on pews, going so far as to enter into legal proceedings when a family sought to pass a seat to a family member, rather than allowing it to return to public availability. The piety of the period, allied to broader concerns of morality and philosophical reflection, brought forth the subscriptions and donations on which Blue Coat and many other charitable institutions were founded. One might also suggest that the hegemony of Protestantism meant that the fortunate and affluent were required to put their money where their mouths were and engage in a more active form of philanthropy than had characterised previous decades. It should be noted here that there is a political element to the conformity that Bluecoat springs from: though Protestantism at this time extended beyond established and exclusive Anglicanism, there was a social exclusion of other Protestant denominations in Bluecoat's origin, as each congregation represented a distinct 'social network', later manifested in commercial and social works.

Between 1708 and 1709 the first school was built on land opposite St Peter's, thereby naming School House Lane, later School Lane. The conceptual model on which it was established was that of the Society for the Promotion of Christian Knowledge (SPCK), which emerged in the late 1600s as a publisher of religious texts whose profits supported missionary work in Virginia and other North American colonies. The provision of its books and pamphlets to Christian charity schools in the south of England led to the encouragement of similar institutions in the provinces, where there was comparable need, in turn delivering profits to the publisher (providing the backbone of these schools' curricula) which would result in its own 300-year survival. The school was one of around sixty Blue Coat institutions, charity schools so named from the colour of their uniforms, blue denoting charity. They adopted their uniforms – a blue frock coat, sometimes with yellow stockings – from Christ's Hospital, a foundling hospital for poor children established in London in 1552 by Edward VI, the school later moving to Horsham in Sussex. Several Blue Coat schools predate Liverpool's: Wells (1641), Basingstoke (1646), Warrington (1665), York (1705), Nottingham and Sheffield (both 1706) and Thatcham (1707), with Durham (1708), Bath (1711) and Coventry (1714) founded before the School Lane building was dedicated in 1717, the same year that Chester Blue Coat was established. In Ireland, there were schools in Dublin (1669), Cork (a 'Green Coat' school, 1700), Limerick (1717), Derry (1773) and Waterford (1740).

Funding of the Liverpool school was provided initially by Blundell himself, who built the smaller school of 1708 at a cost of around £35, and subsequently supported its running from his own pocket and with funds raised from subscribers and church collections. Though Blundell was already well connected in Liverpool business, the creation of these subscription rolls joins together the historic social networks of the Corporation and freemen of 'old' Liverpool with the aspirational businessmen to be found fighting for spaces on the pews of the new metropolitan church of St Peter's. Buying one's way into an emerging social circle might seem a characteristically eighteenth-century way of doing business, yet it clearly has its parallels in contemporary times. Access to established mercantile circles for those who had bought their way to freeman of Liverpool was facilitated by the pre-existence of church social circles and committees, all of which required an additional financial commitment, for which the subscribers' roll of the Blue Coat serves as an admirable template. Blundell himself would contribute £3,500 to the school during his life – 'a tenth part of what God had blessed him with'[3] – and his sons, Richard and Jonathan, would follow his example.

Like much of eighteenth-century Liverpool, the founding and maintenance of Blue Coat was enabled by funds derived from transatlantic slavery, which had started in 1699 when the first ship sailed from the port to Africa. In this 'triangular trade', British goods were transported to Africa in exchange for enslaved Africans, who were forcibly taken to the Americas and the Caribbean, before the ships returned to Liverpool laden with goods from the New World. Research by Sophie Jones has begun the process of analysing the extent of funding thus derived for the charity school. Interrogating the record of donations between 1714 and 1725 in the Blue Coat ledger accounts (Fig. 4) – the period of the building's planning, construction and opening – she identified four main sources of income: annual subscriptions, regular donations, one-off donations and earned income: rent from its properties and goods produced on site by the pupils, whose labours included cotton spinning, stocking weaving and pin making. Annual subscriptions provided the most stable stream, and Jones's research, focusing on 17 individuals and families who were the most consistent sponsors, concludes that 65 per cent of these subscriptions 'were funded either from proceeds of the slave trade, or from trades reliant on the use of slave labour'.[4] Although it is difficult to disaggregate the precise percentages of these two sources, it is clear that substantial funds contributed to the school were derived from the trade in sugar, tobacco and slaves themselves. Some subscribers, such as William Clayton, Richard Gildart and Sir Thomas Johnson, were heavily involved in the trade – all of them Liverpool MPs and the latter two also serving as Lord Mayor – while for others it was a peripheral part of their business. Throughout the eighteenth century and into the start of the nineteenth, merchants also left legacies to the school, including one in 1829 from one of Britain's wealthiest slave traders, Captain Hugh Crow, who also donated to the Liverpool Deaf and Dumb Institution, the Seaman's Hospital in Whitehaven and the Hospital for the Poor Black Slaves in Kingston, Jamaica. In the introduction to the 2007 republication of Crow's unrepentant autobiography, John Pinfold observes that the most striking thing 'about eighteenth-century Liverpool is how few people felt any qualms at the town's involvement in the slave trade'.[5] And the contradiction in the town between philanthropy and the barbaric nature of the business whose profits helped enable it is thrown into sharp focus by the institution of the Blue Coat Hospital.

Blundell himself has been described as puritanical, his tenure as Mayor of Liverpool being distinguished by his attempts to curb drinking on Sundays, yet such British puritanism was rooted in a pietism of personal deportment, not in any dogmatic adherence to external strictures. Blundell was a 'prisoner' in France in 1709 and remarked on the diligence and piety of the French Catholics he was able to observe as he attended church. Irrespective of the truth of Blundell's own personal drivers as recorded by history, it is reasonable to presume as a whole that the many subscribers to the Blue Coat over the years operated somewhere between the poles of outright philanthropy and social and commercial opportunism. While the creation of the Blue Coat served the needs of the poor children of the parish, it had a critical secondary function – that of drawing together in business and conversation the emergent mercantile class of the city. In doing so, it became a social hub for new relationships that endured through much of the eighteenth century, with co-owners of trading vessels and partners in building projects having regular contact through the functions and meetings of the school's various funding and administrative arrangements. This role as social hub is very much mirrored in the twentieth-century Bluecoat building by the social activities of the Sandon Studios Society, which for a time became more critical than the space for practising artists for which the society was set up.

Beyond philanthropy and the connections with work that the school began to provide – graduating pupils often worked in the businesses of the subscribers who funded their education – there is another critical element. The long-established, post-medieval tradition of familial apprenticeship (often to fathers or uncles) and ordered social climbing that enabled access to the status of freeman, and thereby the right to vote in Liverpool, was slowly but inexorably subverted by institutions such as the Blue Coat. As graduating students from impoverished backgrounds, to whom these roles might have been denied, gained apprenticeship outside of traditional family networks (thanks to the benefactor role of the school and its funders), they gained social status. Those successfully completing an apprenticeship to a freeman of Liverpool, irrespective of social background, acquired that status themselves.[6]

The first Blue Coat school is long gone, subsumed by three centuries of development, but it is largely true to say it had outlived its usefulness a few years after it opened. The day school had taken, at its peak, around fifty pupils, both boys and girls (at a ratio of around 3:1), but the rapidly expanding town swelled the needy underclass and there were ever more prospective wards to be taken in. Blundell, on returning from the sea, was dissatisfied at the state of the school and also lamented the return of pupils each day to parents who were indigent, or in some other way incapable of maintaining the high Christian ideals in which their children were being schooled. In 1711, therefore, the board of the school, led by Blundell, sought to expand, and plans were made to create the building we now see.

It should be noted that in the same year that approval for the first school was

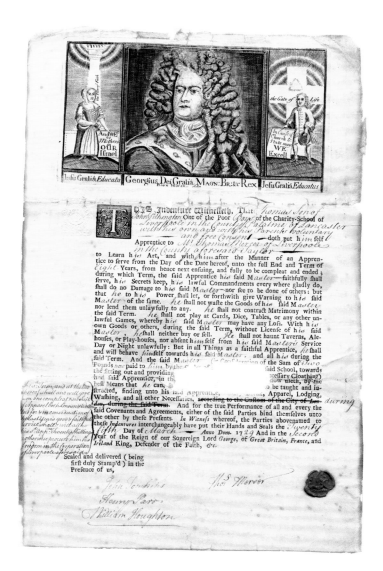

Figure 5. Indenture agreement for Blue Coat pupil Thomas Pilkington, 1729. Image courtesy of the Liverpool Blue Coat School Foundation.

granted, and funds subsequently raised from the wealthy of the parish, other events were taking place in Liverpool that would have a dramatic effect on the port. The Earl of Derby was Lord Mayor, shortly to be superseded by John Earle, and approval was granted for a survey to construct a much-improved town dock. A notable London engineer, George Sorocold, produced and costed a dock scheme, before this role was passed on to another London-based hydraulic engineer, Thomas Steers, who went on to create an enclosed wet dock, far beyond the Corporation's initial quayside plans. This technological innovation – the creation of what became known as 'Old

Dock' – would defy the Mersey's infamous tidal range and enable commercial vessels to unload and load with greatly increased speed and efficiency. This improvement in the port's capabilities was transformational, brought about in no small part by the engagement of Steers, who then settled in Liverpool, going on to become an indelible part of its history.

It is also no coincidence that the second (current) building was begun just as Old Dock was completed in 1715, with the construction of brick kilns on the School Lane site. It was the merchants who would benefit from the dock, and its investors, the land speculators who enabled the dock's excavation and building, its architects and masons, who made up the charity school's first subscription roll and became its early trustees. When Old Dock was completed, it was the world's first commercial wet dock, an innovation that defines the birth of modern Liverpool and would alter the course of its fortunes forever, giving the port a competitive edge over other westward-facing ports such as Bristol. The first ship to enter the dock was owned by Bryan Blundell. Old Dock and the Blue Coat school are therefore intrinsically linked, not only in funders and builders, but in the comparable connections to Liverpool's rising fortunes. A weathervane of a sailing ship atop the new school's cupola was a reminder of the institution's dependence on the port's mercantile maritime success, while old maps of the town show Blue Coat's proximity to the dock and its custom house, just a few minutes' walk away, over land now covering the creek.

The land on which the first school of 1708/09 was built was initially gifted by the Corporation, though the deed granting that land is dated 1722. When the second, present structure was commenced with the laying of the foundation stone in 1716, it followed the acquisition of surrounding dwellings and land that created a substantial estate. This new set of holdings spanned the entire block, from the corner of Manesty's Lane, up School Lane to Hanover Street and back down College Lane at the rear of the current Bluecoat. Though surveys of the building take into account only the 'H'-shaped footprint of the current structure, this belies the scale and influence of the historic school, and somewhat misses one of its key operational characteristics: using every opportunity to offset the charitable costs through financial exploitation of its assets. The whole complex at its peak was described as being 'of a larger extent than necessary for the habitation of boys, girls, masters, mistresses and servants, and some parts thereof are, and have been for some years set off at annual rents to increase the income of the said charity'.[7]

Parts of the complex were let: from 1723, 36 almshouses at the south side of the building; from 1732, Liverpool's first workhouse for the poor, and a free grammar school (repurposing the old 1708 school building), catering to the sons of those not needy enough to fall on the mercies of the charity school. Again, the interconnected nature of Liverpool's social circles is visible. Edward Litherland, of whom we shall hear more presently, worked as mason on both Blue Coat and Old Dock, and was employed in a number of capacities, beyond those indicated by his prominence in the local building trade, by the parish of Liverpool (sidesman, collector of the rector's tax, churchwarden), becoming overseer of the poor and having a direct influence on the interplay between the residents in the almshouses, the population of the workhouse, and the allocation of places at the charity school itself to the needy children of the parish.

As a predominantly brick building, the bulk of the material used in the construction of the school was produced on site, while stone was sourced locally from Brownlow Hill (flagstones), from Wigan (keystones) and from Chester (carved capitals). As an engraving of the school frontage, *The North Prospect of the Charity Schoole in Leverpoole* by H. Hulsbergh (Fig. 6), after an original rendering

Figure 6. H. Hulsbergh, after Joshua Mollineux, *The North Prospect of the Charity Schoole at Leverpoole*, 1718. Image reproduced courtesy of The Right Hon. The Earl of Derby, 2019.

The North Profpect of the Charity Schoole in Leverpoole.
Built at Private Charge, and is to be Sold for the Benefit of the Schoole

by Joshua Mollineux, illustrates, there were features in the original building that are no longer present, notably four statues, three of them representing Faith, Hope and Charity (carved by William Jones) positioned at the corners of the Palladian-derived pedimented centre on the front elevation. Other absent features include bull's-eye windows at the base of the central block, low relief decoration of the pediment, parapet detailing with urns and other ornamentation, and contrasting chequerboard courtyard paving, which was unlikely ever to have been realised as there is no record of such stone being purchased in the accounts book for this period. Also, Hulsbergh's print, sold to generate funds towards completing the building, was produced in 1718 while work was still going on, so it was in effect a visualisation rather than an accurate depiction of the finished building. Much of the original fabric, however, remains, albeit restored or replaced over the past three centuries. This includes distinctive features such as a one-handed clock, cherubs' heads above each window, Liver Birds over the gate and three courtyard entrances, and oval windows that, together with ironwork gates and railings, a cobbled courtyard and stone corner quoins – 'the common currency of buildings after the Great Fire and called "Wrenish"'[8] – make the building such a good example of Queen Anne style architecture (although it was actually built at the start of George I's reign); and while not at the forefront of the period's stylistic developments, its 'complete survival is a considerable rarity'.[9]

In terms of architectural merit, the building's Grade I listed status (designated in 1952) underlines the pleasing nature of its Queen Anne features – broadly typical of English Baroque buildings – though unusual as an outlier of surviving eighteenth-century construction in Liverpool. Joseph Sharples's description of the building in his Pevsner Architectural Guide to Liverpool provides a comprehensive overview of the building and its significance.[10] Other assessments of the building's architectural merits vary. For Janet Gnosspelius and Stanley Harris, the building has a 'mellow beauty', the importance of its design lying in 'the conception of a "U" shaped plan … in a rich 2-storey composition … [whose] 3-storey domestic side wings of 11 bays are much simpler, but then their end elevations close to School Lane repeat the 2-storey treatment of the centre block so holding the whole together'.[11] Quentin Hughes's assessment is, however, more critical:

> Although charming, the Liverpool Bluecoat building is not a very intellectual solution to an architectural problem. There are lots of faults, in particular in the way that semi-circular windows on the end faces of the wings push up through the string course into the windows above, and the complete inability to relate the three storeys of the wings to the two storeys of the main façade.[12]

RECOLLECTIONS of the BLUE-COAT HOSPITAL, LIVERPOOL, St GEORGES DAY, 1843.

Figure 7. *Recollections of the Blue-Coat Hospital, Liverpool, St George's Day, 1843*, 1850. Lithograph by Thomas Picken; published by Skinner, Professor of Water Colouring, Liverpool; printed by G. Webb & Co., London. After a painting by Henry Travis at the Liverpool Blue Coat School.

Howard Colvin, comparing its design to that of Ince Blundell Hall, north of the town, concludes that 'the School is decidedly old-fashioned'.[13] Its form echoes that of similar educational institutions: a symmetrical façade and wings around an open-fronted courtyard, bounded by wall and gate, is reflected by the roughly contemporary schools at Chester or the Green Coat school in Cork. Nor is this style of architecture limited to schools in particular – Worcester's Guildhall is but one example where many of the distinctive features that mark Bluecoat out as unique in Liverpool can be observed as common to construction at this time. Many of these buildings reflect the influence of broader European fashions in architecture that had taken some time to reach Britain in general and the provincial north in particular, but can be seen in precedents, from the domestic architecture of Renaissance Italy to the grandeur of the marble courtyard in Versailles.

For many years, a puzzling aspect of a building as prominent as Bluecoat, 'by far the largest secular building in central Liverpool',[14] has been the identity of its designer. This mystery has been the source of much discussion, and the sense of 'specialness' that the building evokes has led to all manner of speculative attributions, some even going so far as to suggest that it might have been designed by Christopher Wren himself.[15] These lofty associations reflect the regard with which the building is considered, and in themselves ask questions about the drawing together of regional and national elements of building technology and masonry, design and architecture, often with an assumption that these *must* have come in from outside.

One of the great challenges in attaching the name of an architect to the building is the very nature of building construction at this point in history – look through any rate book or trade list for the early 1700s and there will be no mention of 'architects'. Indeed, at the time of Bluecoat's inception, it was far more common to identify the funder or commissioner of a building as the responsible party than the designer or constructor. In analysing the earlier development of the term, Pevsner writes:

> Owing to the absence of professional architects in the Vitruvian sense, the terms 'architectus' and 'architector' were little used during the Middle Ages, and, when used, meant occasionally clerics specially interested or experienced in architecture, but as a rule masons regardless of their particular qualifications.[16]

The revival of the term 'architect' to denote the *designer* of a building rather than specifically the chief builder occurred in Italy from the fourteenth and fifteenth centuries onwards, and spread with the fashionable styles of building into other parts of Europe, though it remained a descriptor of the role that a craftsman or scholar played in the creation of a specific building, and not a description of a trade in the modern sense of 'being an architect'. It did not manifest in Britain until the seventeenth century, the period when the ideals of Vitruvius and Palladio began to see their revival in the works of Inigo Jones and Christopher Wren, yet it remained an unusual term in the world of provincial building until the mid-1750s. As Janet Gnosspelius and Stanley Harris have observed,

> In the seventeenth and eighteenth centuries, apart from a few great designers … the vast majority of architects played dual roles, combining their designing with mastery of craft, generally stone-work, but sometimes carpentry, both of which required skills comparable with those of architecture; many a fine building was designed and erected by someone self-described as a 'mason and architect', and the two professions, socially and professionally, were of equal status.[17]

A number of writers have sought to resolve the question of Bluecoat's architectural attribution and, based partly on regional evidence and partly on an established historical narrative, three names have emerged as serious contenders: Thomas Ripley (c. 1683–1758), Henry Sephton (1686–1756) and Thomas Steers (c. 1670–1750). Relying on the later term for an 'architect' applied retrospectively to a range of other trades, the three contenders can be summarised as 'architect-carpenter' (in the case of Ripley), 'architect-mason' or '-stonecutter' or '-builder' (Sephton), and 'architect-engineer' (Steers). Notably, throughout his life Sephton was described as a 'mayson', yet on his death in 1756 his profession was recorded as 'architect'.[18] Perhaps then, it is a peculiarly modern compulsion that we seek to attach some degree of celebrity to the designer of a building that is now looked on with particular affection.

All three contenders were considered by architectural historian Stanley Harris in his 1957 speculation for the Historic Society of Lancashire and Cheshire, at the time the strongest argument put forward for the identity of Bluecoat's architect.[19] Harris asserts a detailed case for Thomas Ripley, from the London Board of Works, who was present in relevant spheres of influence in the second decade of the eighteenth century, with connections to Sir Thomas Johnson, a Blue Coat trustee and potentially involved in the procurement of the building. Harris's argument – derived chiefly from the somewhat misplaced assertion of 'knowing that the old Custom House was designed by Ripley', the two buildings bearing some common features – also stems from an assumption that a building of the charity school's design or quality somehow did not belong in the Liverpool of the early 1700s, requiring examples from further afield to be drawn upon. This suggestion, however, is in the first instance undermined by Daniel Defoe's contemporary assessment of the state of the town in 1724:

> Liverpool has an opulent, flourishing and increasing trade to Virginia, and the English island colonies in America. They trade round the whole island, send ships to Norway, to Hamburg, and to the Baltic, as also to Holland and Flanders; so they are almost like the Londoners, universal merchants. There is no town in England, London excepted, that can equal Liverpool for the fineness of the streets, the beauty of the buildings; many of the houses are all of stone and the rest (the new part) of brick.[20]

Harris's claim also ignores comparable buildings in the vicinity – Croxteth Hall, or the no longer extant Chester Exchange, which both exhibit comparable Baroque features. There is strong evidence of Liverpool masons working as far afield as Chirk in Denbighshire and Preston in Lancashire in the accounts of the Earl of Derby and comparable estate records from across the region, which gives lie to the suggestion that there was no mason of sufficient capability in the Liverpool vicinity: the geographic range of regional artisans was clearly large at this time. Blue Coat teacher William Trenow's ledger, held at the Lancashire archive in Preston,[21] contains detailed breakdowns of the building's construction, such as the wages for days and half-days worked by the team of carpenters and the division of the many panes of glass required for the windows. Payments are itemised to the level of a few pence, and it would appear strange indeed were the architect also not to be represented.

Harris asserts that 'Volumes I of Leoni's *Palladia* and Campbell's *Vitruvius Britannicus* appeared in 1715. These important works influenced the subsequent "Palladian permeation", but it is beyond the bounds of possibility that the elevations of the Blue Coat Hospital derived from them.'[22] This, however, misses crucial elements of the social network that actually make this highly plausible. These volumes were in the library of the Earl of Derby (Mayor of Liverpool in early 1708, the time of the grant of land to the school), alongside earlier European editions of the works of Palladio. The Earl was also the principal patron of Hamlet Winstanley, who was himself assisted by Joshua Mollineux, the artist who provided the early image of the school from which the fundraising print was produced. It was surely no accident that the engraving for this was undertaken by Hulsbergh, the very engraver who provided the plates for Campbell's work. While these connections are merely incidental, it is certainly not beyond the realms of possibility that the designer of Blue Coat might have had an awareness of, or even direct access to, the volumes on architecture that Harris rules out.

A claim as the architect of the school has also been made for Henry Sephton, whose buildings include Ince Blundell Hall (1720), closest in date to the Bluecoat, but a more self-conscious and serious architectural study that does not employ the latter's round-arched windows, prominent keystones and decoration. Sephton, however, also designed the east wing of Knowsley Hall (1731), which has similarities to Bluecoat and, like it, was illustrated in a painting by Mollineux. Sephton was paid for his plans for St George's church (1720), which though not used, indicates that he was closely involved with early eighteenth-century architectural developments in Liverpool. However, during extensive research in the late 1990s by Bluecoat board member Charles Metcalfe, his consultation with the eminent architectural historians Quentin Hughes and Howard Colvin, and the Historic Society of Lancashire and Cheshire, resulted in a resounding rejection of the case for Sephton.[23]

Writing on behalf of the Historic Society, Janet Gnosspelius's dismissal of Sephton put forward instead a compelling case for Thomas Steers, who had the range of experience needed to design the Bluecoat School ... with its well organised plan and the architectural expression that still gives such pleasure. Steers was a modest man not given to self advertisement ... [and] it is not surprising that his authorship of the design for the Bluecoat did not become part of Liverpool's written history.[24]

Bryan Blundell was a close friend of the Steers family, yet the main evidence for Steers's involvement in building the school is contained in its detailed financial records for the period, meticulously kept by Blundell, who was the school's treasurer. Here, a payment to Steers of £50 is recorded, a considerable sum then, equivalent to his annual salary as Liverpool's Dock Master and Water Bailiff and also to the fee he received for a major project surveying 72 miles of canal in Ireland, from Dublin to Banagher on the River Shannon. Given that the design fee would have been 5 per cent of the construction cost of the school, which was £2,288 by the time it was completed in 1725, and that, as the client was a charity, this fee would most likely have reduced by half, a figure of £50 would be roughly the amount that Steers would have expected. Although Blundell's ledger does not specify what this payment was for, it seems inconceivable that it would have been for supplying materials, for instance, which are recorded in great detail in the accounts. Stanley Harris dismissed Steers from the list of contenders despite the evidential link of his having received a large payment, on the grounds that this might have been for the provision of ironwork, as Steers's family owned a nearby anchor foundry. The accounts, however, are clear in itemising the ironwork elsewhere (£18 for palisades and gates).[25]

The detail of Steers's early life is sparse: he was probably born in Kent in 1672, was present at the Battle of the Boyne (1690) and was listed as a quartermaster in the Fourth Regiment of Foot (The King's Own) in 1702, serving in the Low Countries (where it is possible he became familiar with the principles of hydraulic engineering – piling, land reclamation and various designs of lock gates), before returning to England in 1697. In Liverpool, not only was Steers responsible for Old Dock, but he was heavily involved in the development of the canal network and inland waterway system in England and Ireland, as well as training Henry Berry, who succeeded him as Liverpool dock engineer and was another builder of the waterways. In this context, the Blue Coat seems an anomalous architectural prospect for one so bound up with hydraulic engineering. However, Steers was also capable of architectural renderings, his largest undertaking being the construction of St George's church (1726) on the site of Liverpool's old castle – fashionable enough to recall the Hawksmoor churches in London with which it was broadly contemporary – which featured large, arched, Tuscan windows, with similar detailing to the Blue Coat, though on an altogether different scale.

Further analysis of the school accounts indicates the significance of another figure alongside Steers, that of Edward Litherland (d. 1739), who received in excess of £350, making him the single highest-paid contractor on the scheme. Is this in itself enough to identify Litherland, clearly the chief mason on the project but a name that has not previously been considered among those potentially responsible for the school building, as its 'architect', together with Steers? Both men – Steers as engineer and Litherland as mason – had previously worked together on constructing Old Dock, and one of the interesting patterns that emerges from records of Liverpool building projects in this period is their frequent pairing. They worked together for nearly thirty years: on Old Dock (1710–15); then almost immediately after on the Blue Coat (1716–18); on the entirety of Chorley Street (also known as Squire's Garden on some maps) from 1720, which included a playhouse and coffee house; on St George's church (1726–34); and on what would become the Salt House Dock from 1738. Litherland's other documented works on Merseyside, spanning four decades, include Knowsley Hall, Crosby Hall and West Lane House, Little Crosby, as well as work on bridges and road excavation. Litherland's earliest documented work for Nicholas Blundell (unrelated to the Blue Coat founder) dates from 1702, and he also worked on the first Blue Coat school. He was a competent builder in brick and stone, as evidenced by numerous entries in Blundell's journal and his frequent contracting with the Corporation and local landowners. He was, by any standards, a very successful merchant and was sufficiently well disposed towards the charity school to gift back £50 from his fee. Though a significant figure in the construction of Liverpool, he appears to have held little in the way of public office.

The Corporation of Liverpool, as a controlling authority, set not only the leasing of designated quarry sites, but also the right to quarry or 'gett stone' – records indicate fines for those who sought to take stone for building without this strictly controlled licence. The Corporation effectively created a monopoly that was available on contract, controlling not only the extraction of stone, but also the provision of worked stone products – gravestones, keystones, regular ashlars, gatepost ornaments and columns – and it fixed the rates, in 1699, revised in 1706, at which these could be bought.[26] This appears to indicate that any basic archway, column, pediment or keystone on one building is likely to resemble that of another, not because of a common architect, but because of a common supplier of finished building components, whether by a single mason or by a set of subcontractors providing for him, and one contractually bound to provide those items at a fixed cost. The contract for this was held at this time by Litherland, the 'go to' mason in

Liverpool at this time, who is recorded as repairer of the first school in the account books.

Information on Litherland is fragmentary and confusing, not least as there were at one point numerous individuals of the same name living within a couple of streets of each other (in Lord Street and Pool Lane). Brothers Edward and John Litherland were made freemen on payment of a fine in 1662, and both had sons named after themselves and one another, creating a somewhat tangled genealogical web, yet establishing two dynasties: those descended from John were ships' carpenters, resident in Pool Lane; and those from Edward (Senior) became masons, connected with Lord Street. It is to this latter branch of the family that Edward Litherland appears to have belonged, settling in Lord Street soon after his arrival in Liverpool in 1705, and going on to make a considerable contribution to the development of the town's built environment. By comparison with the other names on Harris's list – Ripley, Sephton and Steers – Litherland, 'Mason of Netherton', has gained none of their celebrity, yet his role in the first half of the eighteenth century in Liverpool appears significant. And in relation to his role in building Bluecoat, he was more than a mere jobbing mason languishing in the shadow of Steers.

The building's architectural significance has been highlighted in a conservation plan that charts the changes to its fabric over three centuries.[27] The most prominent of these began with radical developments a century after the building opened, in the early nineteenth century, when the north-east and south-west wings were widened and extended, and the central block enlarged by taking down the rear wall, whose detail had echoed that of the decorative front façade, and replacing it with a curved wall – a technically challenging task and an early example of façade retention. This created two large central spaces for the growing school. The ground floor, originally split in two by an arch running from the front to the rear courtyard, became a refectory, whose wooden ceiling beams and cast iron columns (see Fig. 8) are again visible (the space having been partitioned and these features covered in the early years of the arts centre) following the 2005–08 capital development. Upstairs became the school chapel, housing – in the centre of the new curve – a Willis organ (Fig. 10), which went with the school to Wavertree when it relocated there in 1906, and which has recently been restored. The space was thereafter used for arts activities – exhibitions and performances – being converted into a proscenium theatre space which, after the Second World War, became an elegant concert hall, hosting many music and other events until reopening as the arts centre's bistro in 2008. An 1881 plan saw the rebuilding of the east side of the south courtyard, the girls' playground, which is now the garden, and the erection of a single-storey building to enclose this space along College Lane. This building housed the school

The school in the late nineteenth century: Figure 8. The refectory. Figure 9. The laundry.

laundry (Fig. 9) and a brewery, currently the home of the Bluecoat Display Centre. Today's popular garden has also undergone many transformations. Variously a courtyard opening on to College Lane, a school playground and a sculptor's yard, it has housed air raid shelters and been landscaped several times – from as early as 1769 it was formally laid out with trees and planting, possibly a herb garden.[28] Resident sculptor Herbert Tyson Smith (known as 'Capability Smith')[29] planted and tended an improvised garden during and after the Second World War, and this was later paved and further planted, maturing into a 'secret garden' that remained until being landscaped into its current configuration in 2008.

Wartime bombing was the cause of substantial change to the building in 1941, fire gutting the concert hall and destroying much of the south-east wing, which was remodelled, with a large section of the south wing having to be demolished and replaced by a caretaker's flat, artists' studios and a small car park. All of these were demolished to make way for the new arts wing, designed by Rotterdam architects Biq Architecten, which opened in 2008, in time for Liverpool's year as European Capital of Culture, a pertinent backdrop and reminder of the global maritime connections of the Bluecoat building's origins. The development saw the most significant change to the building since the early nineteenth century. Alongside creating a new wing to replace the 'lost leg' of the building's capital 'H' formation, the historic fabric was restored – brickwork cement pointing, for instance, being replaced with lighter-coloured lime mortar to match the original – and there were extensive circulation and access improvements, including the installation of three lifts. These changes are the most recent in a succession of internal alternations. Indeed, very little of the original interior fabric remains: a wooden staircase where the north-east wing meets the central block and which, though reconstructed following the war, includes elements of the original structure; and ten fireplaces in small rooms in the north-west wing, dating from the eighteenth to the mid-nineteenth century. These charming details, together with the iconic front façade, belie the fact that Bluecoat is a dynamic building that has witnessed many changes over its lifetime, and continues to evolve, both architecturally and functionally. The four plane trees at the front were planted in the 1920s, yet in their maturity they seem to have a more ancient presence, at least one dating back to the birth of modern Liverpool, of which 'Bluecoat is the only surviving building representing that crucial period'.[30]

To conclude this chapter, which has concentrated on Bluecoat's founding, its architectural significance and the networks of influence in the port that made it possible, a brief overview of the school's impact on educational and pedagogic developments will suggest something of the continuing relationship it had to its

Figure 10. The school chapel, with its Willis organ, c. 1904.

mercantile maritime origins. The school engaged in the education of children from 8 to 14 years of age, many of whom were then apprenticed to maritime trades for eight years as seamen or to the merchants benefiting from maritime trade, some returning as school benefactors themselves. Throughout the accounts, Blundell, as treasurer, invested the school's money in voyages, or saw returns to the school accounts as the result of successful expeditions returning to Liverpool, some of the crews no doubt including former pupils. The two-thirds of a day that children were engaged in manual labour in such tasks as picking oakum, which relies on a supply of used rope from the maritime industries as its raw material and produces an end product intended for use in the same, indicates both the harsh conditions of their 'education' and the commercial imperative for the institution to generate income as a manufactory. This practice continued for many years until the trustees eventually decided it was detrimental to the children's health, although Robin Hewitt-Jones argues that there is 'nothing in the narrow and rigid curriculum of the years which followed to suggest a more liberal attitude', and unprofitability was the more likely reason for this apparent increase in concern for the pupils' welfare.[31]

An account of the school's development is given in *The Liverpool Blue Coat School Past & Present 1708–2008*,[32] which details headmasters, trustees and patrons, the growth in the numbers of pupils, significant old boys who returned to support the school, everyday school life including menus and a calendar of holidays, and the case for departing to new, larger premises in the cleaner air of suburban Wavertree. During its almost two centuries' tenure in the School Lane building, the Blue Coat consolidated its position as an established philanthropic institution at the heart of the life of the growing city. Of particular pedagogical note is the school's adoption in 1812 of Dr Bell's Madras – or monitorial – system of education, in which older and more able pupils became in effect teaching assistants, passing on their learning to other children. Its success apparently attracted teachers from far and wide to observe it.

What significance we draw from these historical links and coincidences in so far as they relate to Bluecoat today is to some extent arbitrary, and we run the same risks of the type of romanticisation or projection noted earlier. What can be seen though, and traced through the history of the building, is a kind of serendipity. Beyond any intentional action, the exceptionalism of Bluecoat has come about, time and again, as the result of it simply being there; and as such, it has drawn people together who have created, for better or worse, opportunity and institution. There is a balance between the intended purpose of the institution and the personal aims of those involved in it, and it is never clear which subverts which. Its genesis facilitated new social networks which transcended its Church origins and went on to create an institution of significant social heft, which made an indelible mark on Liverpool for 200 years, politically and culturally. The emptying of the building when the school moved to the leafy suburbs of Wavertree in 1906 did not end this, and the vacant premises would immediately provide a home for new organisations and communities. Each of these operated with the same mixture of self-interest and necessary collaboration that has always been part of Bluecoat and, as such, have reinforced the significance of the building in Liverpool's history, adding new layers to the strata of Bluecoat's story.

Contemporary artists interrogating the building's school history:
Figure 11. Susan Fitch, *Escape*, 1994. One-day installation on the railings, marking the day in 1800 when pupils ran away.
Figure 12. Geraldine Pilgrim, *Traces*, installation/performance staged on Bluecoat's reopening in 2008. Performed by current pupils, it was inspired by 52 girls who were forced to leave the school when it became boys only in 1949. Photo: Sharon Mutch.

Notes

1   Population sources: 1700: Edwin Butterworth, 'Liverpool', in *Statistical Sketch of the County Palatine of Lancaster*, London: Longman, 1841; 1720: David Brewster, ed., 'Liverpool', in *Edinburgh Encyclopædia*, Philadelphia: Joseph and Edward Parker, 1832.

2   From Liverpool Corporation's 'case' for the bill to build a new parish church, quoted in Janet Gnosspelius and Stanley Harris, 'John Moffat and St. Peter's Church, Liverpool', *Historic Society of Lancashire and Cheshire*, 130, 1980, p. 1.

3   Referenced in John R. Hughes, 'A sketch of the Origin and Early History of the Liverpool Blue Coat Hospital', lecture delivered 5 May 1859, *Transcriptions of the Historic Society of Lancashire and Cheshire*, XI (1858–59), 1859, p. 185.

4   Sophie Jones's research is summarised in a Bluecoat brochure, *Subscriptions, Schooling and Slavery: Bluecoat's Early Years*, 2016.

5   John Pinfold, Introduction to *The Memoirs of Captain Hugh Crow: The Life and Times of a Slave Trade Captain*, Oxford: Bodleian Library, 2007 [1830], p. xv.

6   A surviving indenture document from 1729 in the collection of the Liverpool Blue Coat school outlines the conditions of apprenticeship: 14-year-old Thomas Pilkington, apprenticed to Thomas Mercer for eight years, was forbidden, in that time, to marry, play cards, dice or tables, nor 'haunt Taverns, Ale-houses, or Play-houses' (see Fig. 5).

7   Hospital charter, granted by the Duchy Court of Lancaster, in 1739: cited in Hughes, 'A sketch of the Origin and Early History of the Liverpool Blue Coat Hospital', p. 169.

8   Janet Gnosspelius, letter to Charles Metcalfe, 9 February 2001, p. 3, in the Bluecoat archive.

9   Donald Insall Associates, *The Bluecoat Arts Centre Conservation Plan*, 2002, p. 52, in the Bluecoat archive.

10   Joseph Sharples, *Pevsner Architectural Guides: Liverpool*, New Haven, CT: Yale University Press, 2004, pp. 177–80.

11   Gnosspelius and Harris, 'John Moffat and St Peter's Church, Liverpool', p. 5.

12   Quentin Hughes, letter to Charles Metcalfe, 19 October 1999, in the Bluecoat archive.

13   Letter to Charles Metcalfe from Howard Colvin, 29 October 1999, in the Bluecoat archive.

14   Sharples, *Pevsner Architectural Guides: Liverpool*, p. 177.

15   Charles Reilly, letters to *Liverpool Daily Post*, 28 July 1926, and *Country Life*, 14 August 1926, cited by Stanley Harris in 'The Old Blue Coat Hospital, Liverpool: was it designed by Thomas Ripley?', *Transactions of the Historic Society of Lancashire and Cheshire*, 109, 1958, p. 144.

16   Nicholas Pevsner, 'The term "architect" in the Middle Ages', *Speculum*, 17.4, October 1942.

17   Gnosspelius and Harris, 'John Moffat and St. Peter's Church, Liverpool', pp. 10–11.

18   *The Oxford Journal*, 12 June 1756.

19   Harris, 'The Old Blue Coat Hospital, Liverpool: was it designed by Thomas Ripley?'.

20   Daniel Defoe, *A Tour Through the Whole Island of Great Britain* (1724–26), Harmondsworth: Penguin, 1978, p. 543.

21   Account book, first of William Trenow of the Corporation of Liverpool (d. 1723), 1684–1719. Including accounts of general overseas trade and accounts of Blue Coat Charity School, Liverpool 1684–1712/13, Lancashire Archives, DDBB 8/3.

22   Harris, 'The Old Blue Coat Hospital, Liverpool: was it designed by Thomas Ripley?', p. 145.

23   Letters to Charles Metcalfe from Janet Gnosspelius on behalf of Historic Society of Lancashire and Cheshire, 9 February 2001; Quentin Hughes, 19 October 1999; Howard Colvin, 29 October 1999, in the Bluecoat archive.

24   Letter to Charles Metcalfe from Janet Gnosspelius, 9 February 2001, in the Bluecoat archive.

25   Bluecoat Ledger.

26   Liverpool Town Books (microfilm), Liverpool Record Office.

27   Donald Insall Associates, *The Bluecoat Arts Centre Conservation Plan*, 2002 (with addendum 2005). This document informed the building's capital development, 2005–08.

28   Perry's map of Liverpool, 1769.

29   As dubbed by Sandon artist Edgar Grosvenor, cited in R. F. Bisson, *The Sandon Studios and the Arts*, Liverpool: Parry Books, published on behalf of the Sandon Studios Society, 1965, p. 198.

30   Donald Insall Associates, *The Bluecoat Arts Centre Conservation Plan*, p. 50.

31   Robin Hewitt-Jones, 'A short history of the Bluecoat Chambers', in *The Bluecoat Today and Yesterday*, Liverpool: Bluecoat Society of Arts, 1976, p. 3.

32   Peter Healey, ed., *The Liverpool Blue Coat School Past & Present 1708–2008*, Liverpool: Liverpool Blue Coat School Foundation, 2008.

Chapter 2

Saving the Bluecoat,
Regenerating the City

John Belchem

The Bluecoat is in many ways the most significant building in Liverpool, embodying and epitomising the changing status and image of the place. In the wake of the opening of the first commercial wet dock in 1715, construction of the Blue Coat Charity School (or Hospital as it was known), taking charge of selected orphaned and destitute children, transformed the fortunes of what had previously been little more than an agricultural and fishing village. After 'long centuries of small things', the dock and the Bluecoat laid the foundations for an interlocking and expanding infrastructure of commerce, charity and culture, funded at first in no small part by the infamous slave trade. With the prerequisites for growth in place, Liverpool soon outpaced other provincial towns and ports: as the twentieth century opened, it proudly claimed the status of 'second city of empire'. At this Edwardian high point (and after some considerable delay), the school finally vacated the building to move to new premises in Wavertree (where it subsequently transformed itself into a selective voluntary-aided grammar school). Thereafter the Queen Anne building, the oldest in the city centre, became a contested site, a metonym for the city's fate, as once proud Liverpool transmogrified into the 'shock city' of post-colonial, post-industrial Britain. In grappling with these vicissitudes, the Bluecoat emerged as role model for wider urban renewal. A pioneer exercise in

Figure 13. Bluecoat Society of Arts jubilee plaque, 1977, designed by Julia Carter Preston, set into a gate at the College Lane entrance.

regeneration through conservation, the campaign to save the building prepared the way for Liverpool's inscription as a UNESCO World Heritage Site. As an independent arts centre, the first in the country, Bluecoat showed the value of art and culture in urban regeneration and well-being, laying the early groundwork for Liverpool's successful bid to become European Capital of Culture in 2008.[1] While exemplifying the Liverpudlian approach to urban redevelopment, the Bluecoat owed much of its success to enthusiasts and volunteers, a form of public provision in the city centre beyond conventional municipal services or commercial investment.

***

When the school vacated the premises in 1906, the trustees were apparently unconcerned about its future. The city council, as R. F. Bisson recorded, openly favoured its demolition and replacement by 'some shoddy commercial building' yielding a much higher rateable value. More forward-looking types even suggested using the site, once cleared, as a station for a monorail link to Manchester, an early instance of the oft-repeated but as yet unfulfilled aspiration for improved interconnectivity between the great northern cities.[2] The structure of feeling of the time, Liverpool's Edwardian climacteric, was clearly disposed towards redevelopment rather than conservation. As the celebrations in 1907 of the 700th anniversary of the granting of letters patent to the borough confirmed, Liverpool was 'a city without ancestors', insignificant and obscure until the catalytic impact of civic enterprise in constructing the first commercial wet dock in the early eighteenth century – just at the time of the building of Bryan Blundell's Blue Coat school, the kind of charitable endowment that other towns had long enjoyed.[3] Thereafter growth was exponential, unencumbered by medieval heritage and restriction. 'The history of a place which has lately emerged from obscurity, and which owes, if not its being, at least its consequence to the commercial and enterprizing spirit of modern times', William Enfield observed in his pioneer *Essay towards the history of Leverpool*, published in 1773, 'cannot be supposed to afford many materials for the entertainment of the curious antiquarian.'[4] Liverpudlians, however, came to take an inverted pride in their abbreviated past, looking outwards and away from 'olde England'. As reports of the International Exhibition of Navigation, Commerce and Industry in 1886 acknowledged, 'Liverpool, thanks to modern science and commercial enterprise, to the spirit and intelligence of the townsmen … has become a wonder of the world. It is the New York of Europe, a world-city rather than merely British provincial.'[5] To maintain such global status required constant innovation and redevelopment, demolishing the obsolete and redundant to make way for the new, a dynamic celebrated in Ramsay Muir's *History of Liverpool*, published in 1907 to mark the 700th anniversary.[6]

Against the odds, the Bluecoat escaped demolition before the First World War thanks to the efforts of a not always harmonious coalition of 'radical' Edwardians – advocates and practitioners of 'free art', bohemians, free-thinkers and progressive academics from the newly independent university – marshalled by one of Liverpool's most formidable socially concerned middle-class women, and aided by a plutocratic soap magnate from across the Mersey with a penchant for architectural planning and the acquisition of property. First to move into the vacated building in 1907 were the free spirits of the Sandon Studios Society following the demolition of their premises in Sandon Terrace, the former home of the University Club, itself renowned for its Bloomsbury-like sociability linking academics, artists and wealthy shipowners and merchants with free-thinking cultural and scholarly tastes.[7] There had been considerable dismay in such progressive circles when the university agreed to amalgamate its art classes – at which artists of the calibre of Augustus John had taught in corrugated iron sheds in the university quadrangle – with the proposed Municipal School of Art in 1905. Having proudly welcomed the advent of an independent university in 1903, the city council did not wish to diminish its own sense of civic importance and insisted that painting and sculpture were a municipal preserve. A 'revolutionary band' of art students, joined by tutors Gerard Chowne and Herbert MacNair, established an independent art school and atelier in the old University Club premises in Sandon Terrace, seeking 'to revive the "medieval" practice of master-artists and craftsmen working together with their pupils, as a community'.[8] When the premises were demolished a couple of years later, they moved down the hill into the vacant Bluecoat.

At the Bluecoat, the Sandon hoped to establish an arts centre dedicated to '"free art" in contradistinction to South Kensington and Royal Academy art'.[9] In acquisition and exhibition, as in education, the city council, to the dismay of the Sandon avant-garde, eschewed any embrace of the experimental. Relying on the judgement of aldermen rather than any professional curatorial provision, civic Liverpool sought to establish its cultural credentials (and avoid any suggestion of provincial parochialism) by emulating the metropolitan artistic establishment. Conventional works from Royal Academicians and the like – modest landscapes, genre paintings and unpretentious watercolours – dominated the annual autumn exhibition in the Walker Art Gallery. Profits from this commercial exercise (or 'dumping ground' as critics called it) were the only funds available to the gallery, money which, the Sandon bemoaned, was 'misspent in the acquisition of the mediocre and in the depreciation of the valued in art'.[10] Advocates of the experimental and cutting edge, the Sandon also promoted local artistic talent, a resource eschewed by the city authorities. There were vociferous protests, not least

Figure 14. Sandon Studios Society fancy dress dance, c. 1912, Charles Reilly seated centre.

in a polemic entitled *The Sport of Civic Life, or Art and the Municipality*, when the council awarded the commission for frescoes in the Town Hall, funded by proceeds from the Pageant in 1907 celebrating Liverpool's 700th anniversary, to a London studio: 'It is as ridiculous in our view that the destiny of Liverpool Art should be at the mercy of "the butcher, the baker, and candlestick maker", as it would be to place in the hands of an artist the control of the tramway system.'[11]

While delighting in mocking Victorian convention, the Sandon was imbued with a sense of Edwardian idealism, best expressed by the progressive academics among its ranks, such as Charles Reilly, Professor of Architecture (to whose chair the applied art section had previously been attached). Socialite and socialist, Reilly, a cultural live-wire, moved effortlessly between the 'Latin Quarter' around the Polish artist Albert Lipczinski's 'Schloss' on the corner of Knight Street and Roscoe Street, where artists, academics, actors and trade union activists intermingled, and the progressive inner circle of the New Testament group of academics, so named to imply (not without arrogance) 'that all outside it belonged to the Old'.[12] The group espoused high Edwardian idealism: 'Through its University Liverpool was to be a new Athens saving the country from its materialism by the clearness of its thought, the fineness of its work and the beauty of its buildings.'[13] They hoped to establish 'a complete Faculty of Fine Arts, the first in any English university if not anywhere in the world … Augustus John was to be brought back to Liverpool … and appointments like Epstein and Elgar were to be made to other Chairs'. Plans were perforce abandoned when the city council insisted on municipal control of art education.

After this setback, Reilly sought to relocate the School of Architecture, to move out of Waterhouse's Victoria Building, reviled as a particularly ugly Victorian structure akin to a 'less prosperous Prudential Insurance office'. He looked to follow the Sandon into the Bluecoat, using the chapel block (and adjacent rooms) as prestigious new premises for the university School of Architecture. The rest of the building, he suggested, 'could be very well let out as studios for painters, sculptors and other artists … Thus a community of practising artists and craftsmen centred on the School of Architecture would be formed, the influence of which might be far reaching.' In recommending the scheme to the university authorities, Reilly failed to mention the artists of the Sandon already in residence, an early indication of subsequent difficulties in reconciling his commitments and interests as professional academic, practising architect and cultural entrepreneur. When the university failed to raise sufficient funds, Reilly turned to his friend, the wealthy soap magnate W. H. Lever. A frequent visitor to Lever's 'colony of industry' with its model village at Port Sunlight, Reilly encouraged the industrialist to secure a lease in 1909 for £1,300 a year, with an option to purchase the old Blue Coat school, which he promptly renamed Liberty Buildings in celebration of his victory in the libel courts against the *Daily Mail* and other newspapers. Thanks to Lever's leasehold arrangements, the School of Architecture moved into rent-free accommodation in Liberty Buildings in October 1909.[14]

The following years leading up to the First World War are best described as a complex (not always intelligible) web of intrigue, manoeuvring and misunderstanding between Reilly, Lever and the Sandon. The School of Architecture's move into the Bluecoat prompted the existing tenants, the Sandon, to 'rethink their whole ethos', to begin the transformation from independent art school into a broader, subscription-based cultural society open to art lovers as well as practitioners. The provision of a club room 'which all members can use freely and where meetings can be held for discussion and for social and artistic purposes' served as the hub of the nascent 'arts centre' (as well as city centre rendezvous for radical progressives). Trusting to work in cooperation with Reilly, the Sandon hoped that Lever would refurbish the premises and hand the building over to a body of trustees to be used as 'a free Art Centre'. Independent of all municipal and other official control, the proposed Lancashire Society of Arts was to be 'a permanent

Figure 15. University of Liverpool architecture students in the main studio at Bluecoat, renamed Liberty Buildings by its new owner, William Lever. Photographed during the School of Architecture's time there, 1909–18. University of Liverpool Library Special Collections and Archives, ref. A150.

centre for the interests of art in Lancashire, using the term in its widest sense to include, in addition to the graphic and plastic arts, the arts of Music, Literature and the Drama'.[15]

Reilly soon found irritating fault in some of the rental and housekeeping arrangements of his fellow tenants, and much to their dismay he chose not to join the Sandon committee in handling the negotiations for the proposed Lancashire Society of Arts, claiming that he would be better placed to offer independent (and supportive) advice through his special relationship with Lever, an arrangement which he thought (or so his critics in the Sandon believed) would also have the advantage of securing his appointment as architect to undertake the substantial refashioning of the building. However, once Lever purchased the building in 1913, he espoused far more grandiose ideas for an international 'art headquarters' to rival anything London could offer, a project eulogised in the local press: 'Thus we should have in Liverpool, in addition to the cosmopolitanism of commerce, the cosmopolitanism of art, and, we can imagine a great fame in consequence.'[16] Such a prestigious scheme, Lever insisted, to Reilly's apparent dismay, required an open architectural competition.

At this point, Reilly purportedly put his own interests ahead of those of the Sandon, although research in the university archives by Peter Richmond offers a counterweight to the anti-Reilly tenor of the correspondence reprinted in a lengthy appendix in MacCunn's history of the Bluecoat building.[17] Reilly's priority, it seemed, was to secure new premises for his university department, a building worthy of his achievements in establishing what was acknowledged by his colleague and fellow member of the New Testament, Ramsay Muir, as 'the greatest architectural school in England'.[18] On taking out the lease in 1909, Lever had expressed his willingness, after a term of years, either to purchase Liberty Buildings for the permanent use of the School of Architecture, or to give £25,000 for a new building nearer to the university. According to Richmond, Reilly still favoured remaining in the Bluecoat. It was the university authorities that decided otherwise in 1913:

> When the university elected to take up Lever's cash offer, Reilly may have felt that to associate with any committee dedicated to extracting further money from Lever (in this case to help save the Blue Coat building) might test Lever's generosity too far. Reilly was therefore committed to the university line, leaving him with no option but to withdraw from the Sandon committee scheme.[19]

While friendly relations were subsequently restored, the Sandon were initially outraged by what they considered an act of betrayal by Reilly (and the university), a pursuit of self-interest that threw the future of the Bluecoat back into jeopardy.

This was the point at which Fanny Dove Hamel Calder stepped forward to secure the building for the arts. A member of an honoured Liverpool family, she was the daughter of James Lister, a cotton broker of the old school who retired from the Exchange in disgust at the new practice of 'commercial gambling' and the ruin wrought by 'the Option, Future, and Settlement systems' to devote himself to charitable work and local government.[20] Fanny inherited the commitment to voluntary service, conducted with professional and tireless expertise, a trait with a distinguished – and formidable – pedigree among Liverpool women extending, among others, from Kitty Wilkinson, Agnes Jones, Louisa Birt, Josephine Butler and Margaret Beavan to Eleanor Rathbone. A former art student at the university and a founder member of the Sandon, Fanny extended the agenda of voluntary endeavour beyond health and welfare (the progressive social policy that distinguished Edwardian Liverpool, otherwise backward in political practice) to the promotion of the arts and well-being, concentrating her efforts on securing the Bluecoat following her marriage in 1909 to the lawyer James Calder, scion of another honoured Liverpool family.

In Fanny Calder's eyes, Reilly had 'ratted about the building': the university, she rued, had 'practically dissociated themselves from the old building'. Reilly, she contended, 'would not have cared if it [the Bluecoat] were lost so long as he had a new one to do'.[21] (As it was, owing to the war and unexpected post-war difficulties, the new building for the School of Architecture, designed by Reilly in collaboration with one of his students and fellow member of the Sandon, Lionel Budden, was not completed until the 1930s.) Calder's pique was evident in her negotiations with Lever, as she upheld the prior claims of the Sandon. She was particularly incensed that, having been the first to recognise the value of the building, the Society had been paying rent to the university which itself had enjoyed rent-free accommodation. 'When the old Bluecoat Hospital was derelict and threatened with destruction', Calder reminded Lever, 'it was the action of the Sandon in taking and shewing its value for artistic purpose which first drew the attention of members of the University and other influential persons to the beauty and interest of the old building.' Lever, however, refused to amend the rental arrangements or, with war about to break out, to commit himself to any 'incomplete and immature scheme' for the Lancashire Society of Arts. Liberty Buildings, he insisted with ominous emphasis, 'remains my private property'.[22]

Lever's continued support was an indispensable precondition, as there was little likelihood of any other major source of funding to safeguard the building and promote an arts centre, either from wealthy donors, the city authorities or the broader middle-class citizenry. In projecting itself as the nation's 'second metropolis', Edwardian Liverpool was beginning to exhaust the funds and goodwill of its merchant princes, whose benefaction facilitated construction of the necessarily lavish adornments of civic pride, 'a great cathedral and a great university … twin citadels of the ideal, a citadel of faith and a citadel of knowledge'.[23] Donor fatigue was evident in the initial poor support for a suitable memorial to Victoria. Eventually erected on the site of the medieval castle, later of St George's church, the memorial attested to the Liverpool penchant for serial demolition and reuse, a pattern of urban development more familiar in the United States than in the United Kingdom. There were distinct echoes of Chicago on the Mersey with the radical construction of the Liver Building, opened in 1911, on the most prestigious Edwardian development project, the Pier Head, land reclaimed from the obsolete George's Dock, a new waterfront location suitable for the 'palaces of trade' which attested to Liverpool's commercial pre-eminence.

Figure 16. Sandon Studios Society stalwart Fanny Dove Hamel Calder, 1927, instrumental in establishing an artistic presence in the building and securing its future as an arts centre.

The local authority left the costly business of cultural provision to plutocrats whose contribution to civic pride duly held out the promise of memorialised immortality, as in the museum and library funded by William Brown, a colossus of the Atlantic trade, and the Walker Art Gallery, a more controversial bequest from the eponymous brewer. Corporation resources were concentrated on the provision of basic infrastructure (which necessitated yet further demolition) to tackle the city's notorious problems of public health. Carried forward from the days of the Irish Famine influx, the continuing stigma of the 'black spot on the Mersey' jeopardised the prestige of the 'second city of empire', a much-vaunted and jealously guarded status upheld against growing statistical and demographic evidence to the contrary. There was intense interest in the Town Planning and Housing Exhibition held in Liberty Buildings in 1914. J. A. Brodie, famed city engineer (and inventor of football goal nets), outlined plans for broad ring and radial roads, while F. T. Turton, the deputy surveyor, unveiled a model of Liverpool's new-look tenements with balconies allowing a much-prized asset, individual front doors.[24] The reception accorded to this exhibition was in marked contrast to the lack of attention accorded by the press and civic establishment to the Sandon's groundbreaking exhibition of Post-Impressionist paintings in Liberty Buildings in 1911, a version of the controversial show seen earlier in London, opened by Miss Horniman with a speech that condemned the 'ugliness and dullness' of conventional middle-class life.[25]

Given its delight in the shock of the new, the 'bohemian' Sandon lacked broad constituency support among the Liverpool bourgeoisie, despite efforts to engage with middle-class sociability:

> We want to stimulate the artistic and intellectual life of Liverpool by bringing together those who are interested in something more than fashion and football and bridge and the share market. We want the amateur musical enthusiast to meet the rising professional and the young composer, the collector of taste to meet the promising artist. We want all the bright, appreciative people to meet the clever and original. This ought to give pleasure to them all and make for mutual development quite apart from the actual entertainment at which they meet.[26]

Writing from the stuffy confines of the Athenaeum Club opposite the Bluecoat, Robert Gladstone, chairman of the Mersey Docks and Harbour Board (and an active classical scholar), declined to mix with such company: 'As I am socially a recluse, and artistically a Philistine, I regret to be obliged to confess that the project of the Sandon Studios is altogether outside (or above) my sphere.' Gladstone, however, did become a tenant of the building.[27]

While leading commercial figures kept their distance, an eclectic mix of artistic, academic and political radicals passed through the doors to the club and dining room, including suffragette artists – 'Bohemian feminists' from the Women's Social and Political Union – such as Ethel Frimston.[28] Through his links to Lipczinski, the syndicalist Fred Bower, the 'rolling stonemason', introduced trade union leaders to the Sandon set. 'Lippi' painted portraits of Tom Mann and Jim Larkin, Bower's schoolboy sectarian sparring partner from whom he borrowed copies of the *Clarion* and the *Labour Leader* to wrap around a socialist address placed under the foundation stone of the Anglican cathedral, to remind posterity that 'within a stone's throw from here, human beings are housed in slums not fit for swine'.[29] Encouraged by Bower, 'Lippi' took Larkin and Mann down to the Sandon: on one memorable occasion Tom Mann stood on a chair in the dining room and sang 'The Red Flag' to be followed by ballads by Augustus John and George Harris 'with a sensational rendering of "The Jabberwocky"'. As the historian of the Society recorded with pride:

It is memorable that at Liberty Buildings, by the generosity of Sir William Lever, a tycoon if ever there was one, such men as Bower, Larkin and Mann, John, Lipczinsky [*sic*] and Harris, and those who held the ivory cards of the Wellington Assembly Rooms, and actors and actresses of the Playhouse and the Professors and their wives from the University could gather together more or less amicably.[30]

These were the halcyon days of the Sandon, recollected with embellished nostalgia in the interwar years. As soon as the war ended, Fanny Calder and the committee resumed discussion with Lever, now ennobled as Lord Leverhulme, to institute his 'scheme for an august Institution of United Arts, with endowments and fellowships, to be housed in the reconstructed building, with immense additions and improvements, all on the generous and lordly scale on which Lord Leverhulme's beneficent schemes were always planned'. To their astonishment, Leverhulme announced that he was 'not now disposed to carry out the Scheme as originally proposed', nor, as Fanny Calder discovered to her dismay, would he agree to a more modest proposal, a suggestion that offended his 'Napoleonic' mind.[31] Irascible and irritable, Leverhulme then evicted the School of Architecture, seemingly in a fit of pique at the university's mean treatment of Sir Ronald Ross on his departure from the School of Tropical Medicine, another of his endowments from his libel victory.[32] In the troubled years immediately after the First World War, the future of the old Bluecoat building was again in doubt.

***

The uneasy transition from war to peace hit Liverpool hard – Harrods dropped its plans for a Liverpool store in 1920, a symbolic precursor of the city's downward spiral in the interwar decades. Times were particularly difficult at Liberty Buildings, now entrusted to agents who took little interest in its architectural merit and accepted 'most unsuitable tenants', including umbrella menders and purveyors of women's lingerie. Then in 1925 Leverhulme died, leaving a will that made no provision for the building's preservation. Immediate fears about the future of the building were hardly allayed by an article in the *Liverpool Echo* in July, despite its headline, 'Art and Commerce. No Need for Anxiety about Old Blue Coat School'. New tenants, the Voss Motor Company, had moved in, with Mr Voss explaining that the central hall was 'to be transformed into an up-to-date motor show-room without altering in any way the old world charm of the building as it faces Church-street, all alterations being confined to the *rear* of the building and College-lane'.[33] A few months later advertisements appeared announcing that Liberty Buildings was up for auction, as Leverhulme's executors sought to raise funds to defray death duties. There was no attempt to conceal the obvious consequence: demolition was considered inevitable as the guide price of £40,000 was based on the commercial potential of the site.[34]

This time the city's MPs, local dignitaries and worthies stepped forward, joining the Lord Mayor in a public appeal to raise sufficient funds to save the building ahead of the auction. The architectural case for preservation could be simply stated: 'In a city where everything speaks of modern progress, where practically every monument of the past has been swept away, there remains a building of which any city ought to be proud, a gracious and charming example of one of the most delightful architectural styles.'[35] Sir Leslie Scott, Tory MP for Exchange, warned of the adverse impact on the city's image and reputation should the building be demolished. 'Liverpool is not ancient-history proud', he rued; there was already embarrassment when strangers said, '"Show us something of old Liverpool"':

> If the old Blue Coat School building goes, we shall have nothing of old Liverpool worth showing, except odds and ends laid by in museums. We shall be proved a city so careless of our heritage in old buildings that we allowed the last substantial visible link with our past to disappear.[36]

In a telling contrast with London, a group of prominent academics in the School of Architecture (Charles Reilly, Patrick Abercrombie and Lionel Budden, along with Seymour Conway from the University of Manchester) underlined the singular importance of the Bluecoat in their submission to the Ancient Monuments Society to schedule the building as an ancient monument or at least issue a protective order which would deter purchasers intent on demolition:

> the general effect is of a small college court of most dignified and restful architecture in the early Georgian manner. Placed where it is near to [the] busiest streets in the town and surrounded by modern offices and warehouses it makes a delightful oasis. The buildings themselves are the oldest in the City. If London loses the Foundling Hospital it will still have other Georgian Buildings like parts of the Inns of Court & Queen Anne's Gate. If Liverpool loses Liberty Buildings it will have nothing of the domestic architecture of the eighteenth century left to it.[37]

In the continuing absence of post-war economic recovery, Liverpudlians took a greater interest in the past, a source of inspiration and hope for a better future. In this new appreciation of heritage, safeguarding the best of its past served to reaffirm and encourage the city's commitment to forward-looking civic virtue, enterprise and transformation. J. G. Legge, former Director of Education, deployed an array of what were to become familiar Merseypride tropes, weaving the campaign to save the Bluecoat into a narrative of all that was best (and not merely commercial) in the city's rapid trajectory from obscure past to innovative and enterprising future:

> The more vigorous the life of a modern centre of commercial and industrial enterprise, such as Liverpool, the more valuable any surviving monument that points to a philanthropic or social enterprise in a bygone day, and proves that all through its history there has been the consciousness in the community that man does not live by bread alone. In this regard Liverpool can surely claim to have a record which is unique. Is there any great city in the world where at one moment two such undertakings are in hand as the Mersey Tunnel and the Liverpool Cathedral, each of them bound to be carried forward to completion, and to stand for ever as an achievement of which any capital city might be proud. These will be the works of the twentieth century.[38]

Forsaking retirement in Bath to chair the appeal committee, Fanny Calder trusted that Liverpool's commitment to the future, as attested by the latest great architectural adornments, would ensure a better appreciation of its heritage: 'I cannot believe that Liverpool, who has shown such faith, idealism and love of beauty in building the Cathedral for future generations will at the same time be robbed of this lovely heritage of the past.'[39] In similar manner, E. Guy Dawber, president of RIBA, drew an historical line linking the cathedral back to the Bluecoat: 'It would be a strange anomaly if, at the very moment that Liverpool is erecting a Cathedral, which is attracting world-wide attention, a building of another and earlier page in its history, of great charm and interest, should be destroyed.' Liverpool, he continued,

> is home of one of the best training schools of architecture in the country. What an irony it would be if the citizens of this wealthy city were unable to prevent the sale of such a unique specimen of eighteenth century architecture, an example of good building to all our young architects.[40]

The blending of past and future infused the pamphlet that launched the appeal. The Bluecoat was portrayed as the initial architectural embodiment of the Liverpool spirit, the inspiration for an ever-improving built environment, giving substance and presence (worthy of metropolitan comparison) to civic virtue and commercial enterprise. To jettison such heritage would compromise the city's future:

> we have, set right in the heart of a business community, a building which has, though small in scale, much of the dignity as well as charm of Sir Christopher

Wren's famous east and south fronts of Hampton Court Palace. Thus, the Blue Coat School is historically of great value as the first of the long line of fine buildings, culminating in the Cathedral, that have marked the rise of Liverpool to greatness. In the interests of art and of historical association the loss of so perfect a Queen Anne building cannot be afforded. There would be a certain grim irony in the situation if an ornament to the city, coeval with its first dock, should disappear at the moment Liverpool is embarking on its greatest civic enterprise of the twentieth century, the Mersey Tunnel.[41]

This early articulation of a forward-looking role for conservation and heritage, however, failed to elicit the required financial response.

The economic context in the aftermath of the General Strike was not propitious, as Sir Leslie Scott noted: 'The dislocation of industry through the coal dispute and the long and aggravated depression of shipping makes it a difficult time to raise money.'[42] When Leverhulme's executors agreed to postpone the auction until 17 November to allow more time for funds to be raised, Scott and others intensified their lobbying of the Office of Works for a protective order. 'The case is quite exceptional', Scott assured Lord Peel, 'there is a moral justification for scheduling the building which as a rule is absent.' Although not unsympathetic, Peel was unable to oblige lest it prejudice the auction in a manner unfair to the owner.[43] In a last-ditch effort to prevent the building being sold for demolition, the Lord Mayor arranged for the committee to meet the new Lord Leverhulme in the hope of renegotiating terms. 'It was a disaster', Fanny Calder reported to Scott, noting how Leverhulme was flanked by Sir Edward Sanders and an agent, who were 'cast iron' in their refusal to consider any further delay or reduction in price:

> Instead of a 'friendly talk' LdL [sic] came like a handcuffed prisoner between two policemen evidently quite miserable but saying only what he was told to say … I nearly reduced Leverhulme to tears poor little man by the plea that they had no moral right to do it & that it was a duty to preserve it as his father intended.[44]

Patrick Abercrombie reported in similar manner: '"not a moment's delay in the auction & not a penny off the price" (a sort of Miners' attitude)'.[45] Leverhulme himself was unrepentant about the price, based on £9 10s (£9.50) per square yard, since, as he pointed out to Peel, the Ecclesiastical Commissioners had secured £40 per square yard for the adjoining pro-cathedral site (St Peter's church) on Church Street:

> It is true that the Blue Coat School site is not equal to the pro-Cathedral site but its commercial value per square yard is undoubtedly more than one

quarter of the other. Some other property in the immediate neighbourhood has recently changed hands at £18 per square yard. I mention these facts to show you that the price which we are asking is a reasonable one.[46]

The committee fell into deep dismay and held out little hope, but there were dramatic developments on the very eve of the sale; no sooner had Leverhulme agreed to a further and final three-week delay in the auction date than news arrived of an anonymous donation of £17,100. The donor was subsequently identified as Liverpool solicitor William Ernest Corlett, the very same 'Lover of his Native City' who had donated the first £1,000 to the appeal.[47] After deduction of expenses the appeal had raised about £32,000, so a large mortgage (£8,000) was required to cover the shortfall on the purchase price and to undertake the necessary alterations and repairs (£2,000) to enable the building, renamed as Bluecoat Chambers, to function as an arts centre.[48] The final arrangements for the sale and mortgage were undertaken in January 1927 by the Trustees of Bluecoat Society of Arts in a Deed of Constitution in which they pledged:

> To maintain, carry on, conduct and manage the School Lane property
> (portion of the said Old Blue Coat Hospital) ... as an Institution for the
> purposes and within the meaning of the Literary and Scientific Institutions

Figure 17. The Sandon dining room, relocated to the music room during wartime disruption, early 1940s. Liverpool Record Office, 367 SAN 5/1/7.

Act, 1854, for the promotion of fine arts, literature and science for adult instruction and the diffusion of useful knowledge generally.[49]

Throughout the appeal campaign the emphasis had been placed on safeguarding the building, with little mention of promoting its use as a free or independent arts centre. There was concern that potential donors might be discouraged by the bohemianism associated with the Sandon, whose tenancy and activities continued throughout the crisis period. While still regarded with disdain by some civic worthies, the Sandon had met with greater approval – and not a little metropolitan condescension – when the Society, 'a kind of Three Arts Club composed of people with an urge to do things', put on a concert of music by Holst in the capital: 'There are many little communities of the kind to be found in cities and suburbs, but the Sandon people are a happier collection of talents and pursue better and rarer

Figure 18. Entertainer, writer and musician George Melly (left), who attended Sandon children's parties in the 1930s, with Adrian Henri at the opening of *The Art of Adrian Henri 1955–1985* in 1987. Image courtesy Estate of Adrian Henri.

ambitions than most of their kind.'[50] By this time, however, the Society was starting to lose its radical edge, a process that was to accelerate throughout the interwar years and beyond. A kind of amateur concert society and luncheon club for some members, it was no longer 'a meeting place for those exclusively connected with the arts'; by the 1920s, as George Melly recorded, an 'alleged interest' in the arts was considered 'sufficient justification' for membership. The annual children's party was the highlight of his childhood, while his parents (like other middle-class members) relished the opportunity to take to the boards in review sketches and cabaret saturnalia. When 'in town', his mother would often take young George to lunch at the Society, where he 'was fascinated to meet painters and sculptors in their rough tweed suits, blue or rust coloured shirts and knitted ties. It was proof of another world unconnected with business.'[51]

The initial radicalism and artistic mission still resonated in some quarters, serving to underpin the appeal campaign. The true worth of the Society in pointing the way forward for the rescued building was underlined in a letter to the press by Robert Anning Bell, now a London-based Royal Academician, formerly an instructor in the university's School of Architecture (where Fanny Calder was one of his pupils) and exhibitor in the Sandon's first exhibition of modern art at the Bluecoat in 1908. It was the Sandon, he noted, that had 'first rescued the building from obscurity and since then has demonstrated the value to all the Arts of a focus and centre such as the old Bluecoat building affords'. Furthermore, true to its origins, the Sandon upheld the city's distinctive and original approach to art: 'Liverpool has for long maintained a personality in the world of the Arts, instead of being sucked dry by that octopus, London, and it has increased it in these later years'.[52]

With the building saved from demolition, plans could proceed for a distinctive arts centre. 'The tenants will not be incorporated in a single society, as in the Leverhulme scheme', Fanny Calder explained, 'they will be independent, but, with such a meeting-ground as the building will provide, and with similar tastes and interests to draw them together, there is every prospect that a real and valuable centre will be formed for intellectual and artistic life.'[53] While it was hoped that rental income from the Sandon and other tenants would cover running costs, there was serious doubt in some quarters about the financial viability of an arts centre, given the not inconsiderable burden of mortgage debt and repair costs. With the support of the local press, the Bluecoat appeal was relaunched. 'The late Lord Leverhulme had the fine idea of making Bluecoat Chambers a home of the arts with international connections', the *Daily Post* reminded its readers: 'An institution like that would have given Liverpool a most important metropolitan attribute. There is still time to carry out the scheme. Surely, there are a few wealthy citizens in Liverpool with enough idealism to complete so splendid an enterprise.'[54]

Fundraising for the arts proved even more difficult than the previous appeal to save the building. On the eve of the official opening, Fanny Calder, confident of raising funds, waxed lyrical about the possibilities:

> It has come true, our dream of twenty years ago. We have what we hoped for. The lovely quiet old place has become a true home for all the arts. It is not the old ambitious scheme of 1914, but perhaps none the worse in that the association and combination between the various arts and artists will not be a matter of organisation and rule, but of free and unfettered intercourse, spontaneous and unpremeditated.
>
> Are you realising, oh Liverpool what we have growing in our midst, and that there is nothing anywhere quite like it.[55]

The official opening, however, in March 1929 proved a disappointing launch pad for the appeal, as the guest of honour, Sir William Llewellyn, president of the Royal Academy, was 'not a figure of such outstanding national importance as to attract public interest or catch the imagination of those whose help was needed'.[56] Within a few months the whole project was under serious threat. Amid the financial crisis of autumn 1929 – 'the worst moment in the history of the Society'[57] – donations dried up, income fell short of expenditure, the debt increased as essential repairs and alterations proved costly (the trustees adamantly rejected the charge of extravagance) and there was fear of foreclosure on the mortgage – 'this mortgage is hanging like a thunder-cloud about to burst', Charles Reilly warned in a letter to *The Times*.[58] According to a sensational report in the *Daily Express*, some £8,000 had to be raised 'in one day' if 'Liverpool's "Little Chelsea", the Bluecoat Chambers, is to remain a centre for the artistic and cultural activities of the city'.[59]

With 'characteristic gusto', Reilly (now firmly back in the fold) promoted a range of fundraising initiatives. As money was tight, he called upon erstwhile donors to contribute items to a public auction, 'a great sale of their friends' most precious things' – the gifts, however, W. S. MacCunn, the secretary of the Bluecoat Society, recorded, 'were not of sufficient number or value to justify a public sale by auction'.[60] A cultural polymath with links to the city's main artistic institutions, Reilly arranged for the house receipts of the performance of *Jane's Legacy* at the Playhouse on 18 December 1929 to be donated to the appeal, also boosted by the first of what proved to be fairly regular gifts (normally of £500) from Lord Leverhulme.[61] Reilly also persuaded the owners of Jacob Epstein's *Genesis*, a controversial sculpture of a pregnant woman, to allow it to be exhibited by the Sandon in the summer of 1931 for the benefit of the Bluecoat appeal. A kind of cultural 'freak show', it proved a staggering success, attracting large crowds and returning a profit of £1,026: 'During the month 49,687 people paid sixpence each to gaze at her, some, the newspapers reported, to froth at the mouth, others to be baffled and some, it was said, with reverence.'[62] In an effort to maximise rental income, the concert hall and lecture rooms were let for purposes that fell short of the cultural aspirations of the trustees, as MacCunn recorded in the first *Annual Report*: 'In view of the purpose to which the building is dedicated one would like to see a higher percentage of concerts and a lower percentage of dances, but that, I am afraid, will have to wait until the tastes and social habits of Liverpool show signs of regeneration.'[63]

One of the more eye-catching money-raising initiatives was a fashion display in February 1930 involving some 30–40 mannequins, 400 gowns and £25,000 worth of jewellery, attended by the Lady Mayoress in the afternoon and addressed by F. J. Marquis in the evening.[64] Marquis (later Lord Woolton) was a leading figure in the Liverpool Organization for Advancing the Trade and Commerce of Liverpool, a group of businessman keen to promote much-needed economic diversification as the once great seaport fell further into depression. With a fine commercial instinct for the value of publicity (derived from his promotion of Lewis's department store), he appreciated that 'if we were going to meet with any success in our efforts to interest people in the possibilities of Liverpool as an industrial centre, we had first to interest them in Liverpool'. An early exercise in civic boosterism, the Liverpool Organization promoted a repackaged view of Liverpool history, a track record of hard graft, dynamism and enterprise to attract inward investors. Liverpool's heritage of independent, no-nonsense toughness offered a set of transferable skills, previously deployed to secure commercial pre-eminence, now ripe for industrial application.[65]

While some looked to history and heritage as inspiration for a better future, others relapsed into nostalgia as economic depression deepened. Under the epigraph, 'Liverpool's story is the world's glory', the Society of Lovers of Old Liverpool achieved remarkable unity across socio-economic, political and sectarian divisions. In his lectures, Robert Gladstone tried to imbue a sense of the truly venerable, claiming that Liverpool 'of world-fame as a sea-port, is also a place of very considerable antiquity – though it must be admitted that there are no visible evidences of that antiquity now remaining'. For most members of the society, however, 'old' Liverpool was not antique but within living memory: above all, it signified the good times that were now slipping away. Most lectures reminisced about the practices and characters of yesteryear in commerce, professions and on the docks. Driven by nostalgia, history was being transmuted into heritage, intended for internal reassurance.[66] When Fanny Calder learned from Robert Gladstone that the

Society of Lovers of Old Liverpool had ceased to exist in 1935, 'not for lack of funds or of enthusiasm but simply for lack of material for research', she promptly suggested that subscriptions and funds should be redirected into the appeal to maintain and support the Bluecoat: 'We have but this one treasure left to us to cherish, and surely the antiquarians of Liverpool, either as individuals or as a body, might give a little help.'[67]

The financial plight of the Bluecoat mirrored the deepening economic decline of Liverpool, sadly portrayed in the *Liverpolitan*, the leading local periodical, as 'a stagnant city, commercially, administratively, and culturally'. 'A plague spot of unemployment', the local rate remained resolutely above 18 per cent throughout the 1930s, double the national average.[68] 'Here, in Liverpool', the *Annual Report* for 1932 recorded, 'we are well aware of the depth and magnitude of the depression; it affects every department of our lives and drastically curtails the power of generous giving which has always characterised this city.'[69] Energies and effort were expended principally on trying to cope with debt management and reduction, the essential aim being 'to preserve the old Bluecoat building for all time'. It was little short of a heroic struggle:

> So far we have managed to avert destruction from the only old building of architectural value which Liverpool possesses: we have provided a home for artistic societies and for painters, sculptors and architects who, in their several ways, are enriching the life of the city. The work which we are doing is too valuable to be abandoned until every possible effort has been made to bring it to a successful issue.[70]

Even after the boost of the *Genesis* exhibition, the committee was doubtful of the future:

> Whether we go on depends on our power to collect the necessary money to insure the preservation of the building, and the continuance of the active and varied life which it contains. If we can do this we shall have done much for Liverpool, and, indeed, for the larger world of those who care for the furtherance of the arts and believe that they are of vital importance to the life of a healthy community.[71]

It was not just the continuing 'bad state of trade in Liverpool' that hindered fundraising efforts. A further factor was the ongoing dispersal of the middle classes:

> One of the curious things about Liverpool today was that the proprietors of businesses, perhaps owing to improved transport, were leaving Liverpool as

a residential centre. At first the trend was to Wirral, and now it was to North Wales, and even further. Perhaps that was the reason why the Bluecoat appeal had not so far been as successful as it might be.[72]

There was a similar trend taking its toll on the Sandon as members deserted the sandstone ridge – Liverpool's once fashionable 'high' cultural spine – adjacent to the city centre:

> already before the war those lived nearby with only a quarter of an hour's walk to School Lane from the area of Falkner Square, Canning and Huskisson Streets, Bedford and Chatham Streets, Percy Street and Gambier Terrace gradually moved away as the neighbourhoods deteriorated. Members were getting more affluent and older and living in Wirral or in comfortable retirement further south. When the second war came something had ebbed away for ever.[73]

The financial travails notwithstanding, the committee stuck to its principles and rejected schemes which might clear the mortgage and secure the building, but at the expense of removing or reducing facilities for the arts. MacCunn provides extensive coverage of the somewhat 'delicate' discussions in 1937–38 with the Liverpool Council of Social Service, which offered to pay off the mortgage (then standing at £15,300) in order to take over the building (and the Trust) to bring the various voluntary social services together under one roof. There was some lip service to 'cultural activities', but the scheme required the eviction of virtually all the sitting tenants. Having rejected the proposal (and subsequent modified offers which at least preserved a role for Bluecoat Society of Arts), the committee reaffirmed its commitment to the building as 'a centre for those who practise or are interested in fine arts', with the Sandon as principal tenant.[74] The struggle for funds continued, made all the more difficult by the outbreak of the Second World War in 1939: 'We cannot expect present help in the form of donations or subscriptions, but those who wish to insure the preservation of the building can make provision for help in the future (possibly the remote future) by including in their will legacies to the Bluecoat Society of Arts.'[75]

∗∗∗

Having survived interwar economic adversity, the Bluecoat was damaged during the Luftwaffe raids of May 1941, a blitz that devastated much of the city centre. 'The old Bluecoat Building, that gem of old Liverpool, has suffered from enemy action', the *Liverpool Echo* reported:

but Merseyside folk and others will be glad to know that it can be made secure until the whole building is reconditioned. The cost of these 'first-aid' repairs, however, will be about £1,000 and, as the damage has taken away some three-quarters of the income from upkeep, a further £1,000 a year will have to be raised until the building is restored.[76]

Although relieved that 'the damage has not destroyed the historic interest or architectural value of the building', MacCunn (ever the accountant) regarded the economic consequences as devastating: with three-quarters of the building no longer habitable, rental income was down to 'the very small amount of about £450 a year'.[77] In a no less characteristic reaction, the Sandon displayed its resilience and resolve by organising a 'To Hell with Hitler' party.[78] Ironically and in retrospect, the blitz damage came to be seen in positive terms as revealing the true worth of the building:

> It is a wry commentary on human progress that the Bluecoat should have suffered more from the insidious encroachments of commerce than from the indiscriminate ravishments of war. Indeed, there is a sense in which the air raid of May 1941 may be held to have performed a service, for it blew away a much disfigured part of the building and made such an eloquent shell of much

Figure 19. Bomb damage to the central core during the Liverpool blitz, May 1941.

of the remainder that public consciousness was quickly aroused. Perhaps the beauty at the far end of School Lane had been too much taken for granted, or it may be the flattening of a great commercial block in front of the Bluecoat opened up a new and exciting view of the ruins.[79]

Thenceforth the 'reconditioning' of the Bluecoat was in the forefront of hopes and aspirations for the post-war reconstruction of Liverpool. The most controversial proposal, developed in some secrecy, sought a dramatic extension to the wartime arrangement by which the Bluecoat provided exhibition space for the Walker Art Gallery, closed to the public (until 1951) after having been requisitioned throughout the war and beyond by the Ministry of Food. Having previously criticised the Walker's permanent collection as 'utterly unworthy of the second city of the Empire', Colonel Cotton, city councillor and member of the Bluecoat executive committee, trusted to elevate the city's standing in post-war Britain by developing a new municipal gallery of fine art at the Bluecoat. As the numbers attending the wartime (mainly patriotic) exhibitions had shown, the Bluecoat offered a more accessible and popular location than the Walker.[80] The Libraries, Museums and Arts Committee duly submitted to the Corporation's Post War Planning Committee 'a proposal that the old Bluecoat building (Bluecoat Chambers) should be used as a nucleus of a new Gallery for the fine arts (with possible addition of a Shipping Gallery and Central Lending Library) to be built to the site bounded by School Lane, Peter's Lane, College Lane and Hanover Street'. MacCunn and the Bluecoat executive committee readily appreciated the financial advantages of the plan and promptly informed the Town Clerk of their enthusiasm for the project, 'provided the Corporation on their part will take over responsibility for the existing mortgages', retain the architectural integrity of the building, undertake alterations and additions in sympathetic manner and ensure 'reasonable accommodation for Societies connected with Arts and for individual artists, having special regard to existing tenants'.[81] When the artists themselves finally learned of the proposal, however, there was outrage. 'Architects, painters, musicians and lovers of the arts are seriously alarmed at the prospect of the building being municipalised', the 1946 *Annual Report* recorded: 'in place of being a home of "live" art, the old Bluecoat building would become merely a museum'.[82] In the local press the artists explained that

> they recognise the importance of the Permanent Collection for educational purposes, but stress the necessity to them of having a place 'where we can live together, work and exhibit ... We feel that to divert the Bluecoat Society of Arts, from serving living creative art, to housing that which has been mainly produced by deceased artists would be a disaster.'[83]

As Bisson recorded, the threat of municipal museumification and the consequent delay in repairing the war damage contributed to the mood of austere post-war bleakness among members of the Sandon:

> There was no sudden quickening of the life of the place as there had been following the First World War. Certainly meals were served and periodicals came on time. There were exhibitions of painting and recitals of music and there was always the pleasure of people meeting each other again after an absence of years. The spirit, the tempo, of the years before the war had gone.[84]

For the next couple of years, the executive committee of the Bluecoat, still convinced that Cotton's plan was a financial imperative given the level of debt, waited in vain for negotiations with the city council to commence. Stirred into action by the threat to the site from the proposed inner ring road, they finally took matters into their own hands: architects were instructed to draw up plans to send to the War Damage Commission; pending their approval and the reopening of the entire building, funds were secured from the recently established Arts Council to cover annual deficits, enabling the Bluecoat 'to carry on until the building is earning a full rental'.[85] Thanks to this financial cushion, the prudent MacCunn was uncharacteristically optimistic as he awaited the repairs (somewhat in contrast to the mood Bisson recorded among the Sandon). Three annual exhibitions between 1945 and 1947, entitled 'Recording Merseyside', attracted large numbers and led to a number of acquisitions by local authorities on both sides of the river. 'The great private patron belongs to a past age', MacCunn observed, as he called upon 'the great commercial undertakings that carry on business in Liverpool' to join the local authorities in acquiring art:

> I suggest that they might commission works illustrative of their many-sided activities or of the building (or rebuilding) of their stores, warehouses, factories and offices. Such pictures would have an immediate publicity value and in time to come would provide a most interesting pictorial history of our commercial life.
>
> In this way Liverpool would become the home of a number of valuable semi-private, semi-public collections, and Liverpool painters would be encouraged to remain in Liverpool, recording its life and building up a school of painting characteristic of a great seaport and a great city.[86]

In the *Annual Report* for 1947 he spoke of 'a renaissance of painting in Liverpool comparable to that of forty years ago, when Augustus John and Gerard Chowne were working and teaching here':

Indeed the arts generally are in a more flourishing state than they have been for many years, and there has been a notable increase in public interest in serious drama, in ballet and in music, as well as in painting. Already much of the future accommodation in the building has been allocated to societies and painters who will be most desirable tenants, and it is certain that there will not be room for all who wish to find a home here. Unquestionably Bluecoat Chambers will be the centre of a very vigorous and varied artistic life.[87]

The repair work finally got under way in 1949 alongside the Corporation's scheme for the reconstruction of forty-six and a quarter acres 'in the heart of Liverpool's bombed shopping area, some of the most valuable land in the kingdom', approved by the Minister of Town and Country Planning on condition that 'careful consideration should be given to the old Bluecoat School in order to safeguard its architectural and historic importance'.[88] Thanks to lobbying by the Georgian Group and others, the Ministry of Works agreed that the Bluecoat was of sufficient national importance and historic interest for gold leaf, an item in short and restricted supply, to be made available for the surround and numerals of its single-handed clock. 'Though the clock face is not of structural importance', MacCunn acknowledged, 'its absence has the same effect on the appearance of the main elevation as the absence of a front tooth on an otherwise pleasing human face.'[89] With the release of the gold leaf, the repairs were all but complete in time for the Festival of Britain in 1951, enabling the Bluecoat to take a 'prominent place' in the local festivities coordinated from the office of the festival director located in the building. Around the strapline, '"To-morrow's Tide" – a theme to re-awaken self-confidence, regenerate energy, and so enliven the local scene that our very blitzed sites become symbols of resurrection', Liverpool enjoyed 'a Festival of the people for the people', the 'finest show outside London and one which has attracted visitors from all over the world'.[90]

The reopening of the Bluecoat symbolised the new spirit of self-confidence. Furnished and equipped to the highest standard, the concert hall was opened in April 1951 by Sir Ernest Pooley, chair of the Arts Council, the principal funders of the refurbishment.[91] As the full complement of the 'Bluecoat Chambers art coterie' moved back into redesigned studios and workshops in 'Liverpool's little Chelsea', the trustees contemplated the possible attainment of long-desired financial self-sufficiency:

Now that the building has been reconstructed they hope soon to become self-supporting from the rents of studios and clubrooms and the hiring out of the concert hall. Thus, despite Liverpool's appetite for building sites in the centre of the city, Bluecoat Chambers still stand, a monument to the graces of

Queen Anne architecture and a spur to the artists, craftsmen and architects of Liverpool to-day.[92]

The Bluecoat, it seemed, was on the verge of historic change. 'We start a new chapter with the present year', the executive committee reported in 1951:

> The centre block and the east wing are restored; we have a number of new tenants; and the prospects for the concert hall are good. We can claim, without misgiving, that we are carrying out the purposes of the Trust. The restoration of the architectural beauty of the building is nearing completion; and, with a number of cultural societies and serious, professional painters, sculptors and craftsmen as our tenants, with the provision of a first-class concert hall that will also be an excellent gallery, as well as a small art gallery (leased to the Corporation of Liverpool), we have established a vigorous and fruitful art centre.[93]

In a letter to *The Times*, Lionel Budden, one of the original trustees, sought national recognition for what had been achieved at Bluecoat Chambers in the years of post-war austerity:

> It has now been almost completely restored and is once more fully occupied by a community of architects, painters, sculptors, craftsmen and cultural societies ... the whole centre is again contributing vigorously to the artistic life of the city. This, surely, is an achievement worthy of record in any account of what has been accomplished in Liverpool during years of extraordinary difficulty.[94]

On a subsequent visit to the city, the arts correspondent of *The Times* praised the Bluecoat as 'an institution to which the overloaded term "unique" is surely applicable':

> as the visitor walks round this handsome spacious building and sees all this activity concentrated, in the commercial centre of the city, on practical artistic creation of the most varied kind, he cannot but reflect that Liverpool may have much to teach other cities about those vexed and endemic problems of the relationship between the patron and the artist and of the place of the artist in contemporary society.[95]

After the excitement of the reopening and the activities associated with the Festival of Britain, 1952 marked a return to the more familiar burden of fundraising to meet deficits not covered by the War Damage Commission. The local press helped

Figure 20. Sandon Studios Society Jubilee Exhibition in the refurbished concert hall, 1953. The Sandon was formed in 1905, so this celebration was a little premature. Photo: W. T. Maxfield. Liverpool Record Office, 367 SAN/3/3/13.

launch a new appeal under the heading 'City's Arts' Centre Unique in Europe': 'So far as the trustees are aware Bluecoat Chambers is now the only centre of artistic life of its kind in Europe.'[96] Within a few years, however, the Bluecoat at last became self-supporting, free of the need to apply for Arts Council funding to meet annual expenses. MacCunn's business-like history of Bluecoat Chambers, published in 1956 with the subtitle, 'the Origins and Development of an Art Centre', was a fitting tribute to this hard-won achievement – sadly the long-standing mortgage to Royal Insurance was not paid off until 1969, a couple of years after his death. Capturing the mood of self-congratulation, Viscount Kilmuir supplied a foreword imbued with Merseypride of the highest order:

> To one who enjoyed the high privilege of being a representative of the City in Parliament for nearly twenty years, it has always been an inspiration that our intense civic pride was never limited to political and economic affairs. Liverpool has always been a nursing mother to education in, and the practice of, all the Arts. This book is the story of the preservation in the bomb scarred

centre of our City of a lovely building in its pristine architectural beauty, and
the establishment of a well-equipped centre of the Arts ... the aims were
achieved by a voluntary band of enthusiasts united in their objectives and
united in the determined courage and imagination on which Liverpool can
always call.[97]

Having reached the landmark of financial self-sufficiency, the Bluecoat was able
to move forward through a series of grants secured from the Calouste Gulbenkian
Foundation, awarded on the understanding that funds were to be used for
encouragement of the arts, not for the maintenance of the building or the reduction
of pre-war debt. As the executive committee acknowledged in its 1957 report, the
first such grant 'opens up a new chapter in our history and gives us a magnificent
opportunity of doing what we have always hoped to do – provide help for practising
artists and opportunities for the study of the arts to those who are seriously
interested'.[98] For the next three years, the Bluecoat used the Gulbenkian funds to
mount an annual fortnight-long festival (during which the building was floodlit)
to celebrate the art and culture of particularly important historical periods: 'The
Augustan Age', 'Victorian High Noon' and 'The Turn of the Century'.

Although the Sandon had mounted an exhibition of *Fifty Years of Liverpool Art*
during the Festival of Britain,[99] Bluecoat artists were best known for the embrace
of the contemporary and experimental rather than the retrospective and historical
(hence their earlier rejection of municipal 'dead art'). In the early 1960s, however,
the Bluecoat came under criticism for its continual harking back to the past and
its lack of self-confidence for the experimental. In an undated article in the local
press, Peter Preston bemoaned 'a cultural heart starved of blood', citing the failure
to make best use of either the dynamic potential of the Gulbenkian grants or the
resources of the recently formed Bluecoat Arts Forum.[100] Established in 1961, the
Forum sought to improve contact between the executive committee and the various
cultural societies and individual tenants, 'an important step towards realisation of
one of the original ambitions of the founders of our Society, the establishment of
a true Centre of the Arts in Liverpool'.[101] Preston called upon the Forum to look
outward to 'rout the critics': 'the Bluecoat Forum, if they wish to break through the
closed circle of apathy and conservatism, may have to look outside for the freshness
to capitalise on present material assets and considerable progress'. As it was, *Bluecoat
63*, the next annual celebration funded by the Gulbenkian grant and the city council,
eschewed the historical in order to showcase the artistic production of the Bluecoat
itself, 'making the work of the various cultural societies and individual artists in
the building, and also other members of the Bluecoat Arts Forum, better known to

the public'.[102] By this time, however, the Bluecoat had decided to use a 'substantial portion' of the Gulbenkian grant in more imaginative and forward-looking manner by 'the appointment of an Adviser to consider the whole state of the Arts in Liverpool and the further services this Society might in future afford them'.[103]

By a fortunate coincidence, John Willett, assistant editor of the *Times Literary Supplement*, was appointed to consider the role of 'Art in a City' around the same time that Graeme Shankland, planning consultant to the city, established a separate City Planning Department (headed by Walter Bor) to 'revitalise' the city centre and 'safeguard its future'.[104] Willett responded in synergetic manner, insisting that art in a city such as Liverpool 'should above all be linked firmly to the great schemes for replanning and redevelopment'. While presented to the Bluecoat, his proposals, 'part of the city's plan for reconstruction and redevelopment', were addressed to all those 'concerned about the future of Liverpool, its buildings and its educational system, its reputation and the general sense of life in the city'. The Bluecoat duly found itself the catalyst in pioneer promotion of culture-led urban regeneration: 'although there are many things here that the Bluecoat Society can do on its own I would ask it first to father the whole plan, to sponsor discussion of it and to make it a Bluecoat Plan for the future of visual arts in Liverpool'.[105]

While lagging behind Rotterdam and other continental cities in post-war reconstruction, Liverpool proved a timely test-bed exemplar for Willett's cultural project. In the course of his research – *Art in a City* was not published until 1967 – Liverpool caught the public imagination primarily through the efflorescence of Merseybeat. Encouraged by a number of other developments, such as the space-age architecture of the new Catholic cathedral and the success of the biennial John Moores painting prize, Willett drew up a 'plan of campaign' to 'humanize and beautify the reconstruction of the city', to embellish and strengthen Liverpool's identity 'both to its own citizens and to outsiders':

> It would stimulate national and international interest in Liverpool and reinforce the picture of a genuinely resurgent city. It would arouse a mixture of controversy, pride and delight in the city itself. It would help to attract lively-minded people to Liverpool, as visitors or citizens. It would encourage the younger generation to express itself visually as well as through pop music. It would give work to Liverpool artists and strengthen their position as a distinctive school. It would breathe new life into the existing art institutions: the gallery, the College of Art, the Academy. It would also be a comprehensive operation such as had never been launched before, and it could have historic results for the visual arts.[106]

Already enthused by Minister for the Arts Jennie Lee's plans for provincial arts centres aided by public funds, the Bluecoat, self-proclaimed 'pioneers in the field', responded warmly to Willett's manuscript.[107] Having set the course, the Bluecoat trusted that Liverpool would assume national leadership in the arts through 'a new and socially advanced civic patronage'.[108] However, Willett's priority proposal, the appointment of a public art advisor responsible to the Corporation, went unheeded. Public art and culture were marginalised amid the daunting problems of urban renewal in the 'city of change and challenge'. In the following decades, history and geography turned decisively against Liverpool. Once development aid and other short-term advantages were exhausted, industrial combines were apt to close their new Merseyside plants ahead of branches elsewhere. Here, of course, Merseyside militancy – a myth in the making – helped to justify a boardroom decision taken far away from Liverpool.[109] Thereafter, with the collapse of the colonial economic system and global restructuring – the 'triple whammy' of the end of empire, the introduction of containerisation and eventual entry into the European Economic Community – Liverpool's descent into the 'shock city' of post-colonial, post-industrial Britain appeared unstoppable. During the 1980s employment and population fell by 23 and 12 per cent respectively; by the early 1990s the level of GDP per head stood at only 73 per cent of the European Union average.[110]

Throughout these difficult times, the Bluecoat steadfastly upheld its mission as 'the cultural powerhouse of Liverpool' with 'absolutely nothing merely historical or museum-like about its work'.[111] 'The Bluecoat Society belongs to *the world of culture* in Liverpool', *The Times* reported, 'and to the other world of the culture of Liverpool.'[112] As an arts centre, the Bluecoat was characterised by what Bryan Biggs has described as 'the collision of the worlds of the amateur and high art, the coming together of voluntary effort, collective enthusiasm and the drive of passionate individuals'.[113] Balancing the books remained a problem, compounded by public misconception about the nature of the operation: 'Unfortunately a large proportion of the population regards Bluecoat Chambers as a public building and expects the sort of service which libraries, museums and galleries are in a position to give and this does place a great strain on our overstretched resources.'[114] By appealing to popular tastes, however, the Bluecoat hoped to make ends meet:

> We are always trying to attract commercial bookings, particularly outside
> the normal concert season, hoping as we have in the past, that commerce will
> help to subsidize the arts but we have only made small inroads in this field
> … However, one or two-day fairs of all descriptions, selling books, coins,
> stamps and antiques are very popular and have helped to increase revenue.[115]

> One's only regret is that our usual exhibitions and concerts do not result in such queues in the forecourt![116]

Inevitably rents had to be put up. Already the gallery had increased the cost of hiring its space, leading to protests by Arthur Dooley and other artists, members of the self-styled 'Railings Union' who boycotted the building and displayed their work (and registered their protest) in the open gaze of the public.[117] Thereafter, on Saturdays, the railings at the front of Bluecoat became a sort of salon des refusés for local artists.

As the great 'beat city' of the 1960s transmogrified into the 'beaten city' of the Thatcherite years, the Bluecoat found itself out of place, no longer proud of its city centre location. 'A sad sign of the times was the departure from the Bluecoat of the Liverpool Lieder Circle, whose home it had been since its inception in 1968',[118] the *Annual Report* for 1981 recorded: 'The Circle had found that audiences had declined, partly due to the fact that members were less inclined to come into the city at night.' A 'no-go' area for the suburban middle class, the city centre was prone to crime:

> One of the Bluecoat's double-edged virtues is its prime site in the city centre, and this year we suffered in the wave of burglaries that swept the inner city. Six burglaries within the space of three months, involving repeated shattering of the majority of the internal doors, as well as of the peace of mind of the staff and tenants.[119]

After a succession of ill-fated projects to tackle multiple deprivation, culture-led regeneration – almost a last-ditch option – managed to reverse the downward collapse, at least for city-centre 'Livercool'. By historical irony, Liverpool, a relative latecomer to urban regeneration, was well placed to attract 'creative classes' and cultural tourists, as well as to promote well-being among its residents. While badly damaged by the Second World War blitz, the remarkable waterfront and the commercial and public architecture of England's finest Victorian city subsequently escaped some of the worst excesses of late twentieth-century 'planning' vandalism, perhaps the one advantage of the city's declining fortunes at the time. Following the arrival of Tate Liverpool, the 'Tate of the North', at the refurbished Albert Dock in 1988, culture-led regeneration thrived amid this inherited built environment. The population of the city centre increased some fourfold in the final decade of the twentieth century as the rich legacy of vacated warehouses, lofts and old office buildings were converted into bijou apartments, wine bars and hotels, the latest exercise in the recycling of city-centre space. In 2004 this 'historic' and 'cultural' core gained UNESCO inscription as the Liverpool Maritime Mercantile City World Heritage Site. Alongside the monuments of Victorian and Edwardian grandeur, the Bluecoat is accorded a more venerable place, linked to the warehouses and merchants' houses of the Lower Duke Street area, historic buildings which contribute much to the character of the 'Rope Walks', the parallel narrow streets that now provide the main focus of the city's thriving nightlife and creative industries sector (though now being slowly eradicated by private-sector development).[120]

In the course of this transformation, funded by a variety of agencies and authorities (European, national and regional) with resources beyond those previously at the disposal of the local council, Liverpool acquired Willett's desideratum: a visual arts infrastructure unrivalled in the UK outside London.[121] Here was a crucial asset in securing European Capital of Culture status in 2008. The success of the Capital of Culture year, the occasion for *Art in a City* to be republished and 'revisited', prompted further emphasis on culture, the arts and creative industries, now recognised for their contribution as the principal driver of economic growth in and of themselves in the new 'Livercool'.

One of the jewels of the World Heritage Site, the Bluecoat now finds itself in the most enviable of locations, linking the traditional city centre shopping area with the new Liverpool One development. The premises themselves were extended in most sympathetic and exciting manner by the Rotterdam architects Biq Architecten. 'Muscular in its material qualities and its insistence on usability', this 'robust renewal', much praised in the architectural press, restored the original 'H'-shaped Queen Anne design while providing purpose-built galleries and a performance space. Rough and ready concrete (promptly labelled 'Béton Scouse') attested to the open character of the place: as *Architectural Design* noted approvingly of this arts and community centre: 'There's nothing effete about the Bluecoat.'[122] Opened for the Capital of Culture year, it is perhaps the most important legacy of that transient festival. A most fitting example of the blending of the old and the contemporary, it offers a standing rebuke to a new generation of developers with seemingly little regard for heritage and culture.

Throughout its history since 1907 the Bluecoat has pointed the way forward, showing the value of regeneration through conservation and creative activity. The lesson of the Bluecoat – that redevelopment and conservation should not be polarised in debate – needs to be relearned if Liverpool is to retain its distinctive character and World Heritage status.

Notes

1 As Bryan Biggs has noted, 'there is a strong argument for claiming that the Bluecoat's transformation from school to working arts building represents an early, perhaps even the first, example of arts-led urban regeneration'; see his essay 'Radical Art City?', in John Belchem and Bryan Biggs, eds, *Liverpool: City of Radicals*, Liverpool: Liverpool University Press, 2011, p. 68.

2 R. F. Bisson, *The Sandon Studios Society and the Arts*, Liverpool: Parry Books, published on behalf of the Sandon Studios Society, 1965, p. 37.

3 Walter Dixon Scott, *Liverpool*, London, 1907, p. 6; Ramsay Muir, *A History of Liverpool*, London: Williams and Norgate for the University Press of Liverpool, 1907, pp. 1–6.

4 William Enfield, *An Essay towards the History of Leverpool*, London, 1774, p. 90.

5 'Liverpool: port, docks and city', *Illustrated London News*, 15 May 1886.

6 For an assessment of Muir's history and the 1907 celebrations, see John Belchem, 'Liverpool's story is the world's glory', in *Merseypride: Essays in Liverpool Exceptionalism*, Liverpool: Liverpool University Press, 2nd edn, 2006, pp. 3–30.

7 For progressive Edwardian Liverpool, see John Belchem, 'Radical prelude: 1911', in Belchem and Biggs, eds, *Liverpool: City of Radicals*, pp. 14–40.

8 'Some diversions of a great city. An impression of the cultural life in Liverpool and Merseyside', *The Times*, 5 April 1956.

9 C. H. Reilly, *Scaffolding in the Sky: A Semi-architectural Autobiography*, London: Routledge, 1938, p. 134.

10 *The Sport of Civic Life, or Art and the Municipality*, Liverpool, 1909, p. 12. See also Edward Morris and Timothy Stevens, *History of the Walker Art Gallery, Liverpool 1873–2000*, Bristol: Sansom, 2013, chs 1 and 2.

11 *Sport of Civic Life*, p. 4.

12 Quoted in T. Kelly, *For Advancement of Learning: The University of Liverpool 1881–1981*, Liverpool: Liverpool University Press, 1981, p. 127.

13 Reilly, *Scaffolding in the Sky*, p. 77.

14 W. S. MacCunn, *Bluecoat Chambers. The Origins and Development of an Art Centre*, Liverpool: Liverpool University Press, 1956, pp. 3–10 and Appendix B. See also Kelly, *For Advancement of Learning*, pp. 146–47; and Reilly, *Scaffolding in the Sky*, p. 68.

15 MacCunn, *Bluecoat Chambers*, Appendix B, p. 78.

16 *Liverpool Daily Post*, 27 July 1926.

17 Peter Richmond, *Marketing Modernisms: The Architecture and Influence of Charles Reilly*, Liverpool: Liverpool University Press, 2001, pp. 57–72; MacCunn, *Bluecoat Chambers*, Appendix A.

18 Stuart Hodgson, ed., *Ramsay Muir: An Autobiography and Some Essays*, London: Lund Humphries, 1943, p. 79.

19 Richmond, *Marketing Modernisms*, p. 68.

20 Charles W. Smith, *Commercial Gambling: The Principal Causes of Depression in Agriculture and Trade*, London, 1893, pp. v–vi.

21 Quoted in Richmond, *Marketing Modernisms*, pp. 67–68.

22 Calder to Legge, 12 March 1914, and Lever to Abercrombie, May 1914, quoted in MacCunn, *Bluecoat Chambers*, pp. 71, 10. Correspondence between Calder and Lever, 1914, quoted in Bisson, *The Sandon Studios Society*, pp. 103–04.

23 Muir, *A History of Liverpool*, p. 340.

24 S. D. Adshead and P. Abercrombie, eds, *Liverpool Town Planning and Housing Exhibition*, Liverpool: Liverpool University Press, 1914.

25 'Post-Impressionist pictures and others', *Manchester Guardian*, 6 March 1911. For the exhibition, see Biggs, 'Radical art city?', pp. 62–66.

26 *Sandon Bulletin*, March 1912, quoted in Bisson, *The Sandon Studios Society*, p. 76.

27 Bisson, *The Sandon Studios Society*, p. 59.

28 Krista Cowman, *Mrs Brown is a Man and a Brother. Women in Merseyside's Political Organisations, 1890–1920*, Liverpool: Liverpool University Press, 2004, p. 80.

29 Fred Bower, *Rolling Stonemason: An Autobiography*, London: Jonathan Cape, 1936, pp. 120–22.

30 Bisson, *The Sandon Studios Society*, pp. 99–100.

31 Leverhulme to Calder, 7 November 1918, quoted in MacCunn, *Bluecoat Chambers*, pp. 11–12. Calder's letters in *Daily Post*, 6 August 1926 and 28 February 1929.

32 Bisson, *The Sandon Studios Society*, pp. 104–05.

33 *Liverpool Echo*, 25 July 1925.

34 MacCunn, *Bluecoat Chambers*, p. 14. There is an advertisement for the auction (and a telegram on its postponement) in the Office of Works file at the National Archives, Kew: WORK 14/2030: Liverpool, Lancs: The Bluecoat School: Purchase by public subscription, 1927; advice on war damage restoration.

35 *Liverpool Echo*, 29 October 1926.

36 'Old Blue Coat Hospital. Sir Leslie Scott's Appeal', *Liverpool Post and Mercury*, 1 November 1926.

37 WORK 14/2030.

38   *Liverpool Post*, 6 August 1926.

39   *Liverpool Post*, 6 August 1926.

40   *Post and Mercury*, 3 November 1926.

41   *Save the Old Blue Coat Hospital: Liverpool Appeal*, pamphlet in WORK 14/2030.

42   *Liverpool Post and Mercury*, 1 November 1926.

43   See the correspondence between Scott and Peel, in WORK 14/2030.

44   Calder to Scott, 13 November 1926, in WORK 14/2030.

45   Abercrombie to Scott, 13 November 1926, in WORK 14/2030.

46   Leverhulme to Peel, 12 November 1926, in WORK 14/2030.

47   One-time *Liverpool Echo* editor E. Hope Prince, who was involved in the fundraising campaign, recalled telling Corlett of the situation on the train to work one morning; the solicitor then took him to his office, where he wrote out a cheque for £17,100, saying 'Don't tell a soul.' *Daily Post*, 9 September 1975. This article, 'The cheque in time that saved a school', reports on a commemorative plaque to Corlett, whose family attended its unveiling in the Bluecoat garden that day.

48   MacCunn, *Bluecoat Chambers*, pp. 22–23.

49   Deed of Constitution, 28 January 1927, in WORK 14/2030.

50   Quoted in Bisson, *The Sandon Studios Society*, p. 156.

51   George Melly, *Scouse Mouse*, pp. 72–75 in *Owning Up: The Trilogy*, Harmondsworth: Penguin, 2000.

52   *Liverpool Daily Post*, 9 March 1929.

53   'Old Blue Coat Hospital. Its future use', *Liverpool Daily Post and Mercury*, 29 November 1926.

54   *Daily Post*, 26 February 1929.

55   'A Liverpool dream come true', *Liverpool Daily Post*, 28 February 1929.

56   MacCunn, *Bluecoat Chambers*, p. 29.

57   MacCunn, *Bluecoat Chambers*, p. 29.

58   See Reilly's letter to *The Times*, 22 May 1930, and his article in *Country Life*, 19 April 1930.

59   *Daily Express*, 1 October 1930.

60   *Daily Mail*, 2 November 1929; *Daily Post*, 13 January 1930; and *Liverpool Post and Mercury*, 2 April 1930. MacCunn, *Bluecoat Chambers*, p. 30.

61   *Liverpool Echo*, 11 December 1929; *Daily Post*, 13 January 1930.

62   MacCunn, *Bluecoat Chambers*, p. 31; Bisson, *The Sandon Studios Society*, p. 174.

63   *Bluecoat Society of Arts Annual Report 1930*, p. 4.

64   'Saving the "Bluecoat". Modern fashions in old building', *Liverpool Daily Post*, 14 February 1930.

65   Belchem, 'Liverpool's story is the world's glory', pp. 26–27.

66   See the cuttings on the Society in the Athenaeum Library: Gladstone Miscellaneous Pamphlets, 139.

67   'The Old Bluecoat', *Liverpool Post and Mercury*, 15 May 1935.

68   Among the most serious (and depressing) articles are 'Between ourselves', 'What is wrong with Liverpool?', 'The ebbing tide of Liverpool's trade', 'The struggle for existence', and 'The plight of a great city', *Liverpolitan*, July and September 1932, October 1933, and January 1935.

69   *Bluecoat Society of Arts Annual Report 1932*, pp. 3–4.

70   *Bluecoat Society of Arts Annual Report 1930*, p. 10.

71   *Bluecoat Society of Arts Annual Report 1932*, p. 8.

72   J. A. Tinne, MP, in *Liverpool Daily Post*, 13 January 1930.

73   R. F. Bisson, *Bluecoat Cavalcade: Golden Jubilee Exhibition*, brochure, 1977.

74   MacCunn, *Bluecoat Chambers*, pp. 34–40; *Annual Report 1939*, p. 1.

75   *Bluecoat Society of Arts Annual Report 1940*, p. 6.

76   'Bluecoat building', *Liverpool Echo*, 6 June 1941.

77   'Bluecoat Society: meeting cost of raid damage', *Liverpool Daily Post*, 9 July 1942.

78   Bisson, *The Sandon Studios Society*, p. 199.

79   'Preserving a cultural link with the past: the Bluecoat Chambers, Liverpool', *Manchester Guardian*, 25 November 1952.

80   Morris and Stevens, *History of the Walker Art Gallery*, pp. 66, 196, 201.

81   MacCunn, *Bluecoat Chambers*, Appendix F, 'Colonel Cotton's Scheme'.

82   *Bluecoat Society of Arts Annual Report 1946*, pp. 3–4.

83   'No need for artists' alarm. Col. Cotton explains Bluecoat Chambers proposal', *Liverpool Daily Post*, 14 December 1945.

84   Bisson, *The Sandon Studios Society*, pp. 200–01.

85   *Bluecoat Society of Arts Annual Report 1946* and *Annual Report 1947*. The offer made by Bluecoat Society of Arts to the Town Clerk was not withdrawn officially until April 1948.

86   *Liverpool Daily Post*, 24 April 1948.

87   *Bluecoat Society of Arts Annual Report 1947*, p. 4.

88   'Redeveloping centre of Liverpool: scheme confirmed', *The Times*, 26 January 1949.

89   See the correspondence in the second section of WORK 14/2030.

90   *Manchester Evening News*, 13 August 1951. See also John Belchem, 'Celebrating Liverpool', in John Belchem, ed., *Liverpool 800: Culture, Character and History*, Liverpool: Liverpool University Press, 2006, pp. 44–47.

91   MacCunn, *Bluecoat Chambers*, pp. 60–61.

92   'Liverpool's Little Chelsea. The Bluecoat Chambers art coterie', *Liverpool Daily Post*, 24 May 1951.

93   *Bluecoat Society of Arts Annual Report 1951*, p. 5.

94   *The Times*, 14 October 1952.

95   'Some diversions of a great city. An impression of the cultural life in Liverpool and Merseyside', *The Times*, 5 April 1956.

96   *Liverpool Daily Post*, 25 November 1952.

97   MacCunn, *Bluecoat Chambers*, pp. vii–viii.

98   *Bluecoat Society of Arts Annual Report 1957*, p. 7.

99   Bisson, *The Sandon Studios Society*, pp. 204–05.

100   Undated item among 1963 press cuttings in the Bluecoat archive.

101   *Bluecoat Society of Arts Annual Report 1961*, p. 7.

102   *Bluecoat Society of Arts Annual Report 1964*.

103   *Bluecoat Society of Arts Annual Report 1963*.

104   Jon Murden, '"City of change and challenge": Liverpool since 1945', in Belchem, ed., *Liverpool 800*, pp. 401–02.

105   John Willett, *Art in a City* (1967), Liverpool: Liverpool University Press, 2007, with an introduction by Bryan Biggs, pp. 240–41.

106   Willett, *Art in a City*, pp. 242, 249. See also his articles on 'The arts in Liverpool', *Liverpool Daily Post*, 18, 19 and 20 March 1964.

107   *Bluecoat Society of Arts Annual Report 1965*, p. 6.

108   *Bluecoat Society of Arts Annual Report 1966*.

109   Merseyside Socialist Research Group, *Merseyside in Crisis*, n.p., 1980.

110   Belchem, 'Celebrating Liverpool', p. 53.

111   'What goes on at the Bluecoat', *Liverpool Daily Post*, 13 February 1968.

112   'Two cultures out of muddle', *The Times*, 12 June 1969.

113   Biggs, 'Radical Art City?', pp. 67–68.

114   *Bluecoat Society of Arts Annual Report 1976*.

115   *Bluecoat Society of Arts Annual Report 1977*.

116   *Bluecoat Society of Arts Annual Report 1972*.

117   *The Guardian*, 6 April 1968.

118   The Lieder Circle had been formed by Celia Van Mullem, appointed as joint secretary of Bluecoat Society of Arts with her husband Joe in 1960, and subsequently serving as director.

119   *Bluecoat Society of Arts Annual Report 1981*.

120   John Belchem, 'Introduction: the new "Livercool"', in *Merseypride*, pp. xi–xxix.

121   Bryan Biggs and Julie Sheldon, 'Introduction', in Bryan Biggs and Julie Sheldon, eds, *Art in a City Revisited*, Liverpool: Liverpool University Press, 2009, p. 7.

122   *Architecture Today*, 187, 2008, pp. 58–65; *Architectural Design*, 78.5, 2008, pp. 104–09.

Chapter 3

'A Live Arts Centre'

Bryan Biggs

As the previous chapter demonstrates, the story of Bluecoat's development as a centre for the arts was one of struggle, a seemingly never-ending campaign to raise funds and secure political and popular support to preserve an iconic Liverpool building. What, though, were the creative impulses that drove the establishment of the arts centre? Reading W. S. MacCunn's dry account, written from the perspective of thirty years as Bluecoat Society of Arts' secretary, the perception is of a half-century's involvement in the arts dominated by committees and balance sheets.[1] The book's bald headings – *Origins, Foundations, Consolidation, Survival, Reconstruction* – do not suggest a story of artistic imagination. In contrast, R. F. Bisson's colourful account of the Sandon Studios Society gives a greater sense of the creative achievements of this group of artists and art lovers who transformed the former charity school into a cultural asset for the city.[2] Groundbreaking exhibitions and major figures such as Picasso (who exhibited at but never visited the building) and Stravinsky (who visited but didn't perform there) feature in Bisson's narrative, but how significant is the Bluecoat story in the context of twentieth-century developments in the arts in Britain, particularly in relation to the arts centre movement? And who were the main players with the vision to bring different art forms together under one roof, or whose own artistic or curatorial practices helped distinguish Bluecoat as a place not just run by arts enthusiasts, but for the creation and presentation of progressive art?

Figure 21. Sign above the entrance advertising an exhibition of painting and sculpture, probably during the interwar years.

This chapter will examine how the idea of the multi-art-form arts centre developed and the extent to which Bluecoat was pioneering, not just in terms of its early accommodation of a breadth of art and ideas, but also as a building that combined both the production and consumption of art – working studios for artists alongside programmes of exhibitions and performances for the public. Set against a backdrop of the local and national cultural environment of the time, and the later proliferation of arts centres, the founding of Bluecoat Society of Arts in 1927, born out of a lively artistic presence in the building over the previous two decades, represents arguably the earliest example of a combined arts centre in the UK.

The tenacity of the Sandon Studios Society, and key figures within it such as Fanny Calder or influential allies such as Charles Reilly, represents a radical vision for the importance of art to civic life; but to what extent was this driven by an embrace of new art and creative ambition? There are distinct, sometimes fleeting, moments in the building's history when there was an engagement with modernism, with important exhibitions by the Post-Impressionists in 1911 and 1913 for instance, which exposed Liverpool to European avant-garde art and influenced some of its artists; yet at other times across the last century, Bluecoat – as represented by both the Sandon and the Society of Arts – seemed impervious to new ideas in art, attracting accusations of conservatism, stagnation and parochialism, the venue characterised as an exclusive and genteel club. This uneven trajectory and the, at times, ad hoc way in which the arts were presented – the inevitable result of an organisation essentially run by volunteers, and the arrival or departure of key individuals – makes for a more complicated, contradictory but, undoubtedly, richer history. This is especially so when considered from a contemporary perspective where the relationship of art to place and community, and the value of local distinctiveness in the face of globalisation, have become increasingly important. Bluecoat's evolution as a centre for the arts – its coming into being so early; the circumstances of its founding and survival; its distance from metropolitan taste perhaps; and the sense that it was making it up as it went along – positions it outside mainstream narratives of the growth of arts institutions in this country. Even in Liverpool, the city with which this much-loved building is so closely identified, the question, 'What actually goes on there?' can still be heard.

This chapter will also examine some of the artists who are synonymous with Bluecoat's history, such as Edward Carter Preston, Herbert Tyson Smith and Roderick Bisson, whose art was genuinely innovative yet failed to attract significant recognition beyond the region. Expanding on the themes explored in my essay 'Radical Art City?' in *Liverpool: City of Radicals*,[3] the local arts environment engendered by Bluecoat will be considered in relation to progressive art movements elsewhere. The focus will be mainly on the Sandon, but will go beyond this group and its relationship to Bluecoat Society of Arts to give an account of the venue's later developments, and how the ground was prepared for interdisciplinary arts and a more socially engaged role for the arts centre from the late 1960s onwards, which will be the focus of the next chapter. Much of this came about as a result of changes in national arts policy and a shift from private patronage to public subsidy, yet the overarching story of this chapter is how art and artists have always been at Bluecoat's core, even as the building's survival took precedence, often to the detriment of developing a national reputation as a pioneering and serious centre for the arts.

Bluecoat's relationship to contemporary art begins with the Sandon Terrace Studios, formed in 1905. This became the Sandon Society of Artists in 1908 and then the Sandon Studios Society, which continued formally for seventy years, though it had ceased to be the building's beating heart long before it was wound up. Although instrumental in setting up Bluecoat Society of Arts, the organisation that took

Figure 22. Sandon visitors' book, signed (lower half of second page) by Stravinsky and his musical collaborator, violinist Samuel Dushkin, 23 February 1934, in Liverpool to perform *Duo concertant*. Liverpool Record Office, 367 SAN/1/7/1.

ownership of the building in 1927, the Sandon remained a tenant throughout its life, formally incorporating with the Bluecoat Society in 1979. The Bluecoat nominally led on arts activities, but the Sandon continued to contribute significantly through exhibitions, performances and maintaining the building's vibrant social life, centred around a dining room that attracted a remarkable range of guests passing through the city, particularly in the interwar years when Bluecoat 'became an accepted – even respected – part of the cultural life of Liverpool',[4] before petering out as the Society consolidated its role promoting the arts. As Bluecoat's driving force, it was with the Sandon that the idea for an arts centre germinated, among individuals whose passions can be traced back to their time at art school.

In researching the demise in recent decades of the British art school, Matthew Cornford has described the 'accidental consequences' of these establishments, identifying their role as cultural melting pots for creative (and often disaffected) young locals, for whom art education provided a way into a world of imagination and possibility, with many using the opportunity of art school freedom to form a band, discover a passion for film, engage in political activism, or just think laterally, before going on to make their mark in the world.[5] Although addressed to art schools in the post-war period, Cornford's concept is a useful starting point for considering the Sandon artists, whose arrival at the vacant Bluecoat premises in 1907 was to have unforeseen, and indeed accidental, consequences for the arts in Liverpool.

***

In 1895 University College Liverpool established a Department of Applied Art within its School of Architecture, the first in England, which for the next decade, based in makeshift studios known as the Art Sheds and later complemented by studios in Myrtle Street, exerted a considerable influence on art and design in Liverpool. Offering classes in 'Modelling and Sculpture, Decorative Design, Painting and Drawing from the Life and Antique; Brass and Copper Work, Wrought Iron Work, Stained Glass; Enameling, Wood Carving, and Furniture and Fittings Construction',[6] the seeds of artistic multidisciplinarity were already sown, albeit within a visual arts framework that brought together the decorative arts with architecture and fine art. If not quite the 'Bauhaus on the Mersey' that Quentin Hughes claimed,[7] the Art Sheds nonetheless saw 'decorative artists … educated alongside students of architecture in a multi-disciplinary programme',[8] a skills-based approach in the mould of William Morris and the Arts and Crafts movement that would characterise the arts community that was to develop at Bluecoat.

During the department's brief history it boasted a wealth of teaching talent, including design instructor James Herbert MacNair, whose wife Frances MacNair also taught embroidery, the couple (as part of Art Nouveau group The Four, with Charles Rennie Mackintosh and Margaret Macdonald Mackintosh, Frances's sister) introducing Liverpool to the Glasgow Style; C. J. Allen teaching sculpture; and painting and drawing instructor Robert Anning Bell, who was followed by Augustus John,[9] and then by another New English Art Club member David Muirhead. Mary Bennett describes the Art Sheds as 'the vehicle through which the new in English Art at the turn of the century came to Liverpool'.[10] And with artists from the department involved in major city landmarks such as the Victoria Monument and the Philharmonic Hotel interior, the Art Sheds had a lasting impact on the city, as well as being an inspiration 'to a whole generation of locally based artists and craftsmen who set their standards by it'.[11]

One of the students, Herbert Tyson Smith, later recalled the contrast between the pedestrian teaching he had experienced at the Municipal Art School and the 'free and easy' atmosphere of the Art Sheds, where the charismatic John, with his 'bold and expressive line', had such an impact.[12] It was not perhaps surprising then that a group of students preferring 'free art', led by Fanny Dove Hamel Lister (later Mrs Calder) and Catherine Gwatkin (later Mrs Lascelles Abercrombie), together with their tutor James Herbert MacNair, refused to join the Municipal School of Art when the Applied Arts department merged with it in 1905, and they set up an independent art school instead, Sandon Terrace Studios. They were joined by Gerard Chowne, who had recently been employed as painting tutor by the new art school but 'soon revolted, threw up his appointment and joined (the Sandon)'.[13] In the time-honoured tradition of artists in search of cheap, temporary studio accommodation, the students found premises due for demolition, 9 Sandon Terrace in Upper Duke Street. Now the car park of Liverpool Institute for Performing Arts overlooking St James's cemetery and the Anglican Cathedral, which was then at an early stage of construction, from here they could 'cock a snook at the Municipal School of Art a mere stone's throw away'.[14]

The disaffected artists of the Sandon considered the Walker Art Gallery conservative in its exhibiting and buying policies, closed to Liverpool artists, and the Liverpool Academy of Arts moribund (though several Sandon artists became members, as well as of the Liver Sketching Club). Interestingly, however, the Sandon was not a natural choice for some male students, presumably because they needed to be sure of apprenticeships and employment, which the Municipal School could guarantee more so than the breakaway group. This may explain why so many women were involved in driving the Sandon's early years and had a significant presence in decision making: the first provisional committee had six women and eight men, growing to 15 women and 11 men on the first constituted general committee in 1910. Joining Lister (the only one with a bank account)[15] and Gwatkin as organisers, Fred Dimmick, the group's first treasurer, was a professional dentist who had attended evening classes at the Art Sheds, and was representative of the Sandon's amateur side, an increasingly important element as the group expanded to encompass not just working artists, but those interested in the arts.

The studios opened with 40 members, and within a year there were 100; by 1911 this had risen to 260, over half of them practising artists – in painting, sculpture, music and drama. Bisson describes how the group, once it moved in 1907 to Bluecoat, with its rooms for studios and life classes, 'developed into something of much more consequence to the cultural vitality of Liverpool'.[16] This was especially so after it started staging exhibitions in 1908 and broadened its membership, marking the start of a shift from an independent art school to a society for the arts. By that year, there were insufficient funds to pay Chowne and MacNair as tutors, and they departed, and thereafter it was difficult to maintain anything other than life drawing classes. Yet the art school ethos that determined figures such as Fanny Calder had experienced at the Art Sheds – a combination of independent thought, hard graft and a diversity of practices under one (leaky) roof – underpinned the development of Bluecoat as an arts centre. And the Sandon's predilection for *having fun* was demonstrated by its legendary fancy dress parties, which appear to have had all the decadence of the art school dance, if not on the scale of the famed Chelsea Arts Ball.

Alongside Calder's vision for a highly sociable environment for the city's artistic and intellectual life, there was serious intent to the idea of a centre for the contemporary arts that brought together different artistic practices. In its general manifesto issued at the end of 1909, the Sandon articulated its shift towards becoming an arts society, with a declared aim to 'bring together those working and those interested in all branches of the Arts and afford them a meeting ground and opportunity for discussion and friendly criticism',[17] facilitated by an all-important club room, as well as practical opportunities to study, practise and exhibit art. Charles Reilly, the dynamic Head of Architecture at the university, had already expressed his support for preserving the building when he moved his school into the premises to join the Sandon artists.[18] Together with Lascelles Abercrombie, a literary critic associated with the Georgian Group of poets, they had written a circular in 1908 outlining their plan for the architecture school at Bluecoat, where 'a community of practising artists and craftsmen centred on the School of Architecture would be formed, the influence of which might be very far reaching'.[19] This was the first mention of the idea of Bluecoat as an *arts centre* (though Reilly and Abercrombie did not acknowledge the presence of the artists already there) which, following the aforementioned Sandon manifesto, was starting to become a reality. It was an idea that Reilly developed with his proposal for a Lancashire Society of Arts, which, as outlined in Chapter 2, failed to get the support of the building's owner William Lever, although as Peter Richmond has noted, 'without his [Reilly's] money and social contacts, the Bluecoat's success as a precursor of the arts centre industry would not have been possible'.[20]

Formally constituted as an arts centre in 1927, Bluecoat had already witnessed some remarkable exhibitions and events in the previous two decades, organised by the Sandon, which continued such activities after the establishment of Bluecoat Society of Arts. In examining some of these, there is a strong case for considering the Sandon, both its artists and what it promoted in the building, as 'Liverpool's "Bloomsberries"', a progressive group that was more than just a 'provincial mirror of the Bloomsbury Group'.[21] Though unable to match the intellectual aristocracy of Virginia Woolf, Roger Fry, Lytton Strachey or John Maynard Keynes, the Sandon's energies revolved – unlike its London counterpart – around an iconic building, which acted as an artistic, intellectual and social magnet, and was, importantly (in contrast to the Bloomsbury set's rural retreat of Charleston), a public space in the heart of a bustling city. The Sandon staged 'dances, exhibitions, and entertainments, and invited Liverpool to come. Liverpool did come.'[22] For much of its early history, however, Bluecoat remained inaccessible to all but those with the economic means to become Sandon members or visit the exhibitions, which do not appear to have had free admission. Nonetheless, such exhibitions put down a marker for Bluecoat as a vital place to experience new art, presenting shows that challenged the local art establishment, as represented by the Walker, with a combination of emerging home-grown talent and advanced art from outside.

The first exhibition, *Sandon Society of Artists Exhibition of Modern Art*, in 1908, provided an opportunity to see work by 14 Sandon artists – ten men and four women, some of whom are discussed below – shown alongside honorary members including John, Anning Bell, Mackintosh, P. Wilson Steer and Henry Tonks, and, especially invited, Charles Conder and Claude Monet. Represented by just one painting, *Étretat* (one of several works from the 1880s with this title that depicted a distinctive cliff formation in Normandy), this was probably the first time Monet's work had been seen outside London.[23] The fact that the painting was some twenty years old indicates how far Britain lagged behind much of Europe in terms of modern art, as the next exhibition of significance would resoundingly demonstrate.

I have argued elsewhere that the *Exhibition of Modern Art including Works by the Post-Impressionists*, shown at Bluecoat between 4 March and 1 April 1911, was significant not just for Liverpool but in relation to the story of modern art in Britain.[24] It was a smaller version (less than a quarter of the size) of the controversial exhibition *Manet and the Post-Impressionists*, curated the previous winter at London's Grafton Galleries by critic and artist Roger Fry to 'educate his fellow countrymen on the important shifts taking place in painting in Continental Europe'.[25] The exhibition, shown at the United Arts Club in Dublin (an affiliate organisation of the Sandon) before coming to Liverpool,[26] excluded Manet's work – brought in as a sweetener for the London show – and also featured Sandon artists. This was therefore the first time works by some of the major figures in European modern art were exhibited alongside those of their British contemporaries, thus allowing a dialogue between their respective work for the first time, a model that Fry adopted for a follow-up Post-Impressionist exhibition, which did include British artists.

Next to 46 works by the French School, including five Picassos (whose single painting was a 1909 proto-Cubist portrait of his dealer Clovis Sagot), eight Gauguins, three Matisses, two Derains, three Vlamincks, two Rouaults, two Van Goghs and a Cézanne, the 136 works by Sandon artists must have looked staid, as was demonstrated when the exhibition was commemorated in a restaging, as far as was possible, a century later at the Walker Art Gallery.[27] Yet, as discussed below, the experience of exhibiting with the Post-Impressionists undoubtedly had a profound

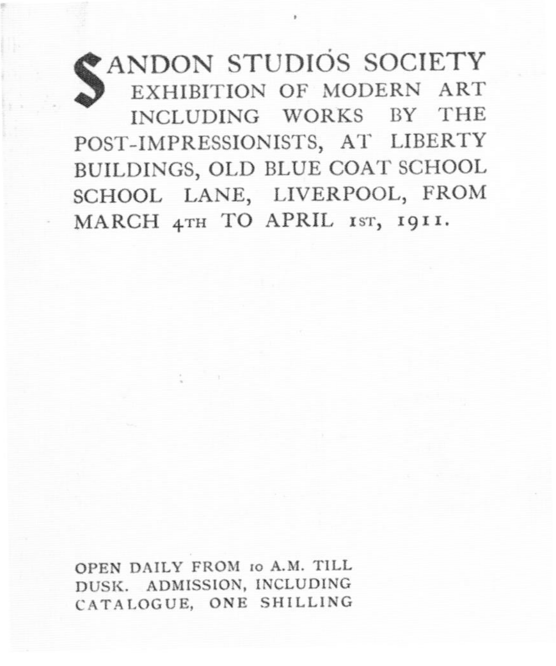

SANDON STUDIOS SOCIETY
EXHIBITION OF MODERN ART
INCLUDING WORKS BY THE
POST-IMPRESSIONISTS, AT LIBERTY
BUILDINGS, OLD BLUE COAT SCHOOL
SCHOOL LANE, LIVERPOOL, FROM
MARCH 4TH TO APRIL 1ST, 1911.

OPEN DAILY FROM 10 A.M. TILL
DUSK. ADMISSION, INCLUDING
CATALOGUE, ONE SHILLING

Figure 23. Catalogue for 1911 Sandon exhibition of modern art including works by the Post-Impressionists. Picasso, Matisse and others showed alongside Sandon artists. Liverpool Record Office, 706.5 CAT.

effect on some of the Liverpool artists, who exhibited again in Fry's *Second Post-Impressionist Exhibition* when it came to Bluecoat in 1913, accompanied by a public lecture by Fry. Reaction to the first show had been generally hostile, the *Liverpool Courier*'s report, 'Anarchy in the Paint Pot', on a debate about the new art organised at the end of the exhibition by the Sandon, concurring with one of the participants that it was all a 'gigantic hoax'.[28] The *Manchester Guardian* meanwhile, in a generally favourable review, praised the Sandon artists, and urged readers to 'readjust the focus of our eye' before judging the Continental artists,[29] whose London showing had had such an impact that, according to Virginia Woolf, 'human character changed'.[30] By the second exhibition, which again featured Picasso and Matisse (though not, according to Bisson, as remarkable a selection as the first show), together with British artists including some from the Sandon 'bold enough to appear in such company',[31] there was greater acceptance, or at least tolerance. But even among the Sandon ranks, opinion was still divided. Its *Bulletin* was scathing in its report of the opening proceedings of the exhibition,[32] but the Sandon committee was pleased with its reception, which 'struck the public fancy and was very well attended and made a profit of £17.2.10. The artists of the club worked wholehearted for its success.'[33]

Sandon artists' involvement in the decorative arts that began in their Art Sheds days was reflected in early exhibitions, notably an *Exhibition of Decorative Art and Handicraft* in 1908. Jewellery was even included by four Sandon artists in the 1911 Post-Impressionist show. Interest in other aspects of design saw an exhibition of the work of eminent theatre designer Gordon Craig in 1913, organised by Sandon members Calder, Henry Carr and Miss M. Bulley, together with the Society of the Theatre affiliated to Craig's school. The following year saw a display of applied art – textiles, furniture and pottery from the Omega Workshop that had been set up by Bloomsbury artists Roger Fry, Duncan Grant and Vanessa Bell.[34] Also in 1914, recent purchases by some of the most significant artists of the day, bought for the nation by the Contemporary Art Society, were exhibited, and included Grant, Bell, Wilson Steer, Augustus John, Gwen John, Walter Sickert, Mark Gertler, Wyndham Lewis, William Roberts and Edward Wadsworth; the latter three artists, who were associated with the new Vorticism art movement, attracted particular ire in the local press.

From these exhibitions, the Sandon evidently had its finger on the pulse of advanced art: while the Post-Impressionist shows were curated by Fry (the Sandon artists included were selected by a hanging committee of the Society), individual members organised adventurous and distinctive exhibitions themselves, continuing right through the interwar years. Carl Thompson, spending time in London, arranged an exhibition at Bluecoat in 1928 of a new generation of artists working in the capital, including Grant, Paul Nash and Christopher Wood (born in Knowsley, he was introduced to the Sandon as a young man by Thompson), which was opened by writer Osbert Sitwell and reviewed by press correspondents who came from all over the country. The following year Edward Carter Preston curated the *Annual Exhibition of Paintings, Sculpture and Etchings*, 'thought to be the best ever'.[35] This included life drawings and a *Reclining Woman* sculpture in concrete by Henry Moore, and works by other artists at the forefront of modern British art including Gertler, David Jones, John Nash, Eric Gill, John Skeaping and Frank Dobson. The fact that there was even a budget line for a curator (a modest £4 shows in the accounts for the year, plus £93 spent on exhibitions)[36] indicates the Sandon's serious intent as exhibition makers at a time when curatorial practice was in its infancy. There were connections to art circles in London through Fry and honorary members such as Tonks, John and Wilson Steer; and the Sandon, which subscribed to a range of periodicals such as *Jugend*, *L'Art et les Artistes* and the *English Review*, and its artists, no doubt immersed in specialist art journals such as the *Studio* and the *Burlington Magazine*, increasingly grew in confidence and independence. By the late 1920s, nowhere 'outside London … could so much contemporary painting and sculpture be seen as at Blue Coat Chambers'.[37] It was not until the Walker Art Gallery appointed a new director in 1932, Frank Lambert (who then became a Sandon member), that the municipal gallery started to 'do for art in Liverpool what the Sandon previously had done'.[38]

The eight editions of the Sandon *Bulletin*, produced between 1912 and 1914, give a sense of the group's early intellectual interests, though the main function of the publication was to provide information on activities, and the tone was mostly light-hearted. Apart from the 1909 declaration of its intent to create a centre for the arts, the Sandon never published a manifesto that either aligned its artists to a particular art movement or articulated the club's broader championing of the arts in the social sphere, a task that was taken up by Bluecoat Society of Arts in its founding constitution. As the *Bulletins* show, the Sandon tended not to take itself too seriously, nor care whom it upset. The inclusion of the *Manifesto of the Futurist Painters* in the satirical publication *A Bushel of Chaff*, produced by Sandon members in 1912,[39] suggests that there was interest early on, at least among some of the group, in radical art thinking from abroad, even though the manifesto's rejection of the past, of good taste and harmony in art, and its celebration of originality and dynamism in the new machine age was already two years old. Given the scurrilous nature of the rest of the Sandon publication, its inclusion may have been intended simply to annoy people.[40] That said, the words of the avant-garde Italian painters are printed in the context of a 'reminiscence' of the debate that the Sandon held about Post-Impressionism, which quotes altogether supportive comments on the new art.

Politically the group appears to have been a broad church. As noted in Chapter 2, political radicals rubbed shoulders with academics, bohemians and suffragists. The Women's Citizens Association, the oldest women's organisation in the UK, presided over by Eleanor Rathbone, met regularly at Bluecoat. Suffragists were, however, ridiculed in one *Bulletin*, even though Sandon women were among those who disrupted James Sexton's play *The Riot Act* – based on the transport strike of 1911 – at the Liverpool Repertory Company (later the Liverpool Playhouse) in 1914, for its unsympathetic portrayal of suffragists during that turbulent period. By the second half of the 1930s, however, the overriding impression is one of conservatism, and with a banker and a department store general manager on its executive committee, it was not perhaps surprising that, having boldly shown the work of Picasso in 1911, the Sandon turned down an offer to exhibit the communist artist's *Guernica* to help the Merseyside Foodship Fund during the Spanish Civil War in 1938, even though 'most people were interested in Spain and many would have been interested in "Guernica"'.[41] One wonders what Sandon members Maud Budden and Ethel Frimston's observations were in their 1932 Sandon talk, 'What we saw in Russia'.

Still largely unrecognised in mainstream accounts of British art's engagement with modernism, the country's regions contributed to this history through groups such as the Sandon in Liverpool and the more advanced, modernist-thinking Leeds Arts Club, whose own Post-Impressionist exhibition in 1913 comprised works by Cézanne, Matisse, Gauguin, Picasso and Kandinsky, borrowed from UK collectors, including several in Yorkshire. These included Frank Rutter, who opened Bluecoat's second Post-Impressionist show that year, wrote a scathing attack in the Sandon satire *The Sport of Civic Life or Art and the Municipality* on the Walker Art Gallery's acquisitions policy in relation to those of other northern galleries, and whose progressive collecting policy as director of Leeds City Art Gallery was the envy of those Sandon artists in despair at the Walker's conservatism.[42] Further research may reveal the extent to which a provincial avant-garde in the years preceding the First World War existed independently from London, and how actively it was networked. Certainly, the Sandon had connections to progressive art circles in Glasgow, Dublin and Leeds, and Fry provided a conduit to what was happening in Europe; however, considering Liverpool's global connections through the port and Reilly's well-established relationship with developments in American architecture, there appear to have been surprisingly few international links, at least in the visual arts (in the Sandon's musical and performing arts activities the picture was a little different). In the interwar years, an exhibition was held of cartoons by Pete Arno, whose distinctive drawings graced the covers of the *New Yorker*, with a catalogue foreword by Paul Nash, but the origins of this 1933 exhibition remain obscure.

The display in 1931 of Jacob Epstein's controversial marble sculpture of a pregnant woman, *Genesis*, described by the *Daily Mail* as 'unfit to show',[43] reflects the ongoing tension between the arts and financial necessity, especially once Bluecoat Society of Arts was responsible for running the building. Proposed by Reilly and fellow architect (and future Sandon honorary secretary) Harold Hinchcliffe Davies to help the Society of Arts' fundraising efforts, 'the event of the year'[44] raises questions about the relationship between these two preoccupations of the arts centre. Was the exercise purely financial, having seen how much interest the same sculpture's public display in London, then Manchester, had previously generated? Fellow sculptor Tyson Smith, who collected the work from Manchester in a truck with a crew of men from his Bluecoat studio (see Fig. 24), would have respected the work and supported its display as a fine sculpture by one of the country's leading avant-garde artists. Yet, presented with concealed uplighting against a black velvet drape and with a rail in front, one wonders why the decision was made to dramatise the sculpture in quite this way. The intention may have been to show 'with dignity and effect' this 'striking and important example of present day sculpture',[45] but

Figure 24. Jacob Epstein's sculpture *Genesis* arriving at Bluecoat, May 1931. *Liverpool Daily Post* photo, with thanks to Peter Hopgood.

its presentation undoubtedly helped fuel the media sensationalism that already accompanied the work, and arguably trivialised it – which surely would have gone against the principles of Sandon members such as Carter Preston and Tyson Smith.[46] As gentle fun, and one assumes in homage, the latter artist made a papier mâché replica of *Genesis* for one of the Sandon cabarets, a sort of 'living sculpture' from within which an actor delivered a soliloquy, written by Sandon satirist Maud Budden, based on her observations of audience reactions to the work. After almost 50,000 visitors – 'Some came away shocked, some laughing, some as if they had been to their first communion'[47] – and comparatively positive local press coverage, *Genesis* at Bluecoat appears to have been a resounding financial and critical, if controversial, success.

Though records of Bluecoat activities in the interwar years are incomplete, exhibitions were, it seems, becoming predominantly local affairs, comprising mainly Sandon artists, and shows from outside were made possible only after the outbreak of the Second World War, when staff from the Walker, whose own gallery had been requisitioned, staged shows such as *Contemporary British Art* (1940) alongside touring exhibitions from the Contemporary Art Society and, after the war, from the Arts Council.[48] From accommodating the Post-Impressionist exhibitions and having notable honorary artist members in London before the First World War, there was now a greater sense of independence from the capital. While this contributed to building a local distinctiveness in art being produced on Merseyside, reflected for instance in three critically acclaimed *Recording Merseyside* exhibitions staged between 1945 and 1947, the disconnect from new art currents of the type that had existed during the Sandon's 'golden years' led to a sense of introspection, partly due, no doubt, to post-war gloom in the shattered Bluecoat building and the inevitable decline within the Sandon itself, as members moved away, grew old or died.[49]

***

Having looked at the impulses that drove the Sandon to develop Bluecoat as an arts centre through consideration of some of its exhibitions, what was the contribution of individual artists? As a working community that started with the Sandon in 1907 and continues today, artists are an essential part of Bluecoat, and a brief look at key figures from these early years reveals their importance, not just in keeping the arts alive in the building, but in their own right.

Bringing external influences from Glasgow and London respectively, J. Herbert MacNair, whose designs had been exhibited at the Vienna Secession in 1900, and the painter Gerard Chowne were among the earliest artists to occupy studios, though their stay was short-lived, and the latter was one of several Sandon artists to die in the First World War.[50] The reputation of Fanny Calder as a tireless advocate for the arts in our story overshadows her practice as an artist who – greatly influenced by her tutor Anning Bell, with whom she also collaborated – painted friezes, illustrated books and designed book plates, and was apparently never without her sketchbook.[51] She was one of a group of at least 17 women selected (by an all-male hanging committee) to make up the 43 Sandon artists who showed alongside the Post-Impressionists in 1911. Calder does not, however, appear to have recognised the significance to her own artistic practice of being included in the exhibition. Her slim autobiography makes no mention of it, nor indeed of the Sandon, of which she became the first president, nor Bluecoat – a surprising omission given her prominent role in founding the former and saving the latter, for which she was recognised with a gold medallion designed by Edward Carter Preston and a parchment signed by all the Sandon members.[52] Art continued as a hobby for her in Bath and the Lake District after she left Liverpool, while other female Sandon members such as Beatrice Herdman felt they 'were not really gifted and … were only passing our time'.[53] It is clear, however, that others, such as Enid Jackson, Kate Sargint, Mary McCrossan, Winifred Phillips and 'the suffragist sculptress' Ethel Frimston,[54] were serious artists, some going on to further study, to teach, or to carry out public commissions. Mostly forgotten and their work undocumented, further research may reveal the breadth and interests of these artists. Whatever the significance of their work, however – and some of it, from the small amount of information available, does appear slight in comparison with better-known contemporaries such as Gwen John or Vanessa Bell – it is noticeable that such a large proportion of the artists exhibiting alongside the Post-Impressionists in 1911 were women (these included four jewellers, representing a craft rather than fine art practice). In contrast, all 20 of the Continental 'modern masters' exhibiting – who would come to dominate the modern movement in art – were men.

An honorary member of the Sandon, Augustus John had left Liverpool by the time the group moved to Bluecoat, but as a regular visitor to the city he participated in social events at the venue and exhibited there frequently. John had a significant influence on Sandon artists, notably the Polish émigré painter he befriended, Albert Lipczinski, whose eventful story we are now aware of as a result of research by David Bingham.[55] His having a studio where he lived, in the 'Schloss' in Roscoe Lane, suggests that Lipczinski did not work at Bluecoat, but he undoubtedly contributed to the life of the Sandon. Politically – if not artistically – radical, 'Lippy' 'perhaps more than any other artist in the city at this time exemplified the convergence of the local and the international, of art and politics, of bohemia and academia'.[56]

Born in Granby Street, Liverpool, Maxwell Gordon Lightfoot attended painting classes at Bluecoat before going on to the Slade in 1907 along with Sandon colleague Winifred Phillips, another promising student who won the summer painting competition with a composition featuring her Sandon and Slade friends, including Lightfoot, playing music at her home, 33 Rodney Street.[57] Influenced by both Chowne and John, Lightfoot – 'the most significant artist to have emerged from the Sandon Studios Society painting classes'[58] – became friends with Slade artists who would make their mark on British art – C. R. W. Nevinson, Stanley Spencer and Edward Wadsworth – joining some of them in the 'Slade coster gang' that apparently terrorised Soho. Influenced by the first Post-Impressionist exhibition, he joined the newly formed Camden Town Group, participating in their first exhibition alongside Walter Sickert. Resigning from the group shortly after, Lightfoot never exhibited again, committing suicide in 1911 at the age of 25. Four of his works were included in an exhibition at Bluecoat the following year.

Direct exposure to Post-Impressionism did have a marked influence on other Sandon artists, as suggested by reviews of their work in *The Spring Exhibition of Pictures* at Birkenhead Art Gallery in 1914, which was 'redeemed from utter mediocrity by the artists hailing from the Sandon Studios, their collective exhibit being the bright particular spot in the show',[59] showing 'the changes of methods and ideas which have entered into the art of today … on what might be termed the "Post-Impressionist wall"'.[60] This impact is seen most clearly in the work of Edward Carter Preston. In 1909 he painted two conventional views in an Impressionist style, looking out from the Bluecoat's front courtyard. By 1911, however, his sketchbooks contain portraits in different Post-Impressionist styles, one jokingly signed 'Spokes Himspressionist'. Cubist-influenced paintings made in the wake of the two Post-Impressionist exhibitions reveal the beginnings of a highly personal style, which he went on to develop in more formal directions.[61] Known principally as a leading medallist (including designing the Next-of-Kin memorial plaque for the First World War) and a sculptor of great distinction for his work in Liverpool's Anglican Cathedral – 'one of the most ambitious programmes of twentieth-century architectural decoration in the country'[62] – engraving and painting were also integral to his practice, but his early works in these media are barely represented in public collections. A 1912 exhibition review in the *Guardian* considered that his work 'shows the most complete assimilation of the simplification and abstract design which characterises the Post-Impressionist movement'.[63] Two abstract landscape drawings from 1911 and a later series of assured and distinctive watercolours based on landscape and still life compare favourably with Vorticist works by Wyndham Lewis and David Bomberg, made around the same time. Carter Preston's non-commercial sculptural work includes the astonishingly futuristic

Arms and the Man (Fig. 25), 'a sultry satire upon modern international and political urges',[64] which recalls the 'consuming inhumanity of machines evoked in Fritz Lang's film, *Metropolis*'.[65] This plaster sculpture of a naked man and woman being crushed by a machine-like figure was exhibited at Bluecoat in 1938 and has since been lost. From photographs, it may have been a maquette for a larger work, which if realised would arguably have had a substantial and menacing presence, echoing the dynamism of Epstein's *Rock Drill* (1913–15) with its dramatic mechanistic/human form, and anticipating Eduardo Paolozzi's robot-inspired Pop Art works in the late-1950s and 60s.[66] Carter Preston left his Bluecoat studio when his sculptural commissions demanded a larger space, but he remained active in the Sandon, which he had helped found, 'hoping thereby to perpetuate a body of people interested in art as an expression of spirit'.[67]

"Arms and the Man," a modern piece of sculpture by Mr. E. Carter Preston, which is being exhibited at the Liverpool Academy of Arts exhibition at the Bluecoat Chambers from May 31 to June 19. A notice appears in another column.

Figure 25. Edward Carter Preston, *Arms and the Man*, 'a sultry satire upon modern international and political urges'. Exhibited at Bluecoat in 1938, the sculpture has since been lost. Unknown press cutting, courtesy of Liverpool Hope University Carter Preston Foundation.

Herbert Tyson Smith was Carter Preston's brother-in-law, and they shared a similarly close relationship to Bluecoat from the start of their careers, both having been Sandon founder members and exhibited with the Post-Impressionists. They were at the forefront of architectural sculpture in Liverpool in the first half of the twentieth century, and they and their families were also synonymous with the Bluecoat building. Carter Preston's daughter Julia rented a studio overlooking the garden for most of her working life, where she developed a distinctive and popular s'graffitto ceramics style (see Figs. 13 and 71) and ensured a century-long family association with the arts centre.

Tyson Smith established a sculptors' studio in 1927, working there until shortly before his death in 1972. From here he established a reputation as Liverpool's most prominent public sculptor, responsible for significant works such as the remarkable reliefs on the Liverpool Cenotaph on St George's Plateau (1930), designed by Lionel Budden, one of several war memorials the artist created on Merseyside and in the north-west. He also carved a tablet on an entrance porch at the Royal Academy of Arts in London (1922) in honour of RA staff and students killed in the First World War. Besides memorials, his well-known works in Liverpool include *The Hod Carrier* and *The Architect* (1950), two large carved figures – the former resembling the heroic workers depicted in Soviet era public art – now in the Museum of Liverpool but originally situated on the outside of Gerard Gardens, one of several Corporation housing schemes (since demolished) designed in a European modernist style under the director of housing, and later city architect, Lancelot Keay. In more playful style, Tyson Smith's reliefs on Spinney House (1951–55, originally Littlewoods, now occupied by Primark) incorporate mermen, dolphins, shells and other nautical motifs that often featured in his work, while at Bluecoat itself, the artist was responsible for the post-war restoration of cherubs' heads, the cartouche over the main entrance, and a commemorative plaque on the north-east wing comprising a Latin inscription relating to the bombing – 'Struck down from the sky by the firebrands of the enemy and partly destroyed on 4th May 1941 restored with dutiful affection in the year 1951' – flanked by the heads of a Bluecoat schoolboy and girl.

Tyson Smith employed sculptors and letter cutters, including his son Geoffrey, in his Bluecoat studio overlooking the back yard, which he nurtured as a garden. He also worked with architects Bernard Miller and Francis Xavier Velarde on many church commissions, and with Budden and Herbert Rowse, for whom he produced interior and exterior works for the former Martin's Bank building (1927–32) in Water Street, together with fellow Sandon artist George Capstick who made the relief over the Queensway Tunnel entrance. Tyson Smith's interests were as eclectic as his practice was versatile, combining Egyptian and Graeco-Roman forms with the modernist experimentation of sculptors such as Epstein (whom he exhibited with and was also featured with alongside other leading sculptors in the 1930 publication *Modern Architectural Sculpture*).[68] A public sculptor who worked to commission, Tyson Smith's work is best seen *in situ*, integrated into buildings or monuments, rather than in museum collections; his 'flat, linear style suited both classical and modern architecture'.[69] By the 1960s, however, architectural sculpture – considered too decorative in the prevailing aesthetic of brutalism – was on the wane and opportunities for Tyson Smith's studio declined.

From the 1930s Bluecoat became home to a new generation of Merseyside painters and engravers who had studied at the Royal College of Art (RCA) in London and returned to contribute to studio life and exhibit regularly in the gallery: Norman Martin Bell, Edward Griffith, Jack Coburn Witherop and Geoffrey Wedgwood. After the war, other RCA graduates followed, the 'Wallasey Surrealist' George Jardine taking up residence between 1950 and 1975, and the tradition resurfaced in 1978 when Northern Irish landscape painter Clement McAleer, fresh from the RCA, relocated to Liverpool on winning a prize in the John Moores painting competition, working in his Bluecoat studio continuously until 2003, when he returned to Belfast.

Yet the painter with the longest studio tenure – over fifty years – was Roderick Bisson, who was self-taught. He, perhaps of all the artists associated with Bluecoat, is its 'hidden gem'. Had he moved to London and been more actively commercial about his work, 'he would surely', believes Ann Compton, 'have earned national recognition for his extended dialogue with international modernism and the vivid imagination, wit and sensuous treatment of form which typifies his paintings'.[70] Joining the Sandon in 1931, Bisson's fresh approach to painting, informed by late Cubism, Vorticism and then by Surrealism and de Stijl, served to highlight the relative conservatism of his fellow artists, who were still preoccupied with Roger Fry's 'significant form' or variations on Post-Impressionism, or had returned to more traditional painting. The contrasting reactions to modernism among Sandon artists in the 1930s is humorously reflected in a painting by Donald Lynch, *So, You Won't Talk, Eh?* (1936), a pastiche of William Frederick Yeames's 1878 painting *And when did you last see your father?*, in the Walker Art Gallery. Also referred to as *And when did you last see your oculist?*, the painting shows the Painters' and Sculptors' Group of the Sandon interrogating Bisson, whose 'offending' painting is being presented as evidence of his embrace of modernism. A startlingly original composition, this painting, *Red Woman, Black Man* (Fig. 26) has recently been rediscovered; with its bold, simplified geometric forms, vivid red and black contrasts, and the 'primitivism' of its figures, it is uncompromisingly modern, not just for a painting in Liverpool, but within British art at that time.

In the 1960s one of Bisson's paintings was mistaken by a commercial London gallery for a work by the Cubist Albert Gleizes; the story was picked up by the *Observer*, which declared 'Undiscovered Genius Shocks Art Gallery'.[71] A subsequent offer of a show in the capital, declined by Bisson, could perhaps have led to a serious appraisal of an artist who had absorbed Surrealism well before its first English showing in London in 1936, and developed an individual style that would sit well in the company of Paul Nash, Edward Wadsworth, Tristram Hillier or the work of other British artists of the interwar years recently reconceptualised as 'romantic moderns'.[72] Bisson forsook his art, ostensibly to avoid any conflict of interest when he started writing exhibition reviews for the *Daily Post* (these were usually generous and always original and insightful, informed by his international outlook), yet he continued to maintain his Bluecoat studio and could apparently be heard on occasion playing Erik Satie hesitatingly on the Sandon Room piano.[73] As chronicler of the Sandon's history, Bisson remained a vital conduit to the avant-garde currents that had flowed through the building.

Figure 26. Roderick Bisson, *Red Woman, Black Man*, oil on board, 1932, private collection.

At the same time, Bisson, whose day job was as designer at Lewis's department store, reflects the importance of design to the artists who made Bluecoat their home in the first half-century. It is an aspect of their work that can perhaps be traced back to the applied arts training of the Art Sheds, and is common to much of their output, seen for instance in Carter Preston's medals, Tyson Smith's architectural sculpture, and the presence of other artists who made their living through craft skills, such as furniture maker William Burden. As Chapter 7 demonstrates, decorative art and craft activities, including the establishment of the leading UK designer-maker gallery, the Bluecoat Display Centre, continued to be prominent in the building after the Second World War, a dimension that should not be overlooked in assessing Bluecoat's visual arts story. To view the work of these practitioners purely in the context of fine art diminishes the building's significance as a centre where applied art and architecture interacted with painting, sculpture and graphic art, often through commissions for the public realm. Architects Miller and Velarde, for instance, both employed Sandon tenants to work on their schemes, including Burdon, Tyson Smith, Mary Adshead, George Mayer-Marton and W. L. Stevenson, who later became head of the School of Art and who decorated Bluecoat's expansive concert hall ceiling with a mural of Bluecoat life. Mayer-Marton was a Hungarian Jewish émigré, who had been significant in Viennese art between the wars and who pioneered the technique of Byzantine mosaic in the UK, creating work for many schools and churches.

Another branch of the visual arts with a presence at Bluecoat was photography, the Liverpool Amateur Photographic Association being based there from 1928, while professional photographers were involved in the Sandon. Most prominent among them was portrait and landscape photographer Edward Chambré Hardman, who joined in 1923, accompanying other Sandon members on foreign trips that resulted in some of his best-known works, such as the evocative *A Memory of Avignon* (1928). The membership included two other wealthy individuals involved in photography, George Rawlins, inventor in 1904 of the oil print, and George Davison, who lived off his early investment in Kodak film and would invite Sandon members to spend weekends at his mansion, Waenfawr, in Harlech, North Wales. Davison's achievements as 'probably the most influential figure in the development of the Pictorialist movement' in the late nineteenth century, and as a passionate exponent of the philosophy of art in photography,[74] have been overshadowed, perhaps due to his ostracism over his political beliefs, which embraced anarchism, syndicalism and pacifism, put into practice by his funding of grassroots political ventures in Wales and Scotland, and his giving over Waenfawr to political and cultural gatherings for, among others, Fabian summer schools and Welsh miners. Though not apparently very active in the affairs of the Sandon, or indeed Liverpool, where fellow Sandon artist Malcolm Arbuthnot ran Davison's Kodak shop in Bold Street, his membership of the Society does illustrate its embrace of photography as an art form and its tolerance of, if not necessarily sympathy with, radical political ideas. Bisson (whose own political affiliation, certainly in the interwar years, was with communism) suggests that the Sandon was also keeping up with the times when, in 1922, it organised an exhibition at Picton Hall of 'Slow Motion Pictures taken by the Ultra Rapid Camera and accompanied by "a light symphony orchestra"',[75] this some twelve years before the Merseyside Film Society became Bluecoat tenants.

***

Until now this chapter has focused on visual art, in its broadest sense, taking in fine art, architecture, photography, applied arts and design, which was the arts centre's initial driving force; however, its combined arts character became embedded in the Bluecoat Society of Arts' constitution, which is discussed below, providing a foundation on which the organisation was able to build, and pointing the way towards new dialogue between the visual, performing and literary arts. This breadth of activity accelerated in the second half of the century, but a brief look at how the main strands developed will demonstrate that, from the beginning, the building was home to different areas of creative practice, the sort of mix that would come to characterise British arts centres after the Second World War; yet it was a recipe that also manifested itself in very different ways from these later institutions.

The Sandon's interest in different art forms was reflected in the various sub-committees it established to develop programmes that Bisson considered 'astonishing'.[76] Its Dramatic Group ensured the prominence of theatre, with events such as a week-long drama school for the more committed thespians in 1933, tutored by influential theatre director Tyrone Guthrie. Bisson claims that the Dadaist-like pranks of painter Syd (Spike) Merrills in the 1930s anticipated the Theatre of the Absurd;[77] however, the Sandon's performance tastes were more middle of the road, with productions meeting Liverpool's appetite for amateur dramatics. Events took place in rooms on the ground floor, using a donated temporary stage, and then in the former school chapel upstairs; however, when this space was restored after wartime bombing there was no proscenium, and Bluecoat as a theatre venue effectively ended, this space being geared instead towards concerts.

The Sandon's love of the theatrical stretched back to its early cabarets when the sketches of Maud Budden (who, with her husband Roland Clibborn, created the popular *Liverpool Echo* comic strip 'Curly Wee & Gussy Goose') became a staple. Parties too were always elaborate affairs, from the university's annual architects'

Figure 27.
Sandon Studios
Society member
Henry Carr,
'painter, farmer
and philosopher',
and participant
in cabarets
and parties at
Bluecoat.

ball, when Charles Reilly would appear as a Roman emperor (or in some similar proprietorial role), his chariot drawn by willing students, to the children's parties later recalled by the entertainer George Melly, who described the Sandon as carrying 'an aura of immense sophistication'.[78]

There were early connections too with Liverpool Repertory Theatre, founded in 1911 by, among others, Reilly, and where in 1913 one of Sandon member Lascelles Abercrombie's plays, *The Adder*, was performed in blank verse. The relationship to theatre is, however, perhaps best exemplified by George Harris, a distinctive but unobtrusive Sandon character who had 'the haunted look that is in the eyes of a good comedian'.[79] Studying under Augustus John in Liverpool and in Paris, he established a fruitful working relationship with the Repertory Theatre's director and Sandon member Basil Dean, designing stage sets, costumes and programme covers for productions at the Williamson Square venue. He then accompanied Dean to London and worked with his Reandean Company in what became a highly successful career as scenic designer in the West End, as well as in New York, until his untimely death in 1929. Harris's contribution to the development of English scenic art has never been fully acknowledged; he bridged the gap between scenic painting traditions and the interwar revolutionary experiments in theatre, which he experienced first-hand in the 1920s on a trip with Dean to Berlin and Moscow to visit the Bolshevik theatre of Vsevolod Meyerhold, whom they met personally.

Harris was 'probably the first modern designer to graduate as a scenic painter',[80] and he had a full understanding of the craft of theatre design and the mechanics of production. He had a 'remarkable ability to put *coldness* on stage',[81] while stylised naturalism was his forte. Yet in spite of his achievements, he possessed a 'sublime indifference to applause',[82] spurning opportunities to promote his work, which he felt spoke for itself in the ingenuity of his designs on stage; those for *Hassan* at His Majesty's, for instance, were described as rivalling 'Bakst in their vigour'.[83] Few would have known that Harris had shown three drawings and a painting in the first Post-Impressionist exhibition at Bluecoat. Whether in London or on his various sojourns to North Africa or Scandinavia, his 'grubby' Bluecoat studio, which he described as 'a workshop, not a boudoir', remained home:

> It never occurred to me that he lived anywhere but in his studio, and I should not have been astonished if I had been told that he was born in the Sandon Studios, that he grew up in them, that he ate and worked and recreated and slept in them. I daresay he would have liked to have died in them.[84]

Here, Harris could experiment with dyes or bookbinding, design furniture, make fancy dress, fashion a mask, craft fine engravings and woodcuts and produce voluminous drawings, many of which he discarded. The Sandon's social life provided ample opportunities for Harris's artistic exuberance, including creating costumes and decorations such as a mural for a party in the life room that remained until 1951 (Fig. 28). His acerbic wit was demonstrated in drawings that graced the satirical *Bushel of Chaff* publication. The tradition of scenic painting at Bluecoat established by Harris was continued in the 1930s by Winifred Humphreys, who became designer at the Playhouse and whose mural decorations included the children's room on the Cunard liner RMS *Mauretania* and the café of Lewis's department store.

Music has been an important ingredient of the arts centre from the beginning, the Sandon establishing an active music group, staging concerts, inviting speakers (including musicologist Cecil Sharp in 1912 to talk on English folk songs and dances) and hosting in its dining room the likes of Stravinsky in 1934. Also home to musical societies, music teachers and instrument makers, and later host to music festivals and exams, Bluecoat became an important venue for classical and early music in the city, as outlined in Stainton de B. Taylor's *Two Centuries of Music in Liverpool*.[85] The story is further explored and brought up to date by Roger Hill in Chapter 6 of this book.

The Sandon's enthusiasm for dance could not be met by staging productions at the venue, whose performance space was limited to music and theatre, a situation

Figure 28. Watercolour sketch by George Harris for a frieze used in a Sandon cabaret, 1920s.

that only changed in the 1980s with the arrival of raked seating and a lively dance programme. However, after-theatre suppers were arranged for companies visiting Liverpool, notably the Ballet Russes in 1928 (including its choreographer George Balanchine), whose legendary ballerina Anna Pavlova had been honoured by the Sandon with an 'at home' in 1912.

While calls for the Sandon to develop as a literary centre were never realised,[86] writing was part of the group's early interests, its members including Margaret Bulley, author of books on art and history, and Lascelles Abercrombie, who was appointed to the first lectureship in poetry at the University of Liverpool after the First World War. Advocated by members such as G. H. Parry, the city's deputy chief librarian, literary activity grew between the wars, with a particular interest in Russian authors. The Wirral-based philosopher and writer Olaf Stapledon, regarded as a pioneer of science fiction and equally prolific in his philosophical writing on ethical subjects and politics, was a Sandon member when his first novel, *Last and First Men: A Story of the Near and Far Future*, was published in 1930. It was reviewed by another Liverpool author, John Brophy,[87] whose description of the bomb-damaged Bluecoat in his novel *City of Departures* (1946), set in wartime Liverpool, suggests a familiarity with the arts centre. Following her involvement in its theatrical productions, Sandon member Irene Rathbone gained a reputation in London for her interpretations of Chekhov's plays and went on to have a career as a novelist; her anti-war novel *We That Were Young*

(1932) is told from the perspective of a former suffragist. It is likely that these writers' connections to Bluecoat were little more than social, but the fact that the Sandon continued to attract members, many of whom were, in their professional lives, engaged in creative and intellectual activity, while others were simply passionate consumers and patrons of the arts, indicates the diverse and fertile environment that developed in the building. No doubt for some of these people, the chance to be part of something exclusive – to dine, party and network – was central; for others, what mattered was active participation in the music or drama group; others rented studio spaces, or joined for the opportunity to exhibit their art.

Bluecoat's first twenty years' involvement in the arts can be summarised as a close-knit group of progressive artists, aligned with a wider group of enthusiasts with differing cultural interests, coming together through their affection for an old building considered worth hanging on to in a rapidly changing city. This period was, in effect, a pilot for the arts centre that was to follow, but different in one important respect: once Bluecoat Society of Arts was established, the building would become accessible to a far wider constituency. While the Sandon would remain a members' club, another tenant alongside new incoming organisations, there would be other voices in the School Lane premises and, for the new Bluecoat Society, new responsibilities and accountability.

***

Figure 29. Sandon life drawing class at Bluecoat, probably 1950s. The artists include, from second left, William Stevenson, Herbert Tyson Smith and Jack Coburn Witherop.

The degree to which Bluecoat can claim to be a pioneering arts centre, and not just the first in the UK, can be assessed by studying the Deed of Constitution drawn up by Bluecoat Society of Arts in 1927, and then considering what it was able to achieve against its stated purposes. But first, how do we 'define an arts centre, and were there similar organisations elsewhere at this time? A 'functional community centre with a specific remit to encourage arts practice and to provide facilities such as theatre space, gallery space, venues for musical performance, workshop areas, educational facilities, technical equipment, etc.' is a typical description of an arts centre today.[88] According to the same source, they began in the UK after the Second World War.

Had the trustees of the Bluecoat Society, which included a Lord Mayor, four MPs, a newspaper proprietor and an editor, two shipowners and a bank manager, chosen to name the new organisation an arts *centre* instead of an arts *society*, Bluecoat's role in the arts centre movement, which developed after 1945, gathering pace in the 1960s and 1970s, might have been more widely recognised. Given that the Sandon and Reilly had conceived the idea in 1908/09, and that the term 'arts centre' was frequently used in public discourse in Liverpool concerning the future of the 'old Blue Coat Hospital', both then and during the appeal to save it after Leverhulme's death, it seems surprising that the term was not adopted as a bold statement for a new type of arts enterprise. The use, however, of 'society' – continuing the Sandon's status as a club and echoing the earlier proposals for a Lancashire Society of Arts – perhaps lent an air of respectability, felt to be necessary in helping to secure the building and enable its future sustainability. There were allusions to the language and role of earlier societies established in the eighteenth century, such as the Royal Society of Arts, whose Enlightenment values and mission to 'embolden enterprise, enlarge science, refine art, improve our manufacturers and extend our commerce'[89] find an almost archaic echo in the Bluecoat Society's constitution, which provides for 'scientific demonstrations' alongside the artistic, literary, musical and 'kinematographic' pursuits that one would expect of a centre for the arts. This was to be achieved within an overarching purpose of 'advancing or giving adult instruction and the diffusion of useful knowledge'.[90]

This concept of *useful knowledge*, harking back to the public dissemination of scientific and other learning in the nineteenth century,[91] has re-entered public discourse in recent years, with the idea that the arts could be *useful* being again interrogated.[92] Art's 'usefulness' manifests itself in an instrumental sense – in a governmental or other funder's measure of art's impact within social or regeneration agendas – or as 'engaged' arts practice, or work 'embedded' in a local context, as represented, for instance, by the architecture collective Assemble's winning the 2015 Turner Prize for its work restoring rundown housing in Liverpool's Granby area. In 1927 'useful art' would have made sense in the utilitarian context of the Sandon's strong applied arts origins, art created for a purpose beyond the purely aesthetic.

The objective to *diffuse* useful knowledge registers education in the arts centre's founding ethos, and although no specific mention is made in the constitution of an obligation to significantly broaden audiences for the arts – the principal beneficiaries of the new ownership being the Society's own circle – there is an indication that the new Bluecoat would also be used and enjoyed by other kindred spirits. Rooms would host 'exhibitions, receptions, lectures, conferences, entertainments, re-unions, dramatic or musical performances', and spaces would be rented to individuals or associations that followed artistic, intellectual or scientific pursuits. This guaranteed the continuation of the artists' studios and cultural organisations already in the building, with an ambition to increase them and generate more income through rents, desperately needed in the days before the building was in receipt of any public funding.

The majority of objects in the 1927 constitution relate to maintaining the building, a reflection of the trustees' priorities. The new organisation was essentially still dependent on private patronage and now required other commercial income streams; any surplus generated from hiring out spaces and from studio rents, including the Sandon's, would go first on the building and then on the arts. With this emphasis on bricks and mortar, the document nonetheless enshrines the arts at the heart of the new organisation, establishing it as a centre unique in the UK. Though there was a proliferation of art clubs and societies across the country, and single-art-form buildings such as galleries and theatres, no evidence has come to light of a similar multi-art-form venue existing at this time that housed studios and working artists, an arts programme of exhibitions and performances, and social spaces. In Devon, Dartington Hall Trust (founded 1925) 'attempted to bridge the gap between creative artists and the community in which they lived ... an inspired model of the arts-centre idea', yet Dartington remained essentially an educational initiative. It was not until after the Second World War that the combined arts model of an arts centre that Bluecoat had pioneered emerged: a year after the Arts Council of Great Britain published a modest blueprint, *Plans for an Arts Centre*, for cultural hubs in small-to-medium towns, Bridgewater in Somerset became the first such centre in 1946, followed by Swindon the same year.[93] One has to look abroad for other centres of multidisciplinary practice earlier in the century, and these are principally to be found in educational models such as the Bauhaus (1919) in Germany, or Black Mountain College (1933) in America.

The arts centre model that Bluecoat was to develop over the following decades, of a cultural umbrella accommodating artists and complementary organisations as tenants, letting out spaces for a range of social and artistic activities, encouraging the public's appreciation of the arts, and providing opportunities for learning, has its foundation here. Bluecoat's capacity for partnerships, participation and reaching a diversity of audiences that we see today stems from that 1927 document. Bluecoat's new aims, however, could not be put into effect immediately, as there was pressing structural work to be done to the building. Following the School of Architecture's tenure between 1909 and 1918, there had always been architectural expertise on hand, and tenants Shepheard & Bower were appointed to carry out this refurbishment, as well as later renovations, including repairs after the Blitz. In the less conservation-conscious 1920s there was an implicit appreciation, reflected in the Society's constitution, of the building's historical and aesthetic architectural importance, at least its distinctive Queen Anne-façaded front section. The plan accompanying the deeds divided the building into two properties – a more historic section (School Lane) and a later, unharmonious assemblage of buildings at the back (College Lane). The former would be maintained at all costs, while the latter, at the Society's discretion, might be sold. Clearly the 'capital H' architectural integrity of the whole ensemble was not yet valued, but thankfully the trustees did not have recourse to put any of this part of the property on the market, and the whole building was eventually protected through the awarding of its Grade I listed status in 1952.

This chapter has looked at some of the arts programmes leading up to the Second World War, with significant exhibitions and the loan of *Genesis* demonstrating an appetite among the wider Liverpool public for new art, albeit, in the case of Epstein's sculpture, under the guise of controversy. With building work and the burden of debt constituting a constant drain on what were essentially voluntary resources, realisation of the vision enshrined in the Bluecoat constitution was further delayed by wartime disruption, which continued well after 1945. It was only in the following two decades, after the building's restoration, when new energies were involved, that the full potential of the arts centre could start to be realised.

Notes

1   W. S. MacCunn, *Bluecoat Chambers: The Origins and Development of an Art Centre*, Liverpool: Liverpool University Press, 1956.
2   R. F. Bisson, *The Sandon Studios Society and the Arts*, Liverpool: Parry Books, published on behalf of the Sandon Studios Society, 1965.
3   John Belchem and Bryan Biggs, eds, *Liverpool: City of Radicals*, Liverpool: Liverpool University Press, 2011.
4   Norman Martin Bell, quoted in Peter Richmond, *Marketing Modernisms: The Architecture and Influence of Charles Reilly*, Liverpool: Liverpool University Press, 2001, p. 73, note 57.
5   Matthew Cornford, conversation with the author, October 2015. See also John Beck and Matthew Cornford, *The Art School and the Culture Shed*, Kingston upon Thames: The Centre for Useless Splendour, Kingston University, 2014.
6   Mary Bennett, *The Art Sheds 1894–1905*, exhibition catalogue, Liverpool: Walker Art Gallery, 1981, introduction, n.p.
7   Quentin Hughes, 'Before the Bauhaus', *Architectural History*, 25, 1962, where he sees the School of Architecture and Applied Arts as a forerunner of the pioneering German design school.
8   Maureen Bampton, 'Craftsman and Client: The Official Commissions of Edward Carter Preston', unpublished PhD thesis, University of Liverpool, 2007, p. 23.

9   Recommended by D. S. MacColl, the young John taught at the Art Sheds between 1901 and 1902. His brief sojourn there had an impact on him, befriending university librarian and Romany scholar John Sampson, developing his skills in etching and creating some key portraits, though he tired of teaching at the university and declared 'I become more rebellious in Liverpool' (quoted in Michael Holroyd, *Augustus John*, Harmondsworth: Penguin, 1974, p. 163).
10 Bennett, *The Art Sheds 1894–1905*, n.p.
11 Bennett, *The Art Sheds 1894–1905*, n.p.
12 Bisson, *The Sandon Studios Society*, pp. 11–16.
13 C. H. Reilly, *Scaffolding in the Sky: A Semi-architectural Autobiography*, London: George Routledge & Sons, 1938, p. 131.
14 Bisson, *The Sandon Studios Society*, p. 21.
15 Bisson, *The Sandon Studios Society*, p. 26.
16 Bisson, *The Sandon Studios Society*, p. ix.
17 Bisson, *The Sandon Studios Society*, p. 56.
18 For a colourful account of the School's time at Bluecoat, see Reilly, *Scaffolding in the Sky*, pp. 130–36.
19 Richmond, *Marketing Modernisms*, p. 59.
20 Richmond, *Marketing Modernisms*, p. 201.
21 See John Tiernan, 'Liverpool's "Bloomsberries": The Sandon Studios Society', *Liverpool History Society Journal*, 6, 2007, pp. 105–11.
22 Fanny Calder, 'Genesis', *The Bulletin of the Sandon Studios Society*, 1, March 1912, p. 2.

23   Bisson, *The Sandon Studios Society*, p. 46.

24   See Bryan Biggs, 'Radical Art City?', in John Belchem and Bryan Biggs, eds, *Liverpool: City of Radicals*, Liverpool: Liverpool University Press, 2011, pp. 63–66.

25   Biggs, 'Radical Art City?', pp. 64–65.

26   See Róisín Kennedy, 'Transmitting avant-garde art: Post-impressionism in a Dublin context', *Visual Resources*, 31.1–2, 2015, pp. 61–73, https://www.tandfonline.com/doi/full/10.1080/0 1973762.2015.1004780, accessed 4 January 2020. There was a mutual agreement between the Sandon and Dublin Arts Club that allowed members to be admitted to each other's club for half-a-crown monthly (Bisson, *The Sandon Studios Society*, p. 83).

27   Walker Art Gallery, *Art in Revolution: Liverpool 1911*, exhibition, 2011.

28   *Liverpool Courier*, 31 March 1911, p. 9.

29   *Manchester Guardian*, 6 March 1911.

30   Virginia Woolf, *Mr Bennett and Mrs Brown*, London: Hogarth Press, 1924, p. 4.

31   Bisson, *The Sandon Studios Society*, p. 88.

32   *Sandon Bulletin*, 5, June 1913.

33   Sandon Studios Society minutes, 30 June 1913.

34   Nearly seventy years later Bluecoat organised a substantial exhibition of Grant's decorative work, *Duncan Grant: Designer*, curated by Richard Shone (1980), which may have contained some of the same work as the Omega show.

35   Bisson, *The Sandon Studios Society*, p. 167.

36   Sandon Studios Society accounts 1929.

37   Bisson, *The Sandon Studios Society*, p. 161.

38   R. F. Bisson, *Bluecoat Cavalcade Golden Jubilee Exhibition*, brochure, 1977.

39   George Harris, W. Noel Irving and Arthur Watts, *A Bushel of Chaff: A Frolic*, privately published, printed by Handley Brothers, Liverpool, 1912, p. 7.

40   This was Bisson's view (Bisson, *The Sandon Studios Society*, p. 86). Although he refers to the *Futurist Manifesto*'s inclusion, it was not in fact Marinetti's founding document from 1909 but the final section of the *Technical Manifesto of Futurist Painting*, written by Umberto Boccioni, Carlo Carrà, Luigi Russolo, Giacomo Balla and Gino Severini, and published in *Poesia*, Milan, 11 April 1910.

41   Bisson, *The Sandon Studios Society*, p. 195.

42   Rutter's attack was included in *The Sport of Civic Life or Art and the Municipality*, 1909, pp. 9–12. See Tom Steele, *Alfred Orage and The Leeds Arts Club 1893–1923*, Aldershot: Scolar Press, 1990. Early modernist exhibitions at Bluecoat had works for sale, but it seems no one, not even Liverpool's municipal gallery, took the opportunity to buy a Picasso for ten guineas, for

instance. It was not until 1964 that the Walker purchased a Cézanne.

43   Review of the sculpture's first showing, Leicester Galleries, London 1931.

44   Bisson, *The Sandon Studios Society*, p. 174.

45   W. S. MacCunn, *Bluecoat Society of Arts Report for Year ended 31st March*, 1932, p. 4.

46   'Whatever the actual reasoning behind the choice, the outcome was highly successful and caused a sensation', Richmond, *Marketing Modernisms*, p. 74. Genesis later joined other works by Epstein at Blackpool, presented at Madame Tussauds in less dignified circumstances, a sort of 'freak show' introduction to modern art.

47   Reilly, *Scaffolding in the Sky*, p. 243. The actor was David Webster who later became general manager of Covent Garden.

48   The exhibitions were held in the concert hall. After that suffered bomb damage they moved downstairs. See MacCunn, *Bluecoat Chambers*, p. 44.

49   See Bisson, *The Sandon Studios Society*, p. 201.

50   Bisson, *The Sandon Studios Society*, pp. 101, 103. Three were killed including Donald Maclaren, and several others reported missing.

51   See Bennett, *The Art Sheds 1894–1905*, catalogue entry on Lister (later Calder). Calder continued in her retirement to paint: see Jane Renouf, *The Lake Artists' Society, 1904–2004: A Centenary Celebration*, Ambleside: Lake Artists Society, 2004.

52   *Autobiography of Fanny Dove Hamel Calder (née Lister)*, self-published, Bath, May 1950. The parchment was destroyed in a fire at Bluecoat in 2008. The medallion is in the Carter Preston collection at Liverpool Hope University. I am grateful to Calder's relative, Nigel Brocklehurst, for supplying information about his great aunt and showing examples of her work.

53   Quoted by Bisson, *The Sandon Studios Society*, p. 9.

54   Bisson, *The Sandon Studios Society*, p. 73.

55   See David Bingham, *1911: Art and Revolution in Liverpool: The Life and Times of Albert Lipczinski*, Bristol: Sansom, 2011.

56   Biggs, 'Radical Art City?', p. 69.

57   The painting is in the collection of University College London.

58   Timothy Stevens, preface to catalogue, *An exhibition of the works of Liverpool artist Gordon Lightfoot*, Liverpool: Walker Art Gallery, 1972, p. 3.

59   *Liverpool Daily Courier* review, March 1914.

60   *Liverpool Daily Post & Mercury* review. Quoted in Bisson, *The Sandon Studios Society*, p. 98.

61   I am grateful to Alan Whittaker and Susan Beck

at Liverpool Hope University for allowing me access to the Carter Preston special collection.

62 Joseph Sharples, 'From signwriter to cathedral sculptor', in Ann Compton, ed., *Edward Carter Preston 1885–1965: Sculptor, Painter, Medallist*, Liverpool: University of Liverpool Art Collections, 1999, p. 19.

63 'A Liverpool picture exhibition', review of Sandon Studios Society annual exhibition, *The Manchester Guardian*, 20 April 1912.

64 George Whitfield, 'What's wrong with the world? – Liverpool artist's metal "monster"', review of Liverpool Academy of Arts' annual exhibition at Bluecoat, *Liverpool Echo*, undated.

65 Cecilia Crighton, 'Private pleasures', in Compton, ed., *Edward Carter Preston*, p. 61.

66 Under a photograph of the sculpture in a press cutting (see Fig. 25), most likely accompanying the *Liverpool Echo* review (see note 64), there is a handwritten note, 'This is plaster about 24" high', which suggests that the exhibited piece was a plaster model, possibly painted metallic.

67 Quoted in George Whitfield, 'Liverpool artists III: Edward Carter Preston', *Liverpool Review*, 2, 1927, p. 423.

68 W. Aumonier, ed., *Modern Architectural Sculpture*, London and New York: The Architecture Press and Scribner's, 1930.

69 Joseph Sharples, *Pevsner Architectural Guides: Liverpool*, New Haven, CT: Yale University Press, 2004, p. 33.

70 Ann Compton, exhibition catalogue essay, *Roderick Bisson: Telling Tales*, Liverpool: University of Liverpool Art Gallery, 1999, p. 2.

71 *The Observer*, 28 January 1968. The gallery was the Redfern, which had been instrumental in promoting Henry Moore, Barbara Hepworth and other British modern artists and introducing new art from the Continent.

72 See Alexandra Harris, *Romantic Moderns: English Writers, Artists and the Imagination from Virginia Woolf to John Piper*, London: Thames and Hudson, 2010.

73 Recounted to the author by Robin Riley, 10 September 2014.

74 Brian Coe, 'George Davison: Impressionist and anarchist', in Mike Weaver, ed., *British Photography in the Nineteenth Century: The Fine Art Tradition*, Cambridge: Cambridge University Press, 1989, pp. 215–41.

75 Bisson, *The Sandon Studios Society*, p. 115.

76 Bisson, *Bluecoat Cavalcade*.

77 Bisson, *The Sandon Studios Society*, pp. 174–75.

78 Bisson, *The Sandon Studios Society*, p. 192. See also recollections of the Sandon in George Melly, *Scouse Mouse*, London: Weidenfeld and Nicolson, 1984.

79 St John Ervine, 'At the Play', review of *George W. Harris*, London: Nisbet & Co., 1930, *The Observer*, 18 January 1931.

80 Basil Dean, in unnamed ed., *George W. Harris*, London: Nisbet & Co., 1930, p. 7.

81 Ervine, 'At the Play'.

82 Ervine, 'At the Play'.

83 Dean, *George W. Harris*, p. 8.

84 St John Ervine, in *George W. Harris*, pp. 2–3.

85 Stainton de B. Taylor, *Two Centuries of Music in Liverpool*, Liverpool: Rockliff Brothers, 1976, ch. 9, 'Music at the Bluecoat'.

86 Letter in *Sandon Bulletin*, 6, 17 June 1913.

87 *Liverpolitan*, II.I, January 1933, p. 20.

88 Wikipedia, accessed 8 January 2016.

89 Royal Society of Arts mission in its founding charter, 1754.

90 *Deed of Constitution of The Bluecoat Society of Arts*, 28 January 1927, p. 3. 'Society of Arts' would, according to MacCunn, indicate Bluecoat's future use (MacCunn, *Bluecoat Chambers*, p. 23).

91 London's Society for the Diffusion of Useful Knowledge, founded in 1826, 'published inexpensive texts intended to adapt scientific and similarly high-minded material for the rapidly expanding reading public' (Wikipedia). Gertrude Stein published her *Useful Knowledge* in 1928.

92 See The Office of Useful Art, http://www.grizedale.org/blogs/blog/8887/the-office-of-useful-art.1, accessed 4 January 2020. Bluecoat staged an exhibition in 2015, RESOURCE, which curator Marie-Anne McQuay conceived as extending 'its enquiry into its own surroundings, questioning the nature, but also future possibilities of arts centres. Is their value based solely on what is presented publicly or what is produced behind the scenes? What new resources should a 21st century arts venue offer to remain useful to the public which they serve?' (quoted in 'Centre Piece: could arts centres once again be the model for the arts in austerity?', *Arts Industry*, August 2015, p. 14). Since Oscar Wilde declared that 'All Art is Quite Useless' in 1890, this position remains a counter to the argument, and that art, as opposed to art centres, is inherently useless.

93 John Lane, *Arts Centres: Every Town Should Have One*, London: Paul Elek, 1978, pp. 1–3.

Chapter 4

Where Village Hall Meets the Avant-garde

Bryan Biggs

The reopening of its concert hall in 1951, rebuilt after wartime bombing, marked a new chapter in Bluecoat's history. That year the 400-capacity space was used for concerts and meetings, as well as exhibitions, as the venue participated in Liverpool's programme for the Festival of Britain, an expression of post-war optimism which, even in a city as shattered as Liverpool, lifted spirits through a range of cultural activities. Though the Bluecoat Society of Arts' financial worries were far from over, the building's studios were full and exhibitions such as the three-week long *Fifty Years of Merseyside Painting* and the ten-day *America 1951*, documenting the American way of life, proved popular, attracting some 20,000 and 30,000 visitors respectively.

Together with War Damage Commission funding, a grant from the Arts Council of Great Britain had considerably assisted the refurbishment, and this support would continue for a further two years. Help from the Arts Council (which had been established in 1946 from CEMA, the Council for the Encouragement of Music and the Arts) was invaluable in the decade following the end of the war. After the Council closed its Manchester office in 1955, its regional officer Nicholas Horsfield, himself a distinguished artist who had got to know the Sandon artists, relocated to Liverpool to teach at the College of Art and played a role in Bluecoat, as adviser, committee member and exhibitor. From the 1960s onwards the Arts Council would

Figure 30. Robin Blackledge performance, *Sun-spot*, 1990.

become increasingly important – and necessary – for organisations such as Bluecoat, both in terms of funding and policy. The growth of the Council – an integral part of the welfare state – was largely a result of Harold Wilson's appointment in his Labour government of the country's first Minister for the Arts, Jennie Lee, and her 1965 White Paper *A Policy for the Arts – The First Steps*. This radical manifesto pledged a new infrastructure for the arts and ongoing support aimed at ensuring that culture would be accessible to all. The increase in public subsidy for the arts was accompanied by a greater commitment from local authorities to support cultural development, including funding towards the establishment of regional branches of the Arts Council; in Liverpool, Merseyside Arts Association would be set up, renting office space at Bluecoat.

Labour's arts policies were part of a wider democratisation of culture and greater educational opportunity in the post-war period, seen for instance in the country's art schools, where young people from a range of social backgrounds were exposed to a breadth of creative ideas; many of them went on to pursue careers, not just as visual artists, but in the worlds of pop music, fashion, television, film, advertising, publishing, or in teaching or politics. The Coldstream Report of 1960[1] introduced a compulsory academic element to the curriculum, with complementary studies and art history being taught, though 'paradoxically, the lack of structured and rigorous education in art history (or in studio practice) gave room to more marginal groups and critical stances'.[2] In the wake of Coldstream, art schools flourished as places for experimentation, with new media and ideas and connections to other discourses opening up in the counter-cultural environment of the time. Bluecoat's exhibition programme was enlivened in this period by its links to the region's art schools – notably Liverpool and, from the 1970s, Manchester too – with many tutors on foundation and fine art courses, as well as students and recent graduates, showing at the gallery.

Even in northern cities still scarred by the war and economic depression there was disposable income to spend on arts and leisure, fuelling in particular an increasingly confident pop culture. And in Liverpool, as the 1960s dawned, a new cultural renaissance was underway, spearheaded by Merseybeat. But it was not just The Beatles, with their art school credentials, who aroused widespread interest in the city from outside. The growing mass media brought Scouse comedians, entertainers and dramas to TV screens across the country, while the Mersey poets' fresh approach struck a chord and inspired a generation of young writers; the swaying, singing Kop staked a claim for football at the heart of the city's culture; and a new cathedral of controversial brutalist design rose on the skyline. This new confidence belied Merseyside's underlying economic malaise, which would worsen in the following decades; yet the optimism was tangible and Bluecoat's resilience after the 1951 Festival was evident, as it sought more ambitious programming in its restored building in order to develop a greater public presence at the centre of Liverpool's cultural life.

To effect this, in 1961 Bluecoat Society of Arts set up a sub-committee, Bluecoat Arts Forum, with the stated aim of bridging the gap between the artist and society, and fulfilling the Society's constitutional remit to promote the arts, while it got on with the business of managing the building and its finances. With Peter Rockliff as its chair and Celia van Mullem its secretary, the Forum's functions were threefold: to publicise and coordinate its member societies (which totalled 45 by 1968, many of them music societies, hence the Forum's emphasis on this art form); to organise events not being provided for by existing organisations in the city; and to be an 'organisation concerned with the arts today … not just a campaign to promote "art for art's sake", but … [to bring] an appreciation and enjoyment of both new and existing work to a wider cross-section of the community'.[3]

New funds would be required in order to realise this. Up until the Second World War, the Sandon, and then the Bluecoat Society, had been mainly privately supported, and sustained Arts Council revenue was slow in coming; however, Bluecoat's charitable status allowed it to apply to trusts and foundations. In 1957 a sympathetic supporter was found in the Calouste Gulbenkian Foundation, with £2,000 per annum secured for three years (compared to the £400 Arts Council grants earlier that decade). This was pivotal for the arts centre, allowing it to support emerging artists with travel grants; fund a critical inquiry into Bluecoat's future role in the city, which resulted in John Willett's seminal sociology of art in a single city, *Art in a City*; and produce three annual festivals encompassing different art forms.[4] While the themes of these were historical, the week-long *Bluecoat 63* festival that followed brought to the attention of over 15,000 visitors the full range of the arts centre's contemporary offer, delivered by many member societies, and with performances, talks and an exhibition, *Artist works with Architect*, curated by a group chaired by architectural historian Quentin Hughes. As an awareness-raising event, the festival demonstrated the building's value 'as a live Arts Centre in the City and as an effective venue for small exhibitions'.[5]

The Forum's ability to make Bluecoat a 'live' arts centre was, however, dependent on its relationship with the Bluecoat Society, and this came to a head when Rockliff suggested that the Forum could only make progress if the attitude of the trustees – whose duty to maintain in the historic building 'a certain aura of respectability … does tend to inhibit free expression of some of the more enterprising developments in the contemporary arts' – changed.[6] Though tensions remained, the Forum did make a significant leap forward with the appointment in 1966 of Wendy Harpe as its first artistic administrator. This was in the context of wider conversations being hosted by Liverpool Corporation – in response to Jennie Lee's advocacy for regional arts centres – about the establishment of a Liverpool arts centre, which naturally Bluecoat was anxious to be part of, given its historical claim to be precisely that.[7] A Merseyside Arts Centre Committee had been set up and meetings were held with Birmingham's Cannon Hill arts centre (today's mac, previously Midlands Arts Centre) and Clive Barker, formerly of London's Centre 42 (the Roundhouse). A report in 1965 by the Arts Forum outlined what such an arts centre for Liverpool should be, relating this to its existing work and arguing that a professional appointment would help develop a city arts association, building on the Forum's activities of coordination, services and creative work.

Harpe's musical legacy at Bluecoat is discussed in Chapter 6, and it should also be noted that her arrival connected Bluecoat to the Sandon's radical visual arts origins and pointed the way forward to the interdisciplinary and socially engaged art that would become a distinctive element of the arts centre offer in the following decades (and which is discussed below). Harpe was the subject of a double-page spread, 'Trendy Wendy', by John Pilger in the *Daily Mirror*,[8] and her adventurous programme was informed by keeping an eye on new trends in London, frequently visiting the likes of Indica Gallery and attending events such as the Destruction in Art Symposium. Here, she met leading artists of Britain's avant-garde John Latham and Mark Boyle (who had been banned from the Institute of Contemporary Arts for allowing the audience to dismantle a piano); both of them later showed at Bluecoat, and through Harpe, Boyle was introduced to Peter Moores who was active in the Arts Forum and became his patron.

Under Harpe's guidance 'what is probably the best non-municipal gallery outside London'[9] gained greater recognition for its exhibitions – a mix of local and national artists – and the live programme was characterised by its art form breadth, ambition and risk taking. For instance, 1967 saw an installation and performances by Mark Boyle and Joan Hills, an experimental film commissioned from Stephen Dwoskin, a concert using glass sheets and rods by Anna Lockwood, exhibitions of contemporary African art and *Northern Young Contemporaries*, visits by the London School of Contemporary Dance and classical Indian dancers, a summer school in modern theatre, poetry from Christopher Logue, Adrian Mitchell, Tom Pickard and Anselm Hollo, and a performance by Yoko Ono (Fig. 31), as well as off-site exhibitions of sculpture, and film and music collaborations at other venues. The following year Bluecoat maintained its avant-garde credentials with poets Barry McSweeney and Bob Cobbing, crossover music group Indo-Jazz Fusions and many others. That year Rockliff was able to report on the Forum's achievements:

The principal problem in the arts today has been defined as 'bridging the gap between the arts and the vast majority of people'. The Arts Council has recently re-worded its objectives to this end. Whilst it is easy to pay lip service to this need, in fact there are very few people working in the arts with clear ideas as to how it can be achieved in practical terms. I think perhaps Wendy Harp's [sic] greatest contribution to the work of the Forum has been in this particular context, and in acting as a catalyst between the creative artists working here and our established art organisations.[10]

The Forum promoted experimental work off-site, such as new music series *Musica Viva* at the university,[11] directed by Bill Harpe and designed by Rod Murray, but by 1970 much of its work – and its funding from the city council – had been absorbed by the Arts Council's new regional branch, Merseyside Arts Association (the rest of the north-west was served by an office in Manchester). The experimental nature of the Bluecoat programmes thereafter effectively reduced, while the local arts network

Figure 31. Yoko Ono performing in the concert hall, 1967. Photo © Sheridon Davies.

and information role developed by the Forum over almost a decade was taken up by MAA, including a popular listings and news bulletin, which became the monthly *Arts Alive* publication. This had previously been distributed by the Arts Forum through the racing department of Littlewoods, courtesy of Peter Moores.

Moores also purchased a building that would become the UK's first community arts venue, Great Georges Community Cultural Project, known as the Blackie (today the Black-E) in Liverpool's Chinatown, and Harpe left the Arts Forum in October 1968 to join her husband Bill in running the new venture. Her interests had moved towards engaging local people more directly in the arts and she felt that, despite accessible events such as readings by the popular new poets, Bluecoat was not the right venue for the burgeoning grassroots arts environment in Liverpool. The Arts Forum did, however, fund several early Blackie events, noting this as

> probably the first time that an Arts organization such as ours has worked together with a Community organization in this way. In terms of the basic problem of bringing the arts to a wider public, our member societies are becoming increasingly aware of the significance and value of the neighbourhood arts movement … This project, seen objectively in relation to the Bluecoat can only be seen as providing complementary facilities.[12]

While Harpe was formulating a radical approach to making art accessible through her nascent community arts initiatives, the recommendations for a more socially connected art contained in Willett's *Art in a City* were being considered.[13] This discourse went beyond Liverpool, with reviews and comment pieces in the national press, and an associated exhibition at the ICA in London in 1967. Willett's book, which grew from a study commissioned five years earlier by Bluecoat, using its Gulbenkian funding, was – as John Belchem discusses in Chapter 2 – groundbreaking, providing an in-depth analysis of art in Liverpool, from its early patronage to the contemporary scene, discussing issues of taste, education, doctrine and the public realm, and culminating in a blueprint for a future role for art in people's lives, in the city's thinking, and in the development of Bluecoat Society of Arts. The idea for the study – and for Willett to author it – had been suggested by Nicholas Horsfield, who was concerned at the state of Liverpool's visual arts. Harpe, however, considered the report 'too academic',[14] and there appeared to be no synergy between her grassroots community approach, albeit one involving uncompromisingly avant-garde artists, and Willett's calls for a wholesale, policy-driven, civic reawakening through art. Both espoused a more democratic and progressive role for the arts, and greater access for audiences, and it is tantalising to think how Willett's action plan to realise his vision for a 'sociology of the arts', informed by the contemporary thinking in the field that he cited (including Richard Hoggart and Stuart Hall in the UK and thinkers on the Continent such as Umberto Eco and Roland Barthes, and informed by Walter Benjamin and Marx), might have played out had it been adopted by Liverpool, and linked to the more improvised, participatory experiments of the Harpes at the Blackie.

The response to *Art in a City* by Bluecoat Society of Arts, the immediate recipient of Willett's proposals, was welcoming but cautious, while the grand scheme for Liverpool sat on the shelf for thirty years until a more confident city had the ambition to harness art as a driver for regeneration. Bluecoat adopted some of the recommendations – to develop its paintings loan scheme and professionalise its gallery – yet it was not in a position, financially or politically, to drive the plan of action. What the report, together with Harpe's curatorial audacity and thinking around audience, did, however, was to put down a marker for a very different Bluecoat: more outward looking, while being socially engaged and connected to the city, its arts community and local people. Over time, these ideas would become core to the organisation, but in the late 1960s, notwithstanding the efforts of Bluecoat Arts Forum, especially under Harpe, the venue was perceived by some as elitist; and while the Sandon continued to host marvellous parties and run an adventurous music group, the arts centre was not for everyone. Sculptor Robin Riley has recalled the environment when he had a studio in the building in the late 1950s, his arrival being regarded with suspicion by some of the old guard studio holders who had been there since before the war. Despite the encouragement of artists Bisson, Mayer-Marton and Allan Tankard, the atmosphere was of a 'private club', provoking disdain from the younger tutors at the Art School, one of whom, Arthur Ballard, refused to join the Sandon as there were 'no communists' there.[15] A decade later another Liverpool sculptor, Arthur Dooley, self-styled 'Catholic-communist' cultural celebrity, led a protest on the railings about local artists being priced out of exhibiting at the gallery and being snubbed in favour of Londoners.[16] Yet on reflection, in the twenty years after the building's reopening in 1951, Bluecoat was consolidated as a vital hub for Liverpool culture. Where else in the north-west, in one venue, could one experience Festival of Britain events, professional concerts in an elegant auditorium, avant-garde performance art, contemporary art exhibitions, a craft gallery, pop poetry, modern jazz, Lieder recitals, film screenings, a community of cultural societies, artists working in studios, the stirrings of community art, and discourse around art's social role?

The ability to encompass such a range of activity was not without its challenges, yet with a more structured approach in place for accommodating different art form strands under one roof, and with the arrival of Merseyside Arts as a funder, information service and arts advocate (its offices located conveniently in the building), the 1970s brought consistency to Bluecoat's programming and greater visibility as a centre for the arts. The story of the arts centre's newly refreshed gallery is told in Chapter 5, and its music history from this period is covered in Chapter 6. The focus for the rest of this chapter is therefore on how Bluecoat, building on the foundations of the Arts Forum, developed a profile across a range of other artistic practices including dance, literature, live art and site-specific work, leading to a blurring of distinctions and mixing of disciplines, this 'combined arts' nature defining the building's continuing function as an arts centre. From the 1970s onwards, as the arts programming influence of the Sandon Studios Society waned, Bluecoat's role as an umbrella for different partner organisations and festivals grew.

***

Wendy Harpe had been Bluecoat's first paid artistic director, and other specialists were subsequently employed to run the programmes, their passions often directing the focus – contemporary dance, early music or jazz, for instance. This was only possible through increased public subsidy – from the regional Arts Council (Merseyside Arts), of which Bluecoat became a revenue client, a position that has continued ever since (funding now coming through the Arts Council's Manchester office) and, in the next decade, from Liverpool City Council. This also enabled greater risk taking in a programme that – alongside the gallery – comprised performances of music, dance, literature and live art, while some building tenants added to this offer, with cinema being provided by Merseyside Film Institute and contemporary crafts by the Bluecoat Display Centre.

Following Arts Minister Jenny Lee's 1965 White Paper, new arts buildings sprang up across the UK, and by the 1970s an arts centre 'movement' was in full flow, with over 150 open by 1978, half of them less than five years old.[17] Bluecoat's earlier origins, however, set it somewhat apart from this, its ad hoc approach as the arts centre was taking shape and when no other comparable institution existed making for a quirky assemblage of amateur and professional elements; a place where, as later described by Hans van der Heijden, 'village hall meets the avant-garde'.[18] For an institution that had been ahead of the game, there was now a sense that Bluecoat was somewhat anachronistic, out of step with the 1960s arts centre model and as a result perhaps taken for granted. It did not even warrant a mention (other than in an appendix of venues) in John Lane's 1978 study *Arts Centres: Every Town Should Have One*, which charted the history of arts centres and looked at case studies, Great Georges – not Bluecoat – being chosen to represent Liverpool. The Blackie was also the subject of another study into arts centres carried out by the Arts Council the year before, but was omitted from the published report at its own request.[19] The dilemma of the new arts centres was summarised in this study by Peter Stark, then director of South Hill Park in Bracknell, as 'quantity or quality, arts centre or leisure centre … problems which derive from the differing priorities of the Arts Council and local authorities'[20] that funded them.

As Chapter 2 indicates, however, Bluecoat as a model of a working centre for the arts had often attracted national attention and the provocation of *Art in a City* and Harpe's adventurous programming were pertinent to debates about art and access for audiences; yet this critical currency did not translate into public subsidy to the same level as that of emerging arts centres such as Arnolfini in Bristol (founded 1961) and the Third Eye Centre (later the Centre for Contemporary Arts – CCA) in Glasgow (founded 1975), or the much older Institute of Contemporary Arts (ICA) in London (founded 1947). These three venues offered a similar combination of activities as Bluecoat, though with much greater resources, including financial. All had a strong visual art component at their core and, with two of them, Arnolfini and ICA, Bluecoat developed exhibition and other collaborations in the 1980s and 1990s.[21] Bluecoat was closer in terms of an interest in 'issue-based' and interdisciplinary art practice to these venues than to other UK arts centres, where the focus was more on performance, particularly theatre and music, and where the programming staple tended towards bought-in touring work.

Like the three aforementioned venues, and others such as Chapter Arts Centre in Cardiff (founded, like Bluecoat, in a former school in 1971), the multi-art-form nature of Bluecoat made it a focus for a broad mix of interests from both artists and audiences. Its lack of a consistent evening offer with an all-important café and bar put it at a disadvantage in relation to these venues, but like them it was well placed to respond to new tendencies in art and had the necessary gallery and performance spaces, curatorial interests and growing specialist audiences to be able to programme thematically across art forms. Bluecoat's relative revenue paucity meant that such programmes were invariably delivered on a shoestring, or had to be project funded, yet the informality of its spaces, central location and connections built up over many years to arts groups, individual artists and colleges, and its own on-site creative community, made it well suited to develop its combined arts capacity. At the same time, the gallery was becoming part of a national network, connected through touring exhibitions, comprising single-art-form Arts Council-funded venues – galleries such as Birmingham's Ikon, Oxford's Museum of Modern Art and Cambridge's Kettle's Yard – and a growing number of local authority galleries presenting contemporary work, especially in the North and Midlands. With the constant challenge – and sometimes tensions – of accommodating contemporary art in a heritage building,

Bluecoat was fortunate in having on its board key figures who brought increasingly necessary business, legal, financial and other skills while having a passion for art across the spectrum. In the 1980s chairs such as Colin Wilson, Peter Urquhart, Alan Swerdlow, and chair of the gallery committee, David King encouraged initiatives that widened the arts centre's remit in the visual and performing arts to better position it in an increasingly competitive arts environment. In 1987, however, it was necessary to separate the organisation into two companies in order to more effectively run both the building and the arts, through differentiating the costs of each. In 1993 the two companies merged as Bluecoat Arts Centre.

What, then, characterised the 'Bluecoat way' of doing things, with visual art at its core but also an integrated and increasingly prominent live programme; and what identifies the venue in the UK's arts centres environment, which, over time, changed from the preserve mainly of the middle classes, to more alternative centres in the 1960s and 1970s, to serving the wider community in the 1980s? By looking at several programme strands and specific events, a sense of Bluecoat's multidisciplinary development from the late 1970s and into the 1990s emerges. As Roger Hill's chronological survey of music in Chapter 6 reveals, many musical genres have found a home at Bluecoat, from classical to experimental, and its embrace of other performing arts has been likewise broad, with theatre the only main omission. With the reconfiguration of its concert hall after the war, drama presentations became less frequent at Bluecoat, and theatre, with the exception of more experimental forms that, as we will see, did occupy an important part of the live programme, was left to the city's Playhouse, Everyman and Unity theatres.

Through Barbara Foran's tenure at Bluecoat in the early 1980s (as programmer, then director), mime had a short-lived presence, with appearances by Nola Rae, Julian Chagrin, Moving Picture Mime Show, David Glass – who would return several times – and Britain's first all-women mime group, Three Women Mime Company. The Arts Forum had introduced dance in the late 1960s, with artists from the Place in London, and the commissioning of Geoff Moore to make a piece with dancers who went on to become the company Moving Being, but it was Foran's enthusiasm for dance that established the venue as a serious space for contemporary work, and Bluecoat played an important role in nurturing local dance practice and building a dance audience.

There were visits from Fergus Early and Jacky Lansley (with *I, Giselle*), Maedée Duprès and Mantis Dance Company. *Summer Dance '85* included performances that pushed the definition of dance, with Peta Lily, Laurie Booth (with turntable artist Philip Jeck), Howard and Eberle, and Théâtre de Complicité, with their Perrier Award-winning show, *More Bigger Snacks Now*. Gregory Nash was in residence

Figure 32. Bisakha Sarker, *Do not yet fold your wings*, performance installation in the Vide, 2015. Photo: Brian Roberts.

during the festival and developed *Circuitous Routes* with visual artist Jonathan Froud, Bluecoat's music and dance director James Beirne as composer, and young people from Merseyside Youth Association's dance group. The resulting performance moved from the front courtyard to the concert hall and demonstrated Bluecoat's capacity to deliver cross-art-form collaboration that used the building's fabric, and to accommodate youth dance. This went alongside support for emerging local professional dance practice, with companies such as Spiral and Delado regularly performing. The latter, an African dance and drumming ensemble, was reflective of the increasing diversity of the live programme in the 1980s, as Bluecoat worked with other local artists such as south Asian dance artist Bisakha Sarker. She would go on to have a long association with the venue, performing in many festivals, collaborating with artists such as Keith Khan, running *Anga Chetna*, an Indian dance summer school for health awareness, and the first ever international dance for care of dementia conference *Memory*, as well as dementia-friendly performances *Fleeting Moments*. More recently, her installation *Do not yet fold your wings* (in collaboration with Ansuman Biswas and Chris Davies), commissioned for the Vide space in 2015 (Fig. 32), was enabled by funding from the Baring Foundation for 'late style' artists.

South Asian dance became a regular feature through collaborations with the Indian arts organisation MILAP, whose annual festival (which eventually grew into Milapfest) brought high-quality South Indian classical dance and music to the venue for many years and introduced companies such as Chitraleka to Liverpool. Other UK-based companies drawing on non-European traditions such as the Jiving Lindy Hoppers with their recreation of New York's black dance of the 1930s, Union Dance's contemporary mix of jazz and reggae influences, and Afro Caribbean dance theatre Kokuma, were featured alongside traditional dance from Spain (with flamenco favourites Jaleo), Korea, South Africa and, later, the Arab world. This echoed the gallery's increasingly diverse exhibitions programme and the 'world music' starting to appear in the live programme, which was later developed by Jayne Casey (see Chapter 6).

The prominence of dance in Bluecoat's programme in this decade is evidenced by the list of artists who performed at the venue: rising star of British dance Michael Clark and Extemporary (both 1984); Phoenix and Shobana Jeyasingh (1986), the latter returning three more times, including in 1994 with choreographer Richard Alston; Sue MacLennan with Intermedia (1985) and Occasional Dance (1987); and Motionhouse (1989) who returned frequently in the 1990s. Much of this activity was facilitated by the removal of the stage and the installation of a retractable seating unit in the concert hall in the early 1980s, which greatly improved sightlines and made the space more flexible for performers. Over time the unit became a liability, requiring a gang of strong men to manually manoeuvre the groaning apparatus into position for each gig, but it did mean that Bluecoat could host more ambitious dance, music and other live events and tap into national touring networks.

Promoted as part of Bluecoat's 'mime and dance' programme, companies such as Trestle and Teatr Blik, from Poland, fitted neither category comfortably. They were part of an expansion of theatre and dance practice into a more visual realm, and Bluecoat provided a focus in Liverpool for these new companies. The 'devised' visual theatre of Complicité, seen at the venue two years after they had started out, and the world premiere of Trickster's The Memory Gate in 1986, started to build a local audience for this area of experimental performance. The Arts Council's Contemporary Music Network tours that visited also occasionally included live performance elements, such as 1986's Futurities, with dance artists Douglas Dunn and Elsa Wolliaston responding to the poetry of Robert Creeley and Steve Lacy's saxophone. James Beirne's curating of such events in his live programme echoed Wendy Harpe's eclecticism and finger-on-the-pulse intuition, and he could rightly claim that Bluecoat's 1985/86 performance season was an 'unprecedented explosion of activity … [with] the flowering of a programme … comparable to any found in the major contemporary arts centres in the country'.[22] The following year he invited Nottingham's Midland Group to present a weekend of performance, featuring Manact and Intimate Strangers. Together with Call of the Wild (comprising members of Moving Picture Mime, Impact and Lumière & Son) and Anne Seagrave and Oscar McLennan, a strand of performance art was emerging in the programme that would come to be known as 'live art', reinforced by live work presented in the gallery programme. Live art, much of it emanating from fine art practice and drawing in elements of theatre, dance, music and much else, would become a key strand of Bluecoat's programme, as discussed below.

With connections to centres for contemporary dance such as the Laban in London and festivals such as Dance Umbrella, there was a consistent offer of fresh work throughout the 1990s and relationships developed with several leading dance artists. DV8 Theatre co-founder Nigel Charnock's first solo show *Resurrection* was followed by four more visits. European youth dance was showcased and there were performances by, among others, V-Tol, the Cholmondeleys who visited in 1986 and returned with a performance around a car in pedestrianised Church Street, the Featherstonehaughs, Emilyn Claid, Yolande Snaith, The Hairy Mairys, RJC and Wayne McGregor's Random Dance Company. Bluecoat

Figure 33. Paula Hampson, *Track* performance, 1996, with sculptures outside the windows by Faith Bebbington. Photo: Robert Cook.

developed a fruitful partnership with the region's new dance agency Merseyside Dance Initiative (MDI), whose annual LEAP festival found a regular home at the arts centre. The first festival, in 1995, saw performances by Green Candle, Sankalpam's fusion of traditional Bharata Natyam with contemporary dance and jazz, and a community dance project with Peter Badejo. Local dance artist Paula Hampson also participated with her company, and she went on to work closely with the arts centre through imaginative collaborations, including *Track* (1997) with Faith Bebbington (Fig. 33), whose sculptures were suspended dramatically across the front courtyard, and girls from Broughton Hall High School. MDI's *Physically Feminine* programmes took place at Bluecoat from 1996 and included another Merseyside dance artist, Andrea Buckley, who performed solo and with her own company, as well as forming Chapter 4 with Hampson, Tom Roden and Ruth Spencer. The company was frequently at the arts centre, in residence or performing, finally in 2004 with *Gallery*, which was one of the last events in the concert hall before Bluecoat closed for redevelopment.

The LEAP festivals and other collaborations with MDI and Dance North West contributed to a diversity of dance practice at the venue in this decade, including Sean Tuan John, Earthfall, Protein, Corali Dance Company, Emily Burns, Carlson Dance Company, Wendy Houstoun, Bedlam Dance Company, Liz Aggis, Judy Bird's *Growing Old (Dis)gracefully* project, South Asian UK youth dance showcase *Disha* with Chaturang, British Chinese dance company Bi Ma and, from Canada, The Holy Body Tattoo. In 1996 choreographed aerial dance duo Momentary Fusion mesmerised (and terrified) the audience by emerging from inside Bluecoat's one-handed clock before descending the Queen Anne building's façade, their performance then continuing inside. The decade also saw the start of *Nadey al Bluecoat*, a partnership with the Liverpool Yemeni Arabic Club, which would develop into the Liverpool Arab Arts Festival. Its 'weekenders' in the late 1990s featured Arab dance, which became an integral part of Bluecoat's live offer.

When the arts centre reopened in 2008, its performance space no longer had the capacity to accommodate large-scale dance, but, mirroring shifts in artistic practice towards the site-specific and dance as public intervention, the venue was able to host a range of work in its new, smaller performance space and around the building, including the gallery. The old gallery had last been used for dance by Rosemary Lee in 1988 as part of *Gathering Light*, a touring exhibition from Camerawork/ Chisenhale Dance Space. But in 2017 something much more ambitious took place: the new, larger galleries were occupied for a ten-day residency by Siobhan Davies Dance, who rearticulated the different spaces through daily performances and sculptural interventions (Fig. 83). Surprisingly, Davies had never performed at

Bluecoat before, though several of her collaborators had, including Andrea Buckley, who was involved in setting up Liverpool Improvisation Collective, whose dance studio is at Bluecoat. The collective's other members – Jo Blowers, Paula Hampson and Mary Prestidge – are continually active in the building, most recently in a collaborative project, *INHABIT*, to develop their own practice and new audiences and participants for dance.

While dance at Bluecoat can trace its lineage back to the 1980s and 1990s (and an interest in ballet stretching back to the early Sandon days), other areas of performance from these decades are perhaps less well known. In her relatively short tenure as live programmer, Jayne Casey introduced a strong strand of LGBTQ work, making Bluecoat, alongside the musical distinctiveness she brought to the venue, a vital platform in the city for new queer performance, much of it local. Between 1988 and 1990 events included Peter Stack's cabaret *Dead Marilyn*, Ivan's *Where have all the flowers gone?*, local theatre group Hollywood TNT with an all-male version of *Whatever Happened to Baby Jane?*, a film and short plays by writer Shaun Duggan, The Beige Experience – billed as 'live fast, die camp' – and Sex and Violence's 'adult pantomime', as well as film screenings for Merseyside Lesbian and Gay Pride Week, and an Alternative Festival Queen event compered by Lily Savage for Merseyside Festival of Comedy, which Casey went on to direct. This strand of her programming at Bluecoat, together with Graeme Phillips's nurturing of Liverpool's 'electric-eclectic queer underground' of this period, much of it driven by graduates of the Everyman Youth Theatre, was a 'latent catalyst' for the Homotopia festival that young actor Gary Everett went on to create in the city in 2003.[23]

Comedy has had a sporadic presence at Bluecoat, sometimes unintentionally, the highlight here perhaps being when one of its press releases ended up in *Private Eye*'s 'Pseud's Corner'![24] There have even been exhibitions intended to make you laugh,[25] and the gallery has programmed live art as part of Bluecoat's contribution to Liverpool's Festival of Comedy, such as local artists Phil Hu (Hughes) and Bob Connolly's *Executive Golf* in the front courtyard, and John Carson's *Off Pat* in the gallery in 1986, and the Whalley Range All Stars, Steve Purcell & Company, Bobby Baker and Etheldreda in 1988. With visits by radio and TV comedians Jeremy Hardy (1990), John Shuttleworth (1994) and Vic Reeves (2009), as well as artists straddling the worlds of performance art and comedy such as Kim Noble (2010) and Bryony Kimmings (2011), comedy has managed to find its way into the programme.

While the venue has been unsuited to conventional theatre, adaptations of Stephen Berkoff (*West* in 1989 and *Greek* in 1993) and other contemporary writers took place, and Ken Campbell's *Reflections of a Furtive Nudist* and *Hail Eris (Goddess of Chaos and Discord)* – charting the genesis of the Science Fiction

Theatre of Liverpool – in 1988 and 1990 respectively, were a natural fit for Bluecoat. Unconventional theatre alongside other new performance also found a place through several Liverpool festivals that began relationships with the venue in the 1990s, such as the international street festival Brouhaha, which often presented work in the front courtyard.

Live art is a term that superseded 'performance art' to describe work that often comes from but does not fit neatly into either a gallery or theatre context. It has come to embrace a vibrant and disruptive area of art that still defies easy categorisation (other than, paradoxically, the category of 'live art' created for it), through strategies such as 'body art, performances for the stage, cabaret, interactions in public, site-responsive work, invisible interventions, overtly political actions'.[26] What Lois Keidan has described as 'experiential, experimental and ephemeral' is still, twenty years on from when she and Catherine Ugwu established the Live Art Development Agency in 1999, which Bluecoat would work with on several projects, 'a fiercely politicised, provocative, and unruly area of practice'.[27] Live art at Bluecoat developed from two directions: first, the dance/visual theatre of the 1980s, described above, and secondly, the happenings of the 1960s that came from a European and American avant-garde visual art tradition stretching back to Dada. Performances stemming from the former were more conventionally presented in the concert hall at Bluecoat, with many of the most innovative touring companies and artists: Dogs in Honey (1989), Ra-Ra Zoo circus theatre (1991, 1993), Forced Entertainment with *Marina and Lee* (1992) and *Speak Bitterness* (1996), Annie Griffin (1993), Forkbeard Fantasy and Stan's Café (both 1994), Blast Theory (1996) and Reckless Sleepers (1999). The second type of work came from a longer history of experimental practice and also had a specific Liverpool origin. 'Total artist' Adrian Henri pioneered happenings in the UK, presenting the country's first in 1962 in the city, and three years later his *Spring* event with Merseybeat group The Clayton Squares took place at Bluecoat, where he had previously exhibited paintings in 1959. Henri, whose *Environments and Happenings*[28] was the first book to chart the development of this form of experimental art, paved the way for performance art in Liverpool, arguably helping create the openness that greeted Yoko Ono when art school lecturer Dave Clapham brought her 'event' *Music of the Mind*, and the world premiere of *The Fog Machine*, to Bluecoat in 1967. 'London is good', said Ono, 'but its approach to my work is more intellectual, wanting to know reasons for things. The audience here was wonderful, very responsive – beautiful young people.'[29]

Following this and Mark Boyle and Joan Hill's *son et lumière* performances that year, there were other experimental live events from Albert Hunt and John Latham, sponsored by Peter Moores, and G.A.S.P.'s 'audio-visual drinking ritual',

The Society for the Promotion of Creativity in 1972;[30] and the same year a multimedia show, *Gorilla*, from Zoom Cortex that featured local jazz/rock outfit Death Kit, light shows, dancing and a 'hysterical and pataphysical "theatre of foam"'.[31] But it was not until the 1980s that live art returned in what Cathy Butterworth describes in her survey of performance work in Liverpool as a 'sustained and consolidated' element of the programme.[32] With funding from a new live art fund at the Arts Council's Combined Arts Department, the arts centre embarked on a series of commissions, starting in 1988 with *No Quarter* in collaboration with new Manchester performance venue the Green Room, and Halifax's artist-led initiative, Babel. These commissions were an extension of the gallery programme and included Peter McRae's durational installation on the steps of Liverpool's neoclassical St George's Hall (Fig. 34), in which white-robed women brandished white flags on top of large white plinths positioned among statues of largely anonymous Victorian men, a comment on the patriarchal nature of the public realm embodied in such civic sites; the work

Figure 34. Peter McRae, *Avenue of Heroes*, St George's Hall, 1988.

was seen by many bus passengers coming into town. *Baggages* was devised by four Manchester artists[33] who would later morph into TEA (Those Environmental Artists), converging from different parts of the city on the Bluecoat courtyard, where they unpacked their 'baggages' to construct a temporary home in which their bodies formed part of the structure.

As off-site projects, both these commissions marked the start of site-specific performances and installations that connected back to the gallery (in relation to which they are discussed in Chapter 5), where at this time the programme regularly extended into the Bluecoat garden with temporary sculptural exhibitions. Going beyond the building and out into the city had started with the Arts Forum's outdoor sculpture projects in the late 1960s, and these new interventions went beyond simply showing objects in new contexts, engaging instead with sites such as bus shelters, billboard hoardings, empty shops, fly-posted alleyways and nightclub doorways. In two projects, *On Location* (1994) and *Second Wave* (1988), artists Susan Collins, Kevin Logan and Linda Cooke, Cath Moonan and John Plowman made work that audiences encountered unexpectedly, and iconic venues such as the neoclassical Oratory by the Anglican Cathedral (Holly Warburton in 1987) and later the subterranean dankness of Dingle Reservoir (Pacitti Company in 2003) were utilised.

Further commissions were themed to reflect bigger global issues: *Independence* in relation to the 50th anniversary of India's partition (1997), and *Countdown* (1999), when David Tse, ex-Frank Chickens' Kazuko Hohki and local artists Hop Art (Mohammad Khalil Eugene Lange and Paul Clarkson) responded to the imminent arrival of the new millennium. A final commission series in 2000, *Trans:Action* with Mem Morrison and Max Factory (whose Sharon Smith brought several solo projects to Bluecoat), was a collaboration with Arnolfini and Warwick Arts Centre, one of Bluecoat's relationships with live art partners in a national sector that later crystallised into the consortium Live Art UK.

Bluecoat had started connecting to the burgeoning live art promoters' network by hosting regional platforms for the National Review of Live Art in 1987 and 1988 (and again in 2002), which enabled selected north-west live art practitioners to go on to present work at the NRLA, then being staged in Glasgow. A partnership was forged with hÅb, based at the Green Room, which was later rekindled for the *Poolside Emergency* weekend events in the new Bluecoat building after 2008. Despite the foundations laid by Henri and others, the 1980s' performance art scene in Liverpool was relatively small. The presence of Jeff Nuttall, author of counter-cultural chronicle *Bomb Culture*,[34] who had come to head up the Art School from Leeds (which then had a reputation as being among the most adventurous fine art departments in the country), did, however, leave an impact, with the emergence of a new generation of artists, including Robin Blackledge who presented work literally all over Bluecoat: in the concert hall, in the front courtyard – his body painted blue – and, painted red, in the garden and on the roof (see Fig. 30). In 1992, for Philip Courtenay's *LODE* project about globalisation, local young people's art project Yellow House collaborated with the artist on a performance that processed from Albert Dock to the Bluecoat courtyard, bearing symbolic wooden cargo that was then configured as an installation in the gallery.

Live art in the 1990s also embraced multi-art-form projects by Liverpool-based composer Jonathan Raisin, whose 1995 music theatre group Hub presented *Learning to Fly* at the venue, followed in 1998 by *Starving Brides*, which involved dance, music, storytelling and video and was co-commissioned with Blackpool Grand, where it was also performed. Its subject was the bizarre but true story of a sideshow in the seaside resort in the 1930s, in which newlyweds competed in a 30-day fast for prize money that would enable them to purchase a house. With Cathy Butterworth running the live art programme from 1999 to 2005, more strategic support was given to local artists, including through a live art associate scheme involving Spark Collective's Adrian Challis, Rebecca Reid and Mandy Romero, with Mike Carney, Gary Anderson, Lena Simic and others presenting work at regular live art sessions. UK artists such as Grace Surman were invited to explore the site-specificity of the concert hall, a large-scale image of her resulting performance now adorning that space, which houses the bistro.

Bluecoat also helped nurture a generation of young, diverse, Liverpool-based interdisciplinary performers in the 1990s. The Visual Stress collective – then billed as the 'Goat People and Urban Jazz' – staged *Death by Free Enterprise* in 1988, a daring (and today, in an environment of risk assessments and health and safety restrictions, utterly unthinkable) multimedia spectacle that dramatically took possession of Bluecoat's courtyard and decorative façade (Fig. 35). Adopting the 'vimbuza' tradition found throughout Bantu-speaking Africa, in which dance and drumming are used as a way of healing, and which was also employed symbolically and politically during British colonial occupation, the intense and ritualistic performance was intended to 'cleanse' the building of the taint of slavery. It used a combination of music, dance, noise and actions that included mountaineers scaling the building, drummers on the roof and performative abseiling by a sermon-reading vicar, as well as Robin Blackledge ascending perpendicularly to the theme tune of the popular Liverpool television soap, *Brookside*. Taking place the same week as Tate opened its new gallery in Liverpool at Albert Dock, the performance, along with Sokari Douglas Camp's cacophonous exhibition of sculptures in the gallery referencing her Nigerian background (see Fig. 61), unconsciously made a powerful

Figure 35. Visual Stress (The Goat People and Urban Jazz), *Urban Vimbuza: Death by Free Enterprise*, 1988: 'cleansing the building of the taint of slavery'. Photo: Mark McNulty.

statement about Bluecoat's culturally diverse curatorial priorities in relation to its new neighbour, which had landed with what some saw as a heavy Western art historical thud.

Visual Stress coalesced around Keith (Kif) Higgins, whose background included African dance/drumming company Delado, and Jonathan Swain, 'instigator of massive happenings, mobile automissions, gatherings, and disturbances',[35] and it drew in people from the city's activist and performance communities, an unpredictable recipe of rave, rasta, carnival and Situationism. The group's *Trophies of Empire* commission in 1992 took the form of a motorcade through the city in the week before Christmas, visiting twelve 'stations of the cross', sites resonant of Liverpool's imperial past. Another *Trophies* commission was from Verbal Images, a music/dance/spoken word collaboration involving several artists who also participated in Bluecoat's annual showcase of new black performance voices, *Oral & Black*. Continuing until 1996, this initiative grew from a close relationship with the city council's Arts Unit, which had a focus on supporting diversity, and the programmes included Sense of Sound choir, poets Levi Tafari, Muhammad Khalil Eugene Lange, Rommi and SuAndi, and the collective Asian Voices Asian Lives, who presented several spoken word/theatre pieces at Bluecoat including *Cooking Up A Storm* (1996), and were commissioned for the 1997 Independence season,

Figure 36. Keith Khan, *Soucouyan* performance in the concert hall, 1989.

their performances a blend of 'British, Asian and Liverpudlian culture'. The group included Bluecoat live programmer Dinesh Allirajah, whose music contribution is discussed in Chapter 6 and who was equally important to the arts centre's live art and literature developments, giving a platform to many emerging local artists whose work often reflected a global consciousness and roots in Africa, the Indian subcontinent or Latin America. Francisco Carrasco's 1996 commission for *artBlacklive* – a 'national platform for the discussion of Black culture and live art' in Leicester – was also presented at Bluecoat as *Azanian Trilogy* with his company Motsibi.

In 1995 Nina Edge drew together a large number of artists and other participants for her processional performance *Sold Down the River*, articulating the sense of betrayal felt on Merseyside, with its departing industries, punitive central government measures and media vilification. As Cathy Butterworth has observed, 'Such interventionist works were topical, critically engaged and celebratory, and though rooted in the local (which, with the onset of globalisation, was also becoming connected to international contexts), were part of a discourse in the UK and USA around black performance.'[36] Edge's procession, from Bluecoat to Albert Dock, was carnivalesque, drawing on some of the same traditions used by Keith Khan in his 1989 performance *Soucouyan*, a contemporary take on a Trinidadian folk tale, involving local musicians and dancers wearing massive costumes (Fig. 36). Khan returned in 1992 with Juanito Wadhwani in another multimedia performance, *Chawal ki Chaddar*. Alongside locally produced work, the inclusion of Khan brought external perspectives to Bluecoat's live art programme in a decade that also saw memorable visits from Delta Streete, performing in her gallery installation, Martin Glynn, Ronald Fraser-Munroe, Duende and, from America, The Hittite Empire – a collaboration with Black Arts Alliance, whose SuAndi presented her one-woman show, *The Story of M*.

The arrival of Liverpool Biennial brought an opportunity to curate more ambitious live art programmes alongside the UK's first international visual arts biennial. For the second Biennial in 2002, in collaboration with Live Art Development Agency, Bluecoat presented *You Are Here*, an intense four days of live art that 'looked at the complexities of contemporary identities [to ask] whether internationalism is a geographical or a cultural concept'.[37] It was conceived as a dialogue with Mexican-American artist Guillermo Gómez-Peña, whose packed Biennial opening event at Bluecoat, *Ex-Centris (A Living Diorama of Fetishized Others)*, transformed the concert hall into a 'living museum of experimental ethnography', as Gómez-Peña's La Pocha Nostra team, together with UK artists and an interdisciplinary Liverpool crew, created a series of provocative tableaux

Figure 37. Cai Yuan and J. J. Xi, *Mad for Real: Soy Sauce and Ketchup Fight* in the front courtyard, co-commission with Live Art Development Agency, 2002.

that messed around with clichés of 'otherness'. LADA presented a version of this the following year at Tate Modern in its *Live Culture* programme where, in the more controlled museum environment, it lacked the edginess of the Liverpool show, but nevertheless represented an important step towards the institutional accommodation of live art in the UK. Both at Bluecoat and off-site, the artists in *You Are Here* took up the *Ex-Centris* theme of complexifying cultural difference, culminating in Cai Yuan and J. J. Xi's *Mad for Real: Soy Sauce and Ketchup Fight* in a specially constructed enclosed Perspex boxing ring in Bluecoat's busy front courtyard (Fig. 37); here they did what it said on the label, their red-streaked, naked bodies finally retiring, as blood mixed with sauce, an apparent draw in the struggle between East and West.

For the 2004 Biennial, Bluecoat was again the site for opening outdoor performances by two artists whose work was included in the gallery show. In *Rolling Home*, Aleks Danko questioned what gets 'rolled over' in the process of urban regeneration, and in whose interests, as teams dressed in eighteenth-century uniforms similar to those worn at the Blue Coat school rolled large, soft, blue plastic houses through busy Saturday shopping streets, to converge on the courtyard. Amanda Coogan's *Beethoven, the Headbangers* explored collective hysteria and group energy, as 100 volunteers went crazy to the composer's Ninth Symphony. The ten-week Biennial was accompanied by *Liverpool Live*, a packed programme curated by Bluecoat, featuring performances and installations on and off site, including new work from China and Scandinavia and a focus on dance, contact improvisation and film. The programme involved Liverpool artists as well as others invited from abroad such as Sachiko Abe (Japan), Bill Shannon (US) and Sebastian Solari (Peru).

Live art continued while the building was closed for its capital development with *China Live*, a 2005 collaboration with Live Art Development Agency and Live Art UK, presenting new work from China's underground performance scene, and other off-site projects in the streets of Liverpool. In 2006 *Good Diversions* comprised interventions in a city centre under rapid transformation by the huge Liverpool One regeneration scheme. Self-appointed 'Queen of Culture' Mandy Romero visited building sites across a swathe of retail development taking shape as Liverpool's year as European Capital of Culture approached. Foreign Investment mapped the city in transition, working with street musicians and a horse and cart, while Leila Romaya and Paul McCann's photographic billboards captured the architectural changes in process. For the Biennial, Humberto Velez's *The Welcoming* was a collaboration with Refugee Action, involving long-established groups of immigrants in the city welcoming new migrants at the Albert Dock. The theme for *Liverpool Live 06* was 'urban apparition', curated by Tamsin Drury of hÅb, and involved performative walks, radio interventions, guided tours and other interruptions into the already disrupted urban fabric and public realm by FrenchMottershead, Lone Twin, vacuum cleaner, Marcus Young, Action Hero and others.

When the building reopened in 2008, Bluecoat's relationship to its new Liverpool One neighbour was explored by Richard Dedomenici on the day the retail-led development opened. His free black balloons bearing the legend 'Bored of shopping' were eagerly consumed by children in the gleaming new shopping streets; the following day his 'Bored of art' balloons had a similar effect when handed out at Bluecoat. *Liverpool Live* continued in the new building with Geraldine Pilgrim's reopening commission, *Traces*, involving children, mostly girls, from the current Blue Coat school dressed in period uniforms reinhabiting the arts centre on a busy Saturday, their silent presence evoking the building's former use and a largely overlooked female narrative (see Fig. 12). Similarly taking over many of the Bluecoat spaces, *Blackmarket for Useful Knowledge and Non-Knowledge* was another 2008 commission with Live Art Development Agency, from Berlin-based artist Hannah Hurtzig and her Mobile Academy, who presented their ongoing participative inquiry, an intense evening involving local 'experts' in dialogue with an audience (Fig. 38). The following year, two other German artists, Angie Hiesl + Roland Kaiser from Liverpool's twin city of Cologne, presented *TWINS – how do I know I am me ...* off-site at what became the music venue Camp and Furnace (Fig. 39), the bare industrial factory space providing a perfect backdrop for a memorable performance installation involving five pairs of identical twins (two pairs recruited locally). Local live art showcase *If Only* and Cathy Butterworth and Antony Pickthall's *Vinny's Flat* utilised the new performance space, but a reduction in funding made it difficult to maintain a regular programme of experimental work of this kind; not, however, before live programmer Richard Kingdom's idea to recreate John and Yoko's seminal live art action was realised in 2010 on the occasion of what would have been Lennon's 70th birthday and thirty years after his death. *Bed-In at the Bluecoat* was an invitation to create something 'for a better world', occupying a double bed situated in the Hub, the arts centre's busy reception/box office/café area (Fig. 40). There were 62 continuous days of activity involving participants from six continents – poets, musicians, dancers, live artists, activists, community groups, LGBTQ football fans, senior citizens and a campaign against domestic violence, whose members, led by Liverpool City Council leader Joe Anderson and other councillors, all wearing women's high heels, walked from the Town Hall to Bluecoat.

Literature, particularly poetry, has a long tradition at Bluecoat. Future Poet Laureate Cecil Day Lewis read there in 1959, as did Carol Ann Duffy in 2010 and

Figure 38. Hannah Hurtzig/Mobile Academy, *Blackmarket for Useful Knowledge and Non-Knowledge*, co-commission with Live Art Development Agency, 2008.

Figure 39. Angie Hiesl + Roland Kaiser, from Liverpool's twin city of Cologne, presented *TWINS – how do I know I am me…*, off-site at the a foundation (now Camp and Furnace), 2009, performers Mursal and Zohal Wahabzadah. Photo: Roland Kaiser.

Figure 40. *Bed-In at the Bluecoat,* with poet Chuck Perkins, 2011.

Simon Armitage in 2008. As discussed earlier in this chapter, in the 1960s the venue was receptive to the new British poetry, with visits towards the end of the decade from, among others, George MacBeth, Libby Houston, Pete Morgan, Harry Fainlight, Michael Horovitz, Basil Bunting, Brian Patten and most of the other 'Liverpool poets'. So popular were some of these readings, many of which took place in the cramped Sandon music room, that they had to be broadcast through speakers to the corridors and courtyard outside. The Black Mountain poets from the influential North Carolina arts college visited as part of a regional poetry network tour that also included Newcastle, Nottingham and Cardiff. Another American poet, Clive Matson, whose early career was associated with the Beats, also read at the venue. And in 1968 there was an exhibition in the gallery of concrete poetry by some of the practitioners of this international visual poetry movement.

Poetry programmes were more sporadic in the following two decades but blossomed again in the 1990s through local grassroots showcases such as *Oral & Black*, with their mash-ups of 'dub poetry', rap and comedy. Dinesh Allirajah was instrumental in nurturing this while bringing in diverse voices from outside, such as Linton Kwesi Johnson, Jean Binta Breeze, Labi Siffre, Salena Godden and Lemn Sissay, who performed on several occasions including with New York jazz musician David Murray. There were also mixed bills such as *Atomic Lip*, featuring Patience Agbabi, and Mannafest's jazz poetry night, *The Mango Lick*. In contrast to the predominantly male 1960s readings, women were more prominent in these programmes, which often featured emerging north-west talent including Mandy Coe, Jean Sprackland and Cheryl Martin. At the start of the new millennium, Bluecoat was one of several venues to host Liverpool's new and now longest-running literature festival, Writing on the Wall, while at the same time promoting a range of literature itself under the brand 'Bluecoat Verbals' that included Doris Lessing, Alexei Sayle, Ian McMillan, John Hegley and, staged at the Neptune Theatre, Germaine Greer. This breadth of writing, encompassing poetry, novels, comedy and ideas, prepared the ground for the *Chapter & Verse* festivals (2008–11) in the new building, a heady mix of some of the most vital creative writers working across the spectrum, from short stories to journalism, science fiction to philosophy, poetry to digital publishing. A sample of the first festival's line-up – Tariq Ali, Bernardine Evaristo, Paul Farley, Linda Grant, Jan Morris, Michael Symmons Roberts, Raymond Tallis and Helen Walsh – indicates this breadth.

An appetite for high-level debate in the city about burning issues of the day had been demonstrated by Bluecoat's *Liverpool Debates* series, organised across the city in partnership with the *Liverpool Echo* in 2007 while the building was closed, and this area of public discourse came within the new literature programme remit. Curated by Maura Kennedy, from the reopening weekend readings by Tom Paulin and Jeanette Winterson onwards the programme demonstrated how well suited the venue now was for a range of live literature and discursive events: there were evenings in the presence of Jackie Kay, Will Self, Sarah Hall, Ed Vulliamy and many other poets and authors; discussion events such as BBC Radio 3's ideas festival, *Free Thinking*; Melanie Abraham's *Liverpool Liming*, which evoked the spirit of *Oral & Black* through a mix of local and international diverse spoken word and music; local initiative Poetry Café and the Talking Poetry sessions; a radical booksellers' gathering for News from Nowhere bookshop's 40th anniversary; an annual celebration of Wirral writer Malcolm Lowry, the 'Lowry Lounge'; poets-in-residence (Nathan Jones and Sean Borodale); and book launches, collective readings of novels, literary walking tours, poetry slams, reading groups and writing workshops, much of which continues, supplemented now by a baby book club.

This capacity to host multiple activities under one roof has always been a feature of Bluecoat, an undoubted strength but also, at times, a challenge in terms of marketing to several different audiences at the same time, and articulating a complex brand that does not have the advantage of a single focus like a gallery, theatre or concert hall. However, this promiscuity is the nature of arts centres and, in reflecting on the twenty-five years before Bluecoat closed for its capital development, we can say that it is where the programme escaped the boundaries of simply an exhibition or performance, or reached beyond the building itself (as we have seen in much of the live art discussed here), that the idea of *interdisciplinarity* and a 'Bluecoat way' is perhaps best illustrated. Through gallery and live programme staff talking to each other and thinking about crossovers, rather than staying in curatorial 'silos', and treating the whole building (and beyond) as a canvas, imaginative thinking, as well as being in tune with and open to external initiatives, resulted in several 'brand Bluecoat' projects. In 1989, for example, *Perestroika in the Avant-Garde* was an audacious programme, whose centrepiece, a concert at St George's Hall by Leningrad underground band Pop Mechanica, is described in Chapter 6. It also featured an exhibition at Bluecoat by artists from the same Russian underground community (held up at customs, the show had to be installed at improvisatory speed, working through the night), and there was another display and talks at Tate. The project captured the imagination of the *Liverpool Echo*, which produced a supplement for the Pop Mechanica gig headlined with a quote from US President Ronald Reagan. Bluecoat staff, city councillors and other Liverpool creatives were invited to Leningrad in reciprocation by the authorities there. The Cold War was thawing, and later that year the Brian Eno-produced band Zvuki Mu from Moscow played Bluecoat on their first three-date UK tour.

Against another European backdrop – the group and quarter-final stages of the Euro 96 football championships in Liverpool – Bluecoat took up the challenge from the city council to curate a themed programme that would appeal to visiting fans and home supporters alike. The resulting programme, *Football Crazy*, populated every corner of the arts centre with football-related activity, its details given in a brochure printed to resemble a multilingual football programme (in Czech, Russian and Italian – the three teams in the group matches – and in English and German). This comprised a one-man theatre show called *Balls!*, films, banners, an exhibition of football record sleeves, a sporting memorabilia day and a football fashion show, *Tackle*, sponsored by Ann Summers, in which striking Liverpool dockers, local trans artists and a Union Jack-clad male stripper strutted the catwalk in the floodlit front courtyard to cheering crowds including the dockers' wives support group, Women of the Waterfront. The fortnight was animated by poet and 'Eurolaureate' Ian Horn, football band-in-residence Kung Fu, and football artist-in-residence Alan Dunn (Fig. 41).

This connecting of contemporary art to popular culture has been seen most clearly in a pop music-related strand straddling all aspects of the programme since the early 1980s, though the roots of this go back further to artists such as Yoko Ono and Captain Beefheart, who had previously presented work at the venue. There were exhibitions of record sleeves, 'rock family trees' and jazz illustrations, a conference on skiffle music, and several contributions from The KLF's Bill Drummond, who

Figure 41. The courtyard transformed during the Euro 96 football championships by Alan Dunn, Bluecoat football artist-in-residence, with banners on the building by David Jacques, 1996.

had studied at the Art School, including his presentation *How to be an artist* in 2002. Twenty years before, in 1982, a Factory Records event in the concert hall had queues (of what seemed like predominantly raincoated post-punks) stretching down School Lane for a night of the Manchester label's promo videos, the first UK showing following screenings in New York and Brussels. Seven years before the first *Video Positive* festival of moving image art, Bluecoat was hosting a large-scale installation of monitors flickering to the sounds of Joy Division and New Order. Another compilation, *History of the Independent Music Video*, was shown in 1988. In 1984 John Carson's *American Medley* installation and his accompanying performance went in search of places in America immortalised in popular song.

In 1990 a reading by Trevor Miller of his apocalyptic vision of the acid house summer of love, *Trip City*, was soundtracked by A Guy Called Gerald, while two live art commission series, *Live from the Vinyl Junkyard* (1996) and *Mixing It* (1997), responded respectively to the declared death of vinyl in the CD age and to remix culture. Ten commissions in all took place in the gallery, concert hall and off-site:

in Jeremy Deller's *Acid Brass*, house music anthems were reworked by a brass band (Fig. 42); Cornford & Cross turned the gallery into a record fair for a day; Jane Sanders took on the persona of a hermaphrodite Elvis; Philip Jeck's installation of record players created a soundscape from fragments of vinyl sound (Fig. 69); Iain Forsyth and Jane Pollard assembled a superstar tribute band comprising Bowie, Morrissey, Kylie, Jarvis, Damon and Robert Smith; John Campbell and Henry Priestman's room-sized tape loop sampled 96 iterations of 'baby' from pop records; Laurence Lane and Matt Wand slowed the Beach Boys' 'Good Vibrations' down to 1 rpm; Reformat created the total experience of an electronic dance environment; Colin Fallows and J. Naughton explored space's 'vinyl frontier'; and Kevin O'Neill shared anecdotes about his record collection with gallery visitors.

In 1997, to mark thirty years since The Beatles' *Sgt. Pepper* album, Bluecoat recreated in its gallery the LP sleeve's famous tableau, updated to include life-size cut-outs of 80 heroes nominated by invited artists, working with staff from the Art School and other artists including Alan Dunn and South Atlantic Souvenirs, to construct of a new version of this iconic image, emblematic of the collision of

Figure 42. Jeremy Deller, *Acid Brass*, a Bluecoat live art commission presented at LIPA, 1997, with the Williams Fairey Brass Band and MC Tony Wilson.

Figure 43. Recreation of the *Sgt. Pepper* record sleeve tableau in the gallery, with a new selection of cultural heroes, for the exhibition *It was thirty years ago today*, 1997.

the worlds of art and pop in the 1960s (Fig. 43). It was accompanied by a display of Pepper pastiches on CDs, LPs, greetings cards, posters and other ephemera, attesting to the continuing allure of Peter Blake and Jann Haworth's design. When Bluecoat expanded its gallery in 2008, larger exhibitions were possible, and art/music crossovers included Janek Schaefer's solo exhibition *Sound Art*, during which the artist, who works entirely within the sonic realm, presented a live performance in collaboration with another turntable artist, Philip Jeck. And, recognising Liverpool's love of country music and the 'wild west' ambience of many of its city-centre bars, *Honky Tonk* was an exhibition involving Liverpool, Texan and other international artists exploring the cowboy aesthetic. A local film was commissioned, tracing the city's roots in country and its reputation as the 'Nashville of the North'.

***

These examples give a flavour of the combined arts nature of Bluecoat as it has sought to carve out a particular niche in relation to other arts centres and the landscape for the contemporary arts in the post-war period and subsequent decades.

Before concluding with an appraisal of where Bluecoat sits in this wider context and in relation to Liverpool's cultural scene, a summary of key elements – *place*, *audience* and *diversity* – that have helped shape the work described above will perhaps give an understanding of what underpins this position. First, *place*: both the building's convenient location close to the city's busy retail core (which has now left Bluecoat with inconvenient delivery and non-existent parking provision), and the physical accommodation of art in the building. As the building developed after the war, art became more accessibly located in Bluecoat's central core: a gallery on the ground floor that was the first thing you encountered on entering the building; and a performance space directly above, invisible at first but reached by an inviting sweep of stairs where the gallery ended. The two announced themselves as arts spaces and *echoed* each other: they shared a grand curved back wall, punctured by arched windows that overlooked a 'secret garden'. These were, however, generally covered over in the gallery, and temporary walls further disguised the synergy between the spaces, while the concert hall's frequent use for commercial functions sometimes made it appear separate from the arts programme. Yet the two spaces often interconnected: Max Eastley's 1983 gallery exhibition of sound sculptures, for instance, was accompanied by a performance of his 'whirled music' upstairs and he installed a wind chime piece on the balcony outside, its sound filtering back down into the garden and the gallery for years afterwards. Keith Khan likewise continued his *Soucouyan* exhibition into a performance with the same title in the concert hall. The gallery would often remain open for the audience, arriving for an evening music or dance event, to pass through on its way upstairs. Curating live and gallery programmes together thematically was hardly unique, but the frequency of this and the physical connections that were made possible by maximising use of the building's indoor and external spaces made this more evident.

There was a literal echo, too, between the art spaces at the building's core. When installing exhibitions in the gallery late into the evening, a concert upstairs could be heard through the thin ceiling, the light steps of a dancer amplified or a galumphing audience causing the track lighting to shake. Equally, a noisy video installation downstairs would travel upstairs to a complaining accountants' exam invigilator or other concert hall user. Sound bleed was a constant problem: a music gig loud enough to be heard from Church Street or, conversely, the strains of a busker there, audible during a quiet poetry event at the arts centre. Shortcomings such as these, as well as the gallery's space constraints, an overall technical paucity resulting from lack of investment, and limited physical access to the upper floors meant that, by the turn of the new millennium, the venue was ill-equipped to meet the demands of an increasingly professionalised arts sector and audiences' expectations of a modern arts facility. This led to Bluecoat's capital development, which brought an enlarged gallery and a soundproofed, fully equipped performance space.

While today one may less easily stumble upon art as one could in the gallery's old configuration, the new space has an enviable 'shop window' on College Lane for its exhibitions, which are continually glimpsed by a substantial number of passers-by, and the gallery's porosity is further enabled by an elegant cloister of windows on to the garden. The garden, too, entered from the rear, remains an unexpected delight both for new visitors and, transformed for instance into a night-time music venue, regulars too. The front courtyard, despite the apparent downgrading of School Lane into a delivery function for Church Street stores, still offers an impressive entrance, one that has beckoned people in with live events, sculptural installations, colourful café umbrellas, fashion shows, night-time projections and festival launches.

Encountering art in a very direct way in a building that functions as a haven in the heart of the city, more so now in the retail-dominated environment that has encroached on its surroundings (while bringing with it a welcome and appreciably larger, new audience), as well as off-site in highly public contexts, has been a feature of the arts centre, which brings us to the second element to consider in relation to Bluecoat's positioning, its *relationship to audience and to the local*. The wide demographic currently attracted to the building is a long way from the exclusivity of the Sandon's 'genteel society' and is achieving what the 1927 constitution set out to do in terms of making the arts accessible (though going far beyond the middle-class art lovers that the Bluecoat Society undoubtedly had in mind). This breadth can be explained in part by Bluecoat's aforementioned proximity – indeed gateway – to Liverpool One and the increase in tourism triggered by Capital of Culture. Bluecoat's combined arts nature, its resident creative community and the many partners it works with to deliver programmes also contribute to a diversity of audiences, and it is clear from recent surveys that people visit Bluecoat for many reasons, not all of them related to its core arts offer. This 'parallel world' of activity in the building is explored in Chapter 7.

Recent analysis by Bluecoat revealed that 13 per cent of its users are disabled and 18 per cent live in the first decile of IMD (indicators of multiple deprivation) areas of Liverpool.[38] A contributing factor here is arguably the role of arts participation at Bluecoat, a process started in the 1980s. It was expanded significantly during the period of closure when, building on a wide-ranging outreach programme, *Bluecoatconnect*, further work was done as *Out of the Bluecoat* – from a temporary home in nearby Paradise Street, and then in Hanover Street – piloting a new scheme, which became the inclusive arts participation project for learning-disabled adults, Blue Room (Fig. 44). This consolidation of

Figure 44. Members of Bluecoat's inclusive arts project Blue Room with Dan Graham's installation in the front courtyard during Liverpool Biennial, 2012.

Bluecoat's participation work placed it firmly at the heart of the arts centre and helped develop new audiences, specifically targeting hard-to-reach communities. Previously, what were designed as 'education' programmes followed a familiar arts centre model of holiday workshops for children, mainly in dance and visual art, and paid-for classes for adults seeking new practical skills in life drawing or printmaking. With greater funds available for more targeted and bespoke programmes, the emphasis shifted towards 'learning', working more strategically with discrete communities in different neighbourhoods.

Nurturing the artistic community has also been a significant factor in developing Bluecoat's role as a local resource. As demonstrated by the examples in this and other chapters, the arts centre, particularly in the 1980s and 1990s, was supportive of visual art, music, dance, literature and interdisciplinary practice on Merseyside, providing a stepping stone for the region's artists, as well as a place for the local to interact with the national and international. The city's narratives have also provided a rich source of material and contexts for artists to respond to and for the arts centre to theme programmes around, such as maritime trade, transatlantic slavery, philanthropy and education, the city in transition, migrant communities – all pertinent to Bluecoat's heritage – as well as popular music and football. Exhibitions such as *Trophies of Empire* (1992), *Democratic Promenade* (2011) and *In the Peaceful Dome* (2017) brought aspects of the port's history into conversation with the present, and much live art commissioning and literature activity is connected to specific local narratives.

The third key element that has shaped Bluecoat's artistic work is *diversity* – of the artists it works with and the audiences it seeks to engage – and the debates concerning identity politics, multiculturalism and inclusion that have informed the arts centre's programme over four decades. In that period, Arts Council policy has sought to address diversity, starting with Naseem Khan's 1976 report *The Arts Britain Ignores*, through to its *Creative Case for Diversity* introduced in 2011 as a measure of how the organisations it funds contribute to greater equality and inclusion in the work they do, in order to better 'reflect the diversity of contemporary England'.[39] Criticisms such as Clive Nwonka's of a cultural and creative industries sector 'littered with the corpses of failed diversity schemes', with current initiatives by funders pointing to 'a diversity agenda performing as a marketing strategy rather than a method of structural transformation',[40] argue for the need, not for schemes, but for greater collective discussion about what the concept of diversity actually means and the sort of social policies required to bring about real change. Nonetheless, funders' policies relating to equality and diversity, if sometimes lagging behind what some arts organisations already do (and elsewhere paid lip service to by clients reluctant to change), have provided a valuable benchmark for the sector and are now considerably more robust than the 'tick box' varieties of old.

For Bluecoat, the development of more diverse programmes in the period under discussion was driven not so much by funders' policies as by an interest among its programmers in artists who were making *vital* work – in dance, music, literature, performance or visual art: vital in relation to the practice, and vital in relation to wider discourses beyond its own framework. Many of these artists operated outside the mainstream (though some would eventually join it), presenting work in a network of arts centres, galleries and other 'alternative' spaces or festivals that included Bluecoat. Their 'diversity' often connected them to audiences interested in, for instance, the political dimensions of class, race and cultural identity, post-colonial histories, personal and non-Eurocentric narratives, alternative traditions, and cross-cultural and interdisciplinary artistic expressions. Their work was sometimes unpolished but often electric, always pertinent to a given situation: the emergence, for instance, of a new generation of local black voices found expression in the *Oral & Black* performance showcases; anniversaries provided an opportunity to critically interrogate post-colonial legacies (e.g. *Trophies of Empire, Independent Thoughts*); the Bluecoat building's physical inaccessibility demanded a radical perspective (Ann Whitehurst's *On the Map*); inclusive arts provision for disabled people was piloted, then became a reality (Blue Room); the traditional under-representation of women was confronted by greater inclusion across the programme, as well as in staffing.

While much of this diversity was brought about in response to a local context and the needs of artists and partner organisations in the region, national networks and collaborations were vitally important too in both the gallery and performance programmes, and international connections also brought in different perspectives to the European/American worldview. Projects that left a profound impression included a residency collaboration in 1998 with the Citadel in St Helens by Zimbabwean a cappella and dance group Black Umfolosi, and an exhibition collaboration with Senegalese artists in 1995/96. And Bluecoat's European connections have not always been the most obvious: examples include the aforementioned *Perestroika in the Avant-Garde*, and an ongoing exchange with Liverpool's German twin city of Cologne, a major international visual arts centre that has provided an opportunity for a more grassroots, artist-led partnership, more in keeping with Bluecoat's connections to marginal places – an orbit that has taken in Dakar and St Petersburg and, more recently, Bangalore and Indonesia.

In the period under discussion in this chapter, it has arguably been such 'left turns' and unexpected partnerships, and those genuinely combined arts programmes where art forms have crossed or connected with wider discourses in politics or popular culture, that have shaped Bluecoat as an arts centre. As with many other similar venues, a sense of place – the building itself and its location – defines Bluecoat, as does its relationship to, and the diversity of, its artists and audiences. Bluecoat's history also shares with other arts centres peaks and troughs in particular strands of performance activity, often the result of changes in staff or funding streams, or the arrival on the scene of other providers in those art form areas. When Bluecoat reopened after the war, and for a long time thereafter, there were few other arts venues in the city (the long-established Philharmonic, Playhouse and Walker, as well as more commercial theatres and music venues), and the arts centre therefore occupied an important position in hosting or housing much of the city's smaller-scale arts activity. Gradually, however, new agencies, festivals or venues fostered music, dance and literature, or became new partners for Bluecoat to work with.

The explosion of visual art provision, with a succession of new spaces – a revived but relatively short-lived Liverpool Academy gallery in Pilgrim Street, Open Eye Gallery, Tate Liverpool, FACT – and then the Biennial and, later, Metal did not so much challenge the gallery as sharpen its curatorial focus and provide opportunities for collaboration.

This richer cultural landscape, however, brought increased competition for funding, as new institutions in the city and the wider region, such as Cornerhouse (now Home) in Manchester , were able to attract more substantial grants, including Arts Council revenue. It was an inability to secure the levels of subsidy required to maintain a consistent offer across such a wide range of live arts, as well as its gallery exhibitions, that has resulted in Bluecoat reducing, or in some cases terminating, some programme strands. In the environment for arts centres nationally, Bluecoat is not alone in this respect but, in contemplating its future as a more civic and engaged arts centre, it has a rich heritage to draw on in the half-century since the Arts Forum set out a template for encountering the avant-garde in the village hall.

Notes

1 The report, the first by the National Advisory Council on Art Education, takes its name from the Council's chairman, William Coldstream. It introduced a Diploma in Art and Design (DipAD) and represented a shift towards a liberal education in art, with less emphasis on craft-based training.

2 Fiona Candlin, 'A dual inheritance: the politics of educational reform and PhDs in art and design', *The International Journal of Art & Design Education*, 20.3, pp. 302–10, http://eprints.bbk.ac.uk/738/, accessed 4 January 2020.

3 Bluecoat Arts Forum promotional leaflet, Liverpool Record Office, 367BLU/18/8-20.

4 *The Augustan Age; Victorian High Noon;* and *The Turn of the Century.*

5 *Report on Bluecoat 63*, also repeated in *Chairman's Report, May 1964*, both in Liverpool Record Office, Bluecoat Arts Forum archive.

6 *Bluecoat Society of Arts Annual Report, 1966/67.*

7 Lee visited Bluecoat in 1965. The Society of Arts' annual report for that year recognised the increasing interest by national government and Liverpool Corporation in the arts, particularly the move towards establishing publicly funded regional arts centres: 'Liverpool will certainly not be left out of this and since we have always rightly regarded ourselves here as pioneers in this field we shall surely play a prominent part in whatever is ultimately decided. Indeed I think we must ensure that we do. For this reason the visit of Miss Jennie Lee to the building on Sat 13 March was of great value and we think and hope she was favourably impressed by what she saw' (F. M. Herzog, chairman).

8 The date is unidentified but, according to Harpe, the feature appeared in June–July 1968, during *Sculpture in a City*, an Arts Council touring exhibition of outdoor sculpture that Bluecoat coordinated in Liverpool.

9 'A new gallery is born', unidentified press cutting review of Liverpool Academy exhibition, 27 November 1967, in Liverpool Record Office.

10 Peter Rockliff, *Bluecoat Arts Forum Annual Report 1967/68*, unnumbered pages.

11 The *Musica Viva* series had started in the early 1960s with concerts conducted by [Sir] John Pritchard at the Liverpool Philharmonic Hall.

12 Rockliff, *Bluecoat Arts Forum Annual Report 1967/68*, unnumbered pages.

13 John Willett, *Art in a City*, London: Methuen, 1967, republished Liverpool: Liverpool University Press, 2007, with an introduction by Bryan Biggs. Willett's articles on 'The arts in

Liverpool', *Liverpool Daily Post*, 18, 19 and 20 March 1964, had generated local debate and, with the book's publication, there followed national press and a public forum.

14   Conversation with the author, February 2015.

15   Conversation with the author, 10 September 2014. In the late 1950s, however, a drive by the Sandon to attract a younger membership resulted in students from the Art College, as well as music and architecture students, joining, which brought 'some fresh air', according to Alan Swerdlow (email to the author, 14 June 2019).

16   *The Guardian*, 6 April 1968. Dooley had exhibited at the gallery in 1964 and 1965.

17   John Lane, *Arts Centres: Every Town Should Have One*, London: Paul Elek, 1978, p. ix.

18   Van der Heijden of Biq Architecten was lead architect on the capital development that was completed in 2008.

19   Robert Hutchison, *Three Arts Centres: A Study of South Hill Park, the Gardner Centre and Chapter*, London: Arts Council of Great Britain, 1977.

20   Peter Stark, in Hutchison, *Three Arts Centres*, p. 44.

21   These included, with Arnolfini, *Trophies of Empire* (1992/93); with ICA, *Graphic Rap* (1983); and with both, *Art & the Sea* (1981) and *Glenn Sujo – Histories* (1982); as well as touring exhibitions, both to and from Bluecoat.

22   *Bluecoat Society of Arts Annual Report and Accounts 1985/86*, p. 3.

23   Quotes from Gary Everett, from an interview with the author, December 2019.

24   This column in *Private Eye*, which rounds up pretentious writing, included Bluecoat's press release for its 'Whirled Music' concert in 1983.

25   Exhibitions of cartoons are referenced in Chapter 5, and *Double Act: Art and Comedy* was a two-site exhibition (with the MAC, Belfast) in 2016 curated by David Campbell and Mark Durden of Common Culture.

26   Theron Schmidt, *Agency: A Partial History of Live Art*, Bristol and London: Intellect and Live Art

Development Agency, 2019, p. 10.

27   Lois Keidan, in Schmidt, *Agency*, p. 8.

28   Adrian Henri, *Environments and Happenings*, London: Thames and Hudson, 1974.

29   Interview with Gillian Linscott, 'The high priestess of happenings', *Liverpool Daily Post*, 10 March 1967.

30   G.A.S.P. comprised Rob Con, Ron Dutton, Julian Dunn and Harry Henderson.

31   From the flyer to the Zoom Cortex *Gorilla* event at Bluecoat, 15–17 March 1972.

32   Cathy Butterworth, 'Dissenters of the creative universe', in Bryan Biggs and Julie Sheldon, eds, *Art in a City Revisited*, Liverpool: Liverpool University Press and Bluecoat, 2009, p. 194.

33   John Biddulph, Peter Hatton, Val Murray, Lynn Pilling.

34   Jeff Nuttall, *Bomb Culture*, London: Paladin, 1970.

35   Jonathan Swain website, http://lookedatthisway.blogspot.com/, accessed 21 April 2019.

36   Butterworth, 'Dissenters of the creative universe', pp. 197–98. Butterworth refers to Catherine Ugwu, ed., *Let's Get It On: The Politics of Black Performance*, London and Seattle: ICA and Bay Press, 1995, which includes contributions from several artists who presented work at Bluecoat.

37   18–21 September. Artists comprised Guillermo Gómez-Peña, Cai Yuan and J.J. Xi, Kira O'Reilly, Oreet Ashery, George Chakravarthi, Silke Mansholt, Qasim Riza Shaheen, Stacy Makishi, Suki Chan and Dinu Li.

38   Audience Finder analysis for Bluecoat, 2017/18.

39   Arts Council England, *Creative Case for Diversity*, https://www.artscouncil.org.uk/diversity/creative-case-diversity, accessed 8 May 2019. A report, *Equality, Diversity and the Creative Case: A Date Report, 2017–2018*, concluded that despite progress, some organisations were 'treading water'.

40   Clive Nwonka, 'The arts were supposed to champion diversity. What went wrong?', *The Guardian*, 15 February 2019.

Chapter 5

'A Dissident View': Bluecoat Exhibitions, 1967–2005

Anjalie Dalal-Clayton and Julie Sheldon

The footprint of Bluecoat has altered greatly since its inception. The pristine, purpose-built galleries we see today expanded and rationalised what for decades was a 'warren of eccentric spaces'[1] unfurling somewhat surprisingly behind the building's symmetrical Queen Anne façade. Until 2005 displays were organised across four principal rooms, functioning as showcases for individual and group shows, but Bluecoat also optimised its resource so that visitors would often encounter artwork elsewhere on site, including outdoors. This inventive layout of exhibitions characterised the visitor experience for decades, making the encounter one of surprise and informality. Sean Cubitt summarised this effect in 1991 when he wrote about Bluecoat's 'architectural atmosphere of slightly clumsy intimacy [that] seems to encourage a dissident view'.[2] The intimate suite of spaces seemed to give permission to critically engage with the displays, to challenge doctrines, while remaining loyal to the curatorial programme. This chapter takes a vicarious tour of Bluecoat between 1967 and 2005 (with reference to some later exhibitions) and takes a detailed look at several landmark exhibitions that were installed into, projected on to, and played out within the fabric of Bluecoat's historic building, while referencing others that were of significance. It is, of necessity, selective, and a comprehensive exhibition history is available on the organisation's archive website, mybluecoat.org.uk.

***

Figure 45. Permindar Kaur, *Tall Beds* in *Cold Comfort* exhibition (on tour from Ikon, Birmingham, and Mead Gallery, Warwick), 1996.

Between the gallery being extended and modernised in late 1967 and the building's closure for capital development in 2005, it staged more than 490 exhibitions, as well as numerous performances, film screenings and discursive events, installations in the garden and courtyard, and off-site projects. To assess the individual contribution of each is beyond the capacity of this chapter. However, it is possible to create a typology of exhibitions at Bluecoat in this period, drawing together a range of shows that are emblematic of the main thematic drivers of the arts centre's exhibition history and that attest to the institutional imperatives of the nascent gallery. In selecting the exhibitions for review we are attempting to demonstrate a distinctive history in Bluecoat's programming, and one in which representation and identity politics, socially engaged practice and the development of new platforms for artworks, such as new media or site-specific practice, are at the forefront.

Accompanying the gallery's Arts Council-funded refurbishment in 1967, Bluecoat established an exhibitions panel to develop a policy, select programmes and, in 1970, appoint its first gallery director.[3] This reassertion of Bluecoat's visual arts profile and articulation as a serious contemporary gallery took place in the context of international shifts in the means of viewing works of art. The white cube decor of gallery spaces had a long maturation in the twentieth century and, by the time Bluecoat formalised its gallery spaces, it was commonplace for works to be displayed according to an international style of presentation. Works of art were spaciously hung at eye-level in a single row, sculpture was isolated on a white-painted plinth with plenty of room around it, and galleries were generally articulated in order to maximise the visual field of the beholder. Artists expected this consideration in hanging their work; and Bluecoat had to cater for artists who were in pursuit of an optimum perspectival positioning of their work. This was never easy at the building on School Lane. Behind its ordered and geometric façade there was an unexpected and higgledy-piggledy layout, in which four principal spaces functioned as the public gallery. A floor plan of Bluecoat in the 1980s shows an articulation of space that was at odds with the enfilade arrangements of many galleries (Fig. 46). Four rooms in the estate were identified for the formal display of art: on the plan we see room 1, the main gallery; room 2, colloquially known as the 'curved room', springs from its side; and room 3, known as the 'side gallery', was reached from a doorway in the curved room, and extended into a fourth room, the 'top space' leading to the gallery office and stairs to the concert hall. These four rooms, conscripted for exhibition spaces, owed their dimensions and their decor to a bygone function of Bluecoat. In order that they might conform to the dimensions and decor of the white cube, they were variously remodelled, partially concealing the original features with white-painted boards that permit the international modern style of display.[4]

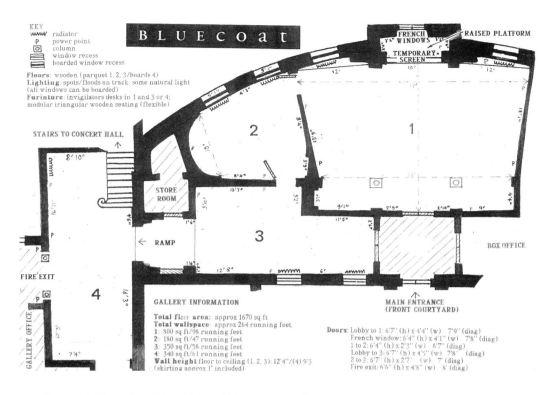

Within the image:

KEY
- ꙨꙨꙨ radiator
- P power point
- ⊡ column
- window recess
- boarded window recess

BLUECoat

FRENCH WINDOWS

RAISED PLATFORM

TEMPORARY SCREEN

Floors: wooden (parquet 1, 2, 3/boards 4)
Lighting: spots/floods on track; some natural light (all windows can be boarded)
Furniture: invigilators desks in 1 and 3 or 4; modular triangular wooden seating (flexible)

STAIRS TO CONCERT HALL

2
1
STORE ROOM
3
RAMP
BOX OFFICE
FIRE EXIT
4
GALLERY OFFICE

MAIN ENTRANCE (FRONT COURTYARD)

GALLERY INFORMATION

Total floor area: approx 1670 sq ft
Total wallspace: approx 264 running feet
1: 800 sq ft/98 running feet
2: 180 sq ft/47 running feet
3: 350 sq ft/58 running feet
4: 340 sq ft/61 running feet
Wall height floor to ceiling (1, 2, 3): 12'4"/(4) 9'3 (skirting approx 1' included)

Doors: Lobby to 1: 6'7" (h) x 4'4" (w) 7'9" (diag)
French window: 6'4" (h) x 4'1" (w) 7'8" (diag)
1 to 2: 6'4" (h) x 2'3" (w) 6'7" (diag)
Lobby to 3: 6'7" (h) x 4'5" (w) 7'8" (diag)
2 to 3: 6'7" (h) x 2'7" (w) 7' (diag)
Fire exit: 6'6" (h) x 4'8" (w) 8' (diag)

Figure 46. Floor plan of the gallery, 1980s: a 'warren of eccentric spaces'.

At the same time that gallery spaces were being remodelled to handle the scale and complexity of artwork of the post-war period, there was a significant shift towards curating as a form of partnership, one in which artists and gallery curators combined their expertise to create the optimum viewing experience. It was not simply the configuration of gallery spaces at Bluecoat that needed to be responsive to developments in contemporary art; its staff also had to facilitate a range of practices, from large-scale painting to installation, performance and moving image. The year that Bluecoat formalised its gallery was a significant one in the history of art and its presentation. In 1968 Harald Szeeman was giving the Christos the opportunity to wrap the Kunsthalle Bern; Pontus Hulten was overhauling the Moderna Museet in Stockholm; Walter Hopps was mastering the art of 'curating outside the box' in Washington; Seth Siegelaub was pioneering ways of exhibiting conceptual art; and Norman Reid was presiding over a massive expansion to the Tate at Millbank. This was a vitalised time for Bluecoat, one in which there was a genuine worldwide spirit of inventiveness and experimentation for curators.

For a period in the late 1960s and early 1970s, artists at the forefront of experimental art practice were evident in the gallery programme, the result of more adventurous programming by Bluecoat Arts Forum (set up to focus on the arts while Bluecoat Society of Arts attended to the business of the building) and then of having a full-time director in post. Sitting somewhat incongruously alongside the likes of the Liver Sketching Club and commercial shows by local artists,[5] it was possible to see work, in 1967, by Mark Boyle and a performance by Yoko Ono and, in 1969, John Latham's *Review of a Dictionary*. The trend in this period towards wider distribution of art and making it affordable through editioned prints and multiples was reflected in shows such as *Multiples* (1969) and *A Concept of Multiples* (1972), in collaboration with Alecto International, and featuring David Hockney, Claes Oldenburg, Eduardo Paolozzi and many others, while the Arts Council was a regular source of inexpensive touring shows of contemporary prints and works from its collection by, among others, Henry Moore.

New directions in British sculpture, representing a move away from the plinth and towards site-specificity, were presented by Bluecoat at outdoor venues in the city centre with two Arts Council national touring exhibitions, *Sculpture in a City* (1968) and *Outdoor Sculpture* (1969), which included Anthony Caro, Kim Lim, Barbara Hepworth and William Turnbull, who returned in 1972 with a geometric tubular metal installation in the front courtyard as part of the nationwide Peter Stuyvesant Foundation-funded *City Sculpture Project*. The same year into that space Fred Brookes manoeuvred an installation of railway sleepers using a forklift truck, as part of his gallery show, and more conceptual approaches by artists whose practices straddled disciplines included solo exhibitions in 1973 by Derek Boshier (*Documentation and Work 1959–72*) and Tom Phillips, and in 1974 by Barry Flanagan. David Saunders, like Brookes a lecturer in Liverpool Polytechnic's Fine Art Department, and a leading figure in the Systems group of artists, exhibited paintings in 1974, as the gallery increasingly showed work by staff from art schools in both Liverpool and Manchester. Women oversaw these developments – Wendy Harpe, programming for Bluecoat Arts Forum, and gallery directors Lucy Cullen, Theresa Collard and Barbara Putt. The latter curated *An Honest Patron: A Tribute to Edward Marsh* (1976), which brought together works, including loans from the Tate, from the collection of Marsh, who had been Winston Churchill's private secretary and a supporter of modern art in Britain. This was one of a series of researched historical exhibitions that also included *Images of War* (1974) and *Duncan Grant: Designer* (1980).

Bluecoat's formalising of its gallery came in the wake of politically charged world events and the emergence of identity politics, including through the women's

Figure 47. The gallery in 1977: Simon Roodhouse and George Drought's exhibition of etchings and drawings. Photo: George Tate.

Figure 48. *The Liverpool Nude* exhibition, curated by Pam Holt, 1978. Photo: George Tate.

movement. An engagement with feminist discourse is one way in which we might measure Bluecoat's reflection of these times. This arguably dates from 1978 with an exhibition entitled *The Liverpool Nude* (Fig. 48), curated by Liverpool-based artist Pam Holt.[6] Not exclusively composed of women artists, it nonetheless paved the way for later, overtly feminist projects, notably *Phoenix: Women artists at work* in 1979, with four London artists – Kate Walker, Monica Ross, Sue Richardson and Suzy Varty – who turned the gallery into a studio, creating an evolving installation related to women's lives (Fig. 50). Though accompanied by a more conventional display by regional artists, *North West Women's Art Exhibition*, the jumbled informality of *Phoenix* anticipated relational aesthetics and making use of the gallery for a more direct public engagement. Also in 1978, London-based Argentinian exile Marisa Rueda showed her highly political ceramic sculptures in a two-person show, and was later included in *Women's Images of Men* (1981) and *Power Plays* (1983). The first of these (Fig. 49), a large group exhibition from the Institute of Contemporary Arts that turned the tables on the male gaze, attracting huge audiences during its national tour and much press ire, was a key exhibition for Bluecoat, whose *Power Plays* exhibition featured three artists from that show – Rueda, Sue Coe and Jacqueline Morreau – with uncompromising paintings, drawings and sculpture exploring the abuse of power. The gallery worked with another artist from this network of feminist artists, Pat Whiteread, on a solo show of mixed-media works addressing environmental concerns, *Conservation Pieces* (1985). Solo exhibitions by women – from Rose Garrard (1984), Jagjit Chuhan and Judith Rugg (both 1985), and Pam Skelton (1988) onwards – became a feature of the programme and would continue in the new gallery, with Jyll Bradley and Gina Czarnecki (2011), Niamh O'Malley (2015) and Larissa Sansour (2017).

The programmatic nature of exhibitions at Bluecoat in the late 1970s was facilitated by the arrival of staff who did more than maintain the operation and began to think about how to realise and contextualise the ideas of artists and works of art in the gallery space. Bryan Biggs, artistic director of Bluecoat since 2006, began working at the venue as administrative assistant in 1975. Appointed gallery director the following year, he became overall director of Bluecoat in 1994. In the 1970s and 1980s he presided over a small team of staff, without specialised job titles, who fulfilled exhibition organising roles. At first Biggs and a gallery assistant shared all the technical and administrative tasks associated with mounting an exhibition, including installation, invigilation, managing private views and publicity, compiling catalogues, and all the other practical tasks that accrue to exhibition making. A recent fine art graduate, Biggs's exhibition methods enabled him to hone his skills as a curator, commentator, installation designer and diplomat.

Figure 49. *Women's Images of Men* exhibition (on tour from ICA, London), 1981, including works by (from left) Eileen Cooper, Marisa Rueda (floor), Mandy Havers and Jacqueline Morreau.

All artists are aware that the allocation of space in a gallery is both tactically and hierarchically significant. Since Bluecoat was not set up as an art gallery, it always posed lighting issues for its curators. For obvious reasons, purpose-built galleries tend to favour skylights, but at Bluecoat, lateral light raked into the spaces, often calling for windows to be boarded (even more necessary with the arrival of video art) and strategic spotlighting to deputise for top light. The main gallery was the premier room, and for many years its importance, as a space apart, was signalled by the fact that it was carpeted. The removal of the carpet in 1989 to reveal the original parquet floor was equally a sign of the prestige of a space, reflecting fashionable flooring in international galleries – as well as its practicality. This was long overdue and followed significant exhibitions such as *Urban Kisses: 7 New York Artists* (1982), on tour from the ICA, when monumental framed drawings by Robert Longo – shown alongside works by Keith Haring, Cindy Sherman and other rising art world stars – were shoehorned into Bluecoat's ill-fitting spaces. Despite the inadequacies that such shows exposed, the 1980s witnessed increasing curatorial ambition. And with incremental improvements – rudimentary strip lighting replaced by a track system, elegant modular wooden seating commissioned as part of contemporary craft show, *Prescote at the Bluecoat* (1983), one of two shows curated by Ann Hartree of craft specialist Prescote Gallery in Oxfordshire – accompanied by more stylish

Figure 50. Poster/flyer for *Phoenix: Women artists at work*, 1979.

Figure 51. *Black Skin/Bluecoat* exhibition poster, 1985.

publicity, production of modest catalogues, and curatorial collaborations with other galleries such as ICA, Arnolfini in Bristol, Orchard Gallery in Derry and John Hansard Gallery in Southampton, the gallery's national profile and network grew. Resources remained limited, yet Bluecoat was able to draw on curatorial expertise on its advisory committee, including from Marco Livingstone (in Liverpool, working at the Walker Art Gallery), whose connections to young artists emerging from London's postgraduate courses brought painters such as Stephen Farthing, Graham Crowley and Tim Jones for early-career exhibitions at the gallery, and facilitated a Bluecoat touring retrospective drawing show by British pop artist Derek Boshier (1983). While maintaining a commitment to the vitality of the local scene, the gallery increasingly produced shows of national interest: Marc Camille Chaimowicz's *Past Imperfect* (1983), which was accompanied by the first serious assessment of his work in a publication; a four-person show, *Tony Bevan, Glenys Johnson, Jefford Horrigan, Jan Wandja* (1984); and toured-in shows by international names such as Ian Hamilton Finlay and Duane Michals (both 1985). The decade also saw Bluecoat's first international exchange exhibition with Liverpool's German twin city of Cologne, *Four Legs to Fly* (1987), arranged with BBK Gallery, which continued for several years and was revived in 1999 as *Eight Days A Week* by German art critic Jürgen Kisters, and maintained as an ongoing exchange programme by artists Pete Clarke in Liverpool and Georg Gartz in Cologne. This initiative, run on a shoestring, has provided opportunities for Liverpool artists to show work in one of Europe's leading centres for contemporary art, and for Cologne artists to discover the delights of England's 'falling down city'.[7]

The arrangement of the gallery's four interlinked rooms was used to good effect in 1985 when Bluecoat staged the watershed exhibition, *Black Skin/Bluecoat* (Fig. 51). Displaying works by four artists – Sonia Boyce, Eddie Chambers, Keith Piper and Tom Joseph – it was the first exhibition at Bluecoat to provide a platform for a burgeoning, self-consciously black British artistic practice.[8] Its title, devised by Chambers, was a clever play on Frantz Fanon's influential book *Black Skin, White Masks* (1952), which interrogates the construction of black identity in relation to colonised peoples. For much of the twentieth century, at Bluecoat and elsewhere, works by black artists were typically displayed in exhibitions of African or Caribbean art, even if the artists had never set foot in either continent.[9] However, towards the end of the 1970s and into the 1980s the first appreciable generation of British-born black artists were graduating from art school, staking their claim for a distinctly black British identity and due recognition from the nation's art institutions. *Black Skin/Bluecoat* was one among many small and large group shows being staged across Britain in the early-to-mid 1980s, either by municipal museums and galleries or by black artists themselves, which sought to bring the existence of this new generation to the attention of an otherwise ignorant public. Much, though not all, of the work of these artists was socially and politically engaged, speaking to issues of unemployment, the collapse of industry, racial tension and the rise of the far right. In the aftermath of the Toxteth uprisings in 1981, it was vital for these artists to have a platform at Bluecoat.

What made *Black Skin/Bluecoat* distinct from presentations of black British artistic practices being offered by other public art galleries was its tighter focus on the participating artists' individual practices. Elsewhere, surveys were the preferred format, evidencing the breadth of artists and practices but failing to engage with the individual concerns and artistic strategies being employed. *Black Skin/Bluecoat* was initially conceived as a small survey, but through a collaborative curatorial approach, both the artists and curator, Bryan Biggs, determined that young black artists had been sufficiently introduced to the art world via the survey model and that it was now time for a deeper engagement with individual practices. The principal exhibition spaces were thus configured so that each artist was assigned their own section to display a more substantial body of work than would have been possible in a survey style show. *Black Skin/Bluecoat* was a masterclass in representational and politically engaged practice, with a range of drawings, sculptures, paintings, collages and installations that depicted the domestic and familial as political, melded grand historical and personal-political narratives, and explored the relationship between slavery and capitalism. Piper's slide-based work *The Trophies of Empire* (1985) took particular advantage of the curved room to underscore its exploration of history as a circular process, by projecting a cycle of images on the rounded wall.

This was a pivotal exhibition for Bluecoat, not simply because it was the first in its programme history to engage with the notion of being both black and British and how that position is reflected through artistic practice, but also because it enabled the organisation to begin a dialogue with Liverpool's black community. Local black artists were delighted to see black artists represented more visibly by Bluecoat, but some also questioned why these artists, based in London and Bristol, had been provided an opportunity to exhibit at Bluecoat before local black artists. In the years that followed, however, there was a proliferation of exhibitions featuring work by locally based practitioners[10] who, together with other UK and international black artists, peppered and punctuated Bluecoat's programme, with many group and solo exhibitions. Some group shows were initiated by Bluecoat, including *Numaish Lalit Kala* (1988), new British Asian work curated for the local MILAP Indian Arts Festival. Others were touring collaborations with other venues and with independent curators, notably Eddie Chambers, starting with *Black Art: Plotting the Course* (1989), a partnership between Bluecoat, Oldham and Wolverhampton art galleries, involving 27 artists.[11] Chambers had participated in *Black Skin/Bluecoat*, and a legacy of that show was the relationships forged with three of its artists, with Chambers, Boyce and Piper returning to curate shows and the latter two exhibiting again several times.

Importantly, there were also solo shows, some at a critical stage for artists starting to make their mark nationally. In 1986 South African artist Gavin Jantjes's painting series *Korabra* in the main gallery, relating to transatlantic slavery, was complemented by a sequence of shows intended to provide an historical and local context: photographs by the Liverpool Black Media Group relating to Liverpool 8 (*Pieces of 8*) and a display from the Institute of Race Relations, *From Resistance to Rebellion*, documenting Asian and Afro-Caribbean struggles in Britain. In 1988 the automated sculpture of Nigerian-born, London-based artist Sokari Douglas Camp created a cacophony in the gallery and, opening the same week as

Tate, could not have contrasted more with the cool aesthetic of the first shows by Bluecoat's new neighbour at the Albert Dock, *Starlit Waters* and the Rothko room. In 1989 Keith Khan's *Soucouyan* project combined an exhibition and performance drawing on Trinidadian carnival traditions, and Liverpool-born Chila Kumari Burman's 1995 survey show, *28 Positions in 34 Years*, took over the whole gallery and was subsequently toured nationally. Complexities around the construction and representation of identity was a continuing thread in the gallery programme. Collaboration with Autograph, the Association of Black Photographers, saw *Mis(sed) Representations* (1992), with work by six artists including Donald Rodney and Maxine Walker, a version of which went, as *Autographed*, to BBK Cologne for the Photokina Festival. The relationship with Autograph was reignited in 2012 when John Akomfrah's three-screen film installation on the life and work of Professor Stuart Hall, *The Unfinished Conversation*, was premiered at Bluecoat, against the backdrop of that year's Liverpool Biennial.

Although accommodation of large-scale artwork such as Akomfrah's was only fully realised with Bluecoat's new gallery spaces in 2008, the adaptability of the main gallery was extended in the 1990s with the successful installation of early- to mid-career solo shows by, among others, Bashir Makhoul (*Al-Hejara*, 1993), Lesley Sanderson (*These Colours Run*, 1995) and Permindar Kaur (*Cold Comfort*, 1996). Makhoul's large paintings, drawing on Arabic pattern and calligraphic motifs in the colours of the flag of his native Palestine had been shown in 1990 group exhibition *Interim Report*, when they were facilitated by boarding the exit to the garden and creating a pleasing trinity that retained the feature of the original pilasters (Fig. 52). Sanderson used the same arrangement to present a triptych of large drawings and rectangular floor pieces, whose vivid yellow hue was repeated in other gallery rooms. The uncanny scale of Kaur's *Tall Beds* (1993) was maximised by their scraping into the space of the high ceilings of the main gallery (Fig. 45).

Kaur's show was initiated by the Ikon, Birmingham, and Mead Gallery, Warwick, and Makhoul's by Huddersfield Art Gallery; for Bluecoat, like many regional galleries, buying in exhibitions, as well as touring their own, was a necessary part of programming, helping spread the costs of originating ambitious shows and increasing their national reach. Like Keith Piper, Sanderson had previously exhibited at the venue, in *New Contemporaries* in 1986, and both they and Kaur were representative of a diverse cohort of British artists being reflected in Bluecoat's programme with increasing regularity.

A commitment to making the gallery, and the whole building, more inclusive was also evident in exhibitions that addressed disability, starting with Ann Whitehurst's *On the Map: Placing Disability* (1994), in which she turned the tables on disabling

Figure 52. Paintings by Bashir Makhoul in *Interim Report* exhibition, 1990.

environments through a large-scale board game with outsized furry dice, in which non-disabled participants always finished last, and which was literally rolled out subsequently as a training tool in architecture offices and planning departments. Whitehurst's interventions in other parts of the building highlighted Bluecoat's physical inaccessibility and informed thinking around its capital development and making the building accessible, which was finally realised in 2008. Tenants moving into the refurbished Bluecoat then included Deaf and disability arts organisation DaDaFest, with which the gallery had fostered a productive relationship through exhibitions such as *Senseless – Art/Bodies/Misfits* during the 2003 European Year of Disabled People,[12] and would continue in the new gallery with *Niet Normaal: Difference on Display* (2012) and *Art of the Lived Experiment* (2014), curated by Aaron Williamson (Fig. 53). The new accessible spaces meant that Bluecoat could be more inclusive as a place for resident artists, and Sally Booth, the 2009 recipient of the Adam Reynolds Memorial bursary award, organised by Shape, would spend several months in a studio drawing and creating lightbox photo works based on Bluecoat's distinctive oval windows.

Despite the shared understanding by artists that there were prime and subprime spaces in Bluecoat, the gallery has always been pragmatic about optimising the sites of display. Hence, visitors to pre-2008 Bluecoat would often encounter artwork in corridors and stairwells, in the café, and in the courtyard and garden. This bleeding into other areas of the building allowed the art to escape the confines of the white cube, while also facilitating a greater accommodation of artistic practices beyond those traditionally featured in galleries. An installation view of *Cover Versions* in 1981, for instance, shows album covers arranged in a dense salon-style hang, arguably the first exhibition to present the new wave of young, then relatively unknown record sleeve designers, such as Peter Saville and Malcolm Garrett. This marked an important inclusion of graphic arts into the programme, although it might be observed that their relegation to the side gallery and top space attested to common perceptions that graphic art was less important than fine art. Nonetheless, Bluecoat organised a number of exhibitions of graphic art, including *Recent Posters from Czechoslovakia* (1981), curated by Gérard Mermoz from his personal collection smuggled out from behind the Iron Curtain. There were several cartoon and comic strip exhibitions featuring the likes of Bill Tidy, Larry, Posy Simmonds, Alexei Sayle and Ray Lowry, and an ICA collaboration, *Graphic Rap* (1983), that presented the new wave of alternative 'comix' from Europe and the US, including Art Spiegelman's *RAW* and *Biff*, while Glen Baxter and John Stalin – two artists who subverted graphic

Figure 53. Tony Heaton, *Gold Lamé* installation in *Art of the Lived Experiment* exhibition, curated by Aaron Williamson for DaDaFest, 2014. Photo: Jon Barraclough.

illustration tropes – were also presented. In 1993 the gallery curated a tribute to the Widnes-born artist Mal Dean, known for his early 1970s jazz illustrations in *Melody Maker* and surreal cartoons in *International Times*, and other graphic representations of popular music were shown in two exhibitions of Pete Frame's labyrinthine *Rock Family Trees*, one charting the development of Merseybeat. Dean's exhibition was one of several substantial, specially researched shows of artists who died young, all of them Merseyside-born and Liverpool Art College-trained, who had made a mark in their respective spheres, and who included Ray Walker (1987), known for his political murals in London's East End, and the 'fifth Beatle', painter Stuart Sutcliffe (1990).

Curating in non-collecting institutions, such as Bluecoat, presents endless challenges as well as opportunities. Working within the constrictions of space requires a degree of collaborative curating, professionalism between artists and curators, and a measure of negotiation on both sides. An early example of the gallery meeting the requirements of collaborative curating was Mark Boyle and Joan Hill's *Son et Lumière for Earth, Air, Fire and Water* of 1967. The pair had pioneered the multimedia techniques of liquid light shows, psychedelic projections of bubbling and swirling coloured dyes combined in the heat of the projector, presenting these at gigs by the darlings of the UK underground music scene, Soft Machine. Equally art installation and performance, *Son et Lumière* utilised spaces accordingly. The performances were in the Sandon Room (Fig. 54), some distance from the gallery, where the exhibition was installed. Here, the curved room was never a space to hang large paintings but it was eminently suited to installations, and to what would later be called black box activity. This early commitment to multimedia, multi-platform presentation remained a stable fixture in the programming of work at Bluecoat.

The commitment was somewhat formalised twenty years later, with the inception of *Video Positive* in 1989, which reaffirmed the gallery as a site that could transform the static, presentational space of the museum into a space for projection and immersion. Bluecoat welcomed the new video medium, and often appeared to be unfazed by the technical and other challenges of presenting pre-digital moving image artworks. There was always a 'can do' spirit at Bluecoat, and an installation such as Mike Stubbs's *Desert Island Dread* was a tour de force of technical wizardry and practical inventiveness. The team filled the main gallery with a heap of sand, fashioned sand castles, installed a slowly rotating glitter ball and created eerily lit stalactites made from black, water-filled condoms suspended from the ceiling. This was in the first *Video Positive*, organised by Merseyside Moviola, the brainchild of Eddie Berg and curated in collaboration with Steve Littman. This biennial festival of moving image/electronic art put Liverpool on the map as a centre for new media art, and over several editions effectively became the UK's premier showcase, working with a range of local venues and gaining an international profile through imaginative commissioning and a pioneering community programme. Moviola's 14-year tenure at Bluecoat started with a modest office in 1989, expanding to take over a whole wing, the organisation finally relocating to a new building in Wood Street, having morphed into FACT (Foundation for Art and Creative Technology) along the way. While based at Bluecoat, alongside six *Video Positives* up to 2000, the gallery hosted many Moviola/FACT exhibitions including Tony Oursler's first solo show in the UK, *Cigarettes, Flowers and Videotape* (1993), the US artist having previously shown at Bluecoat in *Video Positive 91* (Fig. 76).

In the early days of Biggs's tenure few staff were called 'curators' and the activity was better characterised as 'organising exhibitions' than as curating them. Biggs recalls that exhibition organisation 'was pretty two-way – getting to know an artist and

Figure 54. Mark Boyle and Joan Hill's *Son et Lumière* performance in the Sandon Room, 1967.

mutually selecting work, though over time as the curator role developed and became professionalised, I guess my role became more authorial'.[13] The facilitative aspect of Bluecoat was further developed in and through its offer to what we would now term 'socially engaged' artists, individuals and artist groups who invited community participation, or led to interventions into the public realm, throwing the gallery open to political activism, interdisciplinary work with other art forms or engagement with technology. Bluecoat has always recognised that changes in UK and international art practice are reflected – and in some cases pioneered – in the work of artists residing in and around the city;[14] and the commitment to the region's many artists has never simply been a gesture of parochial loyalty. Liverpool and the region has hosted particularly strong artistic groupings, from the Sandon Studios Society and Liverpool Academy to the photo realists championed by Edward Lucie-Smith in the 1970s and the Marxist-inclined Liverpool Artists Workshop in the 1980s.[15] By 'distinctive provincialism', Bluecoat meant favourable programming of exhibitions by regional artists, and particularly large group shows that pulled together well-regarded local artists, including Clement McAleer, Pete Clarke, Nina Edge, David Mabb, Sue and David Campbell, Paul Morrison, Lin Holland, Leo Fitzmaurice, The Singh Twins, Paul Rooney, David Jacques, Alan Dunn and many others.[16]

The Christmas shows, sometimes with over 50 artists, became greatly anticipated celebrations, both for the artistic community and for buyers, building on the seasonal selling exhibitions that started in the 1970s when popular artists such as Don McKinlay, Sam Walsh, Melvyn Chantrey and Peter Mousdale would shift the majority of their work on the opening night. Such was the strength of work being produced in the city's burgeoning independent studios in the 1980s and 1990s – the Bridewell, Arena, Liverpool Artists Workshop and Bluecoat itself – or emerging from the Art School, that more 'curated' shows entirely of home-grown talent were possible. The 1992 exhibition series *A Pool of Signs*, for instance, brought together 22 Liverpool-based artists whose work chimed with current critical discourse in visual art practice around the politics of representation and the representation of politics, media culture and new media, female identity and the public realm.[17] Having local artists working at Bluecoat, such as gallery assistant Chris Kennedy, helped the venue gather intelligence on the local scene, as did employing others as freelance technicians and workshop leaders. The gallery also provided space for Tate Liverpool's Momart Fellowship artists to present a culminating exhibition at the end of their residency: Maud Sulter (1991), Elizabeth Magill (1994), Emma Rushton (1996) and Marion Coutts (2001), and other artists-in-residence such as Robert Soden (1987), whose works on paper, created *en plein air* during his time at Bridewell Studios and capturing a city in transition, were shown.

Alongside being attuned to work produced locally, Bluecoat's programming, especially from the 1990s onwards, was informed by Liverpool's historical global connections. In 1992 a series of 'celebrations' were taking place to mark the 500th anniversary of Columbus's arrival in the Americas. A counter-programme, *Five Hundred Years of Resistance*, had been devised to acknowledge the darker ramifications of Europe's conquest of the Americas and, contributing to the Liverpool campaign, Bluecoat reunited with artist-curator Keith Piper to produce a programme of exhibitions and events titled after his earlier work shown at Bluecoat, *Trophies of Empire*, which ran from 1992 into early 1993 across venues in the port cities of Bristol, Hull and Liverpool.[18] Fifteen artists' commissions were awarded through an open competition to devise responses to the legacies of empire in the context of the Columbus quincentenary, as well as the consolidation of European unification with the advent of the single market taking place that year, which 'symbolically dislocated the old imperial states of Europe from links with their ex-colonies in favour of forging a new, insular "Pan European" consciousness'.[19] Piper and Biggs, along with representatives from the venues in Hull and Bristol, selected the artists in a highly collaborative manner, their choices informed through dialogue and a shared understanding that the programme, with its potential to revolve around issues of imperialism, slavery and decolonisation, would not be circumscribed by the cultural identity of its artists.

While Piper's own video installation, *Trade Winds*, was shown at the Maritime Museum (at a time when Liverpool's role in the slave trade was largely absent from that venue's displays), three of the other seven *Trophies of Empire* exhibitions and events took place at Bluecoat, the first a group show that referenced the relationship between the transatlantic slave trade and contemporary global capitalism. Liverpool/Manchester design collective South Atlantic Souvenirs & Trouble presented *The Trophy Cabinet*, an installation comprising an array of trade commodities enabled by slavery, including tastefully packaged boxes of tea, sugar and tobacco, that were disrupted by ironic captions describing the 'violence, pillage and mayhem' that ensued in the 'European invasion of the Americas, the boom years of the slave trade, the plundering of the Orient, and the scramble for Africa'.[20] Rita Keegan's *Cycles*, a strongly autobiographical video installation with imagery of her family stretching back to her great, great grandmother, the daughter of a white woman and a slave, offered a personal reflection on the relationship between diaspora and the impact of slavery, past and present (Fig. 55). A similarly personal reflection was offered through Liverpool-born artist Paul Clarkson's series of paintings *The Witness & The Observer*, which deconstructed visual representations of official history through his own cultural identifications.

These personal and autobiographical works were contrasted with Veena Stephenson's sculpture *Ring a Ring o' Roses A Pocket Full of Posies*, which reconfigured the Union Flag motif on a dissected boardroom table, beneath images of the London Stock Exchange, the Crown Agents (the body set up to administer Britain's post-colonial interests) and the Gulf War. These various elements, including the work's title, were combined to give a sense of the delicate and precarious balance between global trade, warfare and disease in European history. Imperial legacies in India were explored by Shaheen Merali's film installation *Going Native*, which comprised rows of deckchairs upon which holiday images were projected. The piece related to the conquest of Goa by the Portuguese, and its continuing 'colonisation' through tourism. In Bluecoat's garden, Juginder Lamba's sculpture *The Cry*, constructed and carved from ancient timbers salvaged from barns and quayside warehouses in Lancaster (another slave port on England's north-west coast), stood surrounded by buildings seemingly little changed since they were first erected in the era of the transatlantic slave trade, giving the work a special resonance, a 'shrine … to all oppressed peoples'.[21] The exhibition was complemented by a live art piece from

Verbal Images, a Liverpool-based group of urban griots, Indian dancers and African drummers, whose performance involved rap and dub poetry, dance, visuals and music, reflecting their own individual heritage in a celebration of the wealth of black British culture. Finally, another Liverpool artists' group, Visual Stress, presented *Mobile Auto Mission*, a day-long motorcade cruising the streets of Liverpool in the run-up to Christmas, a 'carnival taking the wrong direction into the uncharted territories of the city … [visiting] … stations of the cross'[22] – patently imperialist buildings and sites considered complicit with the festive season's consumer madness.

Trophies of Empire was an ambitious and expansive programme of exhibitions and live art that became a blueprint for other Bluecoat programmes. Its presentation of work by black artists was particularly innovative. In many other public museums and galleries, works by black artists continued to be grouped together for exhibitions devised on the basis of the artists' ethnicity, which tended to foreground questions of identity and cultural difference and preclude considerations of their practices in relation to broader developments in contemporary art. *Trophies of Empire* departed from the popular black survey or black group show curatorial model by bringing works by both black and white artists together so that practices and objects became the focus of attention, rather than their makers' ethnicities. Although the theme had the potential to favour black artists, who are arguably more invested in the topic of Britain's imperial legacies, it was not considered their preserve. This was, and arguably remains, a novel curatorial approach to displaying work by black artists, given that race-based exhibitions remain a somewhat popular mode through which to present the work of black artists in public museums and galleries.[23]

One such project that did adopt the curatorial model of *Trophies* was *Independent Thoughts*, a complex, large-scale programme of interrelated exhibitions involving nine venues across the North and Midlands of England between summer 1997 and spring 1998 that marked and responded to the 50th anniversary of Indian independence and partition.[24] The programme was initiated by artist Juginder Lamba, who, having exhibited at Bluecoat in *Trophies of Empire* and in the solo show *From the Wood* (1995), proposed to the gallery a series of visual art commissions by British South Asian and other artists that would take a critical look at issues surrounding independence and the wider impact and legacies of partition. Lamba's proposal was developed into a more expansive programme, with a consortium of venues holding an open submission process to encourage a diversity of perspectives on the theme of independence, from literal responses to the events in India in 1947, to looser responses to the notion of personal, emotional, psychological or cultural independence. The resulting thirteen commissioned artworks reflected a wide generational and media range.

The Bluecoat component of *Independent Thoughts* was a series of installations by Mohini Chandra, *Travels in a New World 2*, which explored the history of Indian workers brought to Fiji in the nineteenth century to work on sugar plantations and subsequently forced to migrate elsewhere after independence. The installation comprised several tea chests lit from within and covered with Chandra's family photographs, shown in a room whose floor was covered in dry tea leaves that crunched underfoot, releasing an intensely musty, herbal scent. The piece played on the way Indian workers were moved around under British rule, just as people move their possessions around in tea chests. In the second installation, the backs of photos taken at a family reunion were displayed in frames, their surfaces revealing scant information scrawled in pencil: the dates and places they were taken and names of the individuals in them. By revealing only the backs of the photos, the artist invited viewers to imagine their own stories about her family. In the final installation, interviews with Chandra's family members (all living in different parts of the Pacific Rim but each filmed against the backdrop of the same roaring ocean), talking about their memories of the day the photos were taken, were simultaneously projected on to the walls of the main gallery, creating a virtual family reunion.

Bluecoat continued its independence season with three live art commissions interrogating similar themes of diaspora and migration, selected from open submission and presented in October 1997. Nina Edge's interactive *The Observers Book of Independence* was staged in a popular city-centre bar in which audience members were invited to nominate what they wished to become independent from. Rona Lee's *auto/nomos*, a durational two-day performance/installation of a large Union Flag, bleached of colour, laid out in Bluecoat's auditorium, raised questions about gender, identity and nationhood (Fig. 56). And *Departures* by regionally based performance group Asian Voices Asian Lives combined music, poetry, theatre and comedy to link themes of arrival and departure within an airport setting, a comment on the promises of independence for Indian migrants to Britain.

Independent Thoughts attracted 68,000 visitors to its various exhibitions and offered a vital opportunity for a wide and critical exploration of overlapping concerns about nationhood, cultural identity and the legacies of colonialism, as well as an intergenerational and interdisciplinary dialogue between artists that resulted in the production of significant new work. Some of the artworks were subsequently shown abroad, for example Chandra's *Travels in a New World 2* in *Out of India: Contemporary Art of the South Asian Diaspora* at the Queens Museum of Art in New York the following year. The themes of the project were further developed by a symposium, *Independent Practices*, and an associated collection of essays of the same name.[25]

Figure 56. Rona Lee, *auto/nomos*, performance/installation in the concert hall, 1997, a Bluecoat live art commission.

The Liverpool Biennial was launched in 1999, two years after *Independent Thoughts*, bringing contemporary art from around the world to the city by commissioning leading and emerging international artists to make and present permanent and temporary public artworks, and to work on community-based projects. This initially threatened the place of local artists and, after the first year when Susan Fitch, Bashir Makhoul, Gary Perkins and Amanda Ralph were selected for *Trace*, curated by Anthony Bond, Liverpool-based artists were never fully embraced into the main Biennial international programme, showing instead in an independent 'fringe'. As Bryan Biggs diplomatically observes: 'In such a globalised environment, the local takes on new significance, and within visual art it is the biennial, traditionally based on the model of Venice with its international pavilions, that has become a predominant site through which to consider the local within the new global relationships.'[26]

Bluecoat was involved in the Biennial from its inception, participating in each edition (Fig. 57). It was part of a local curatorial team in 2002 when it programmed work at its own venue and at Tate Liverpool, including Mexican-American artist Guillermo Goméz-Peña, whose Pocha Nostra group also presented a memorable Biennial opening interactive performance, *Ex-Centris (A Living Diorama of Fetishized Others)*, at Bluecoat. This was a collaboration with the Live Art Development Agency (LADA), the first of several performance art programmes,

Liverpool Live, that Bluecoat curated with LADA and independent curator Tamsin Drury, who took the 2006 programme out into Liverpool city centre while the venue was closed for its capital development (see Chapter 4). That year Bluecoat was also invited to curate *Walk On*, an exhibition by Liverpool artists in its Chinese twin city of Shanghai during its own Biennale. It was shown, somewhat incongruously, at Salon Vogue in Citic Square, where Philip Jeck gave a commanding performance at the launch, wringing exquisite sounds from vinyl and electronics that resonated through the upmarket shopping mall.

One artist who exemplified an engagement between the local and international, as well as with the key platforms of the period, was the site-specific artist Janet Hodgson (1960–2016). She was, for many years, a resident of Liverpool and had a long association with Bluecoat, having three exhibitions and contributing to numerous group shows there; and this is significant because it evidences Bluecoat's long-standing commitment to working with artists – and not just locally based ones – over time to develop fruitful relationships. Hodgson responded to the historic legacy of Bluecoat in a number of specially commissioned pieces: *I must learn to know my place* (1994), *History Lesson* (1999) and the renovated building's reopening film, *Re-Run* (2008). Taken together, they form a trilogy that unflinchingly deals with Bluecoat's 300-year history. Hodgson's interest was piqued by the building's original incarnation as a school, and she projected

Figure 57. *Trace*, the first Liverpool Biennial, 1999, with works at Bluecoat by Julie Gough (foreground) and María Magdalena Campos-Pons.

the lines 'I must learn to know my place' on to the exterior (Fig. 58). The work consisted of large cursive writing repeated all over the façade, unnervingly recalling a time-consuming form of punishment (schoolroom lines) that also drilled an 'improving' message into the minds of pupils in receipt of its charitable education. In *History Lesson*, the artist returned to Bluecoat's former school life, simultaneously projecting feature-length film sequences on to nine locations throughout the gallery. The multi-projection artwork fictionalised scenes enacted by figures in nineteenth-century costume, giving glimpses of the school's quotidian life – a history lesson silently delivered by a period-dressed headmaster in a gaslit schoolroom (Fig. 59). At the end of the film he dismisses his class and, acknowledging the conceit of the installation for the first time, gestures to the camera to pan out beyond the scene so that we might discover the technical crew, just about to restore the film set to a white-walled gallery.

I must learn to know my place was part of *On Location*, a series of site-specific commissions, and such off-site projects became a distinct strand of Bluecoat's work in this period, responding to artists' changing practices to escape the confines of the gallery, while seeking a more direct engagement with the public and the city. While many of these interventions were funded as live art commissions (see Chapter 4), the gallery also facilitated off-site projects such as Artangel's nationwide billboard posters *We Don't Need Another Hero* by Barbara Kruger (1987), securing sites in Liverpool, including one at Albert Dock, and thus inadvertently commenting on the imminent arrival of the Tate of the North (Tate Liverpool). As an extension of group exhibition *Second Wave* (1988), John Plowman appropriated a large advertising hoarding site at Canning Place, which was also used by TEA (Those Environmental Artists) for *Living Spaces*, a series of interventions around the city centre. This was commissioned for *New Art North West*, a regional survey in collaboration with Cornerhouse in Manchester in 1991, when Geoff Molyneux also created railway sleeper installations at Oxford Road and Edge Hill stations. Extending its exhibitions beyond the gallery in this way, Bluecoat helped prepare the ground for initiatives such as the annual grassroots visual arts festival Visionfest (started in 1992), which exploited Liverpool's urban fabric and its richness of found spaces and unusual locations, paving the way, seven years later, for the Biennial, whose artists have continued to explore site-specific opportunities across the city. Bluecoat's installation of an immersive slide-tape work by Holly Warburton at the neoclassical Oratory, next to Liverpool's Anglican Cathedral – part of nationwide 1987 public art commissions *TSWA 3D* (initiated by Television South West/South West Arts) – demonstrated the possibility of using this hidden space, with its collection of historic stone sculptures, for many subsequent art interventions. For the ambitious, multi-

Janet Hodgson Bluecoat commissions:
Figure 58. *I must learn to know my place*, night-time projection on to the building, 1994.
Figure 59. *History Lesson*, film installation in the gallery, 1999.
With kind permission of Louise and Wellington Cumberland.

site *artranspennine98* project, spanning the northern region from Liverpool to Hull, Bluecoat stayed on site, contributing a gallery exhibition by American eco-artists Helen Mayer Harrison and Newton Harrison, who imagined this swathe of England as a dragon, reawakened to fight ecological crisis.

Invited curators were central to Bluecoat's programming, enabling it to widen its engagement with current critical thinking, as well as different geographies. John Roberts's *Approaches to Realism* (1990), comprising work by Rasheed Araeen, Art & Language, Terry Atkinson, Sue Atkinson, David Batchelor, Sonia Boyce and David Mabb, was accompanied by an essay that argued for a radical reclamation of realism through a rejection of its characterisation as 'the conflation between realism in art and the *world of appearances*'. Brian McAvera's two-part exhibition *Parable Island* (1991) was a wide-ranging survey of current tendencies in artistic practice in both the Irish Republic and Northern Ireland, which took over the entire gallery and installed sculptures in the front courtyard and garden.

Working with independent curators also enabled Bluecoat to encompass fresh thinking around diversity, the local and the global, and new art networks opening up internationally. In 1994 Nigerian artist and curator Olu Oguibe's *Seen/Unseen* (Fig. 60) presented the work of British-based artists of African heritage – Uzo Egonu, Lubaina Himid, Folake Shoga, Yinka Shonibare (and Oguibe himself) – to interrogate problematic issues around cultural authenticity and the controversy surrounding Susan Vogel's 1991 survey show at New York's New Museum, *Africa Explores: Twentieth Century African Art* (on tour, it ran concurrently with *Seen/Unseen* at Tate Liverpool), whose anthropological classification was seen as reinforcing ethnologically defined stereotypes of 'African art'. A challenge to received perceptions of the contemporary arts from the African continent was reflected in the UK-wide festival *Africa95*, for which Bluecoat hosted *Cross-Currents: New Art from Senegal*, curated by Senegalese artist Fode Camara in collaboration with Jan Cools from de Warande in Turnhout, Belgium, where it was first shown. This led to an invitation to Bluecoat to participate the following year in Dak'Art, Senegal's biennial 'platform for contemporary art with cultural roots in Africa', the arts centre nominating Liverpool-connected artists with such roots to participate in the Tenq workshop in Dakar.[27]

One criticism of Western presentations of African art in exhibitions such as *Africa Explores* was their exclusively sub-Saharan focus. Bluecoat addressed this in several exhibitions, the process initiated largely through dialogue with Bashir Makhoul (who had studied in Liverpool and had his first show at Bluecoat), who helped introduce contemporary art from the Arab world to the venue. This became a significant strand, with exhibitions such as *Veil* (curated by Iniva [International

Institute of Visual Arts], 2003), which would continue in the new, enlarged gallery with *New Endings Old Beginnings* (curated by November Paynter, 2008), *Arabicity* (curated by Rose Issa, 2010) and *I exist (in some way)* (curated by Sara-Jayne Parsons, 2013), connecting to Bluecoat's development of the Liverpool Arab Arts Festival. Makhoul was instrumental in establishing the Centre for Art International Research (cair) at Liverpool John Moores University (LJMU), which developed residencies, including a Henry Moore Sculpture Fellowship for British artists with perspectives from outside the Western mainstream, and these culminated in solo shows at Bluecoat by fellows Bill Ming (1993), Nina Edge (1994) and Juginder Lamba (1995). Another international LJMU resident artist who exhibited was Walid Sadek from Lebanon, whose *Karaoke* exhibition (1998) was accompanied by a catalogue – at 6 x 8 cm, the smallest ever produced by the gallery – with a prescient essay critiquing 'globalization's ravenous mobility … in relation to the "local" as an already co-opted terrain'.[28] Imran Qureshi from Pakistan also showed in a three-person drawing exhibition (2001).

While Bluecoat was able to widen its international embrace of non-Western art through externally curated touring group exhibitions representing new art from Japan, China, Pakistan and India, solo shows were also possible through other partnerships, notably with Sunil Gupta from OVA (Organisation for Visual Arts),

Figure 60. *Seen/Unseen* exhibition curated by Olu Oguibe, 1994: work by Lubaina Himid (left) and Yinka Shonibare.

Figure 61. Sokari Douglas Camp's solo exhibition, *Alali*, 1988.

one of the curators, along with Eddie Chambers and Rasheed Araeen, franchised by Iniva. Two of OVA's solo projects by artists then based in Malaysia were premiered at Bluecoat: Simryn Gill (1999) and Wong Hoy Cheong (2002), who returned to the venue for a 2004 Liverpool Biennial commission, for which he revisited the absurd but true story of Roy Rogers's horse, Trigger, taking a bow from a first-floor window of Liverpool's Adelphi hotel to adoring fans outside during the singing cowboy's visit to the city in 1954. The artist edited this three-screen film into a single-channel video for a group show curated by Sara-Jayne Parsons in 2011, *Honky Tonk*, which drew out the connections between Liverpool and a Country and Western aesthetic. The new gallery spaces proved eminently more suitable than the old 'warren of eccentric spaces' for such ambitious, large-scale, local/global exhibitions, even if something of the old gallery's charm had been lost.

***

What is remarkable about Bluecoat's exhibition history is not just its record of ambitious support for emerging artists, such as Piper's *Trophies of Empire* programme, but also its maintaining of subsequent relationships with artists who had exhibited at the gallery. Its programme, distinguished by mixing the local and the global, live art and site-specific practices, and nurturing culturally diverse artists and 'dissident' art practices, was described by the *Guardian*'s art critic, Robert Clark, as a 'model for provincial galleries':

> They don't just show art based on social issues or purist abstraction or conceptualist multi-media installations or figurative realism. They show the lot. They don't rely on a weedy permanent collection or lazily accept the endless supply of Arts Council touring packages.
> The liveliness comes from the fact that when you go down to the Bluecoat

you don't know exactly what kind of art you will see but you can be sure you'll see art up there on the walls and not some visual dissertation on a theoretical theme by a bunch of over-interfering arts administrators.[29]

What is also remarkable is the way in which each exhibition in the diverse programme was reconciled to, or responded to, the constrictions of space at Bluecoat, demonstrating how the organisation used its estate inventively, and sometimes eccentrically, to host artists' work. As we have seen, working within the constrictions of space requires the diminution of a single authorial voice and vision. Accordingly, the exhibitions discussed reflect the development of *collaborative* curating at Bluecoat, stemming from a dialogue with artists and curators, a sensitivity to changing practices, a 'can do' attitude to technological developments, as well as pragmatic solutions to shifts in the funding environment. What we have tried to do is to reanimate the history of some of Bluecoat's landmark exhibitions. Inevitably, the record of how many tussles over space there were or what egos clashed in the making of exhibitions rests in individual memories. However, behind the scenes interactions between artists and gallery staff are invisible to the viewer; and the eerily quiet, conventional installation shots, shown in this chapter, always record the calm following the storm.

We thank Bryan Biggs for sharing his knowledge, resources and insights in the preparation of this chapter.

Notes

1. Sean Cubitt, 'Eminent Fomorians: Irish art in Liverpool', *Circa*, 57, May–June, 1991, pp. 22–25 (p. 22).
2. Cubitt, 'Eminent Fomorians', p. 24.
3. Michael Oelman was the first gallery director, his short spell at the helm being followed by Lucy Cullen, Theresa Collard, Barbara Putt and Bryan Biggs. Its title changing, the role was continued by Janice Webster, Catherine Gibson, Sara-Jayne Parsons, Marie-Anne McQuay and Adam Smythe.
4. The naming of rooms is slightly conflicting: the old galleries were named 2, 3 and 4 before the larger space was used as the main gallery (Gallery 1).
5. Bluecoat's selling shows provided an important source of income for several Liverpool artists.
6. There had been solo painting shows by Dorothy Bradford (1965, 1972), Margaret Dean (1966, 1971) and Judith Bibby (1968) – the first solo exhibition by a woman in the new space. Other early women's solo shows include Pat Cooke (1971), Anne Külzer (1972) and Susan Sterne

(1972). Pam Holt had shown in two exhibitions of 'hangings' in 1970 and 1972, alongside Paul Neagu, Noel Forster, Roy Holt and others.
7. During exchanges with BBK the German gallery would refer to Liverpool in this way: source Bryan Biggs.
8. Bluecoat had also hosted *Contemporary African Art* (1966), an exhibition of paintings from the Transcription Centre, London, curated by Dennis Duerden; a solo show of etchings by London-based Nigerian printmaker Bruce Onobrakpeya (1972); and *Contemporary Art of Africa, the Caribbean and Liverpool* (1973), an exhibition of paintings, drawings, prints and sculpture by Mohammed Ahmed Abdalla, Uzo Egonu, Margaret Hendrickse, Dumile Keni, Erroll Lloyd and Ronald Moody, organised by John Mapondera and the UKAF Committee. Egonu returned to Bluecoat in the exhibition *Seen/Unseen*. In 1984 London-based artist Jan Wandja showed in a four-person exhibition with Tony Bevan, Glenys Johnson and Jefford Horrigan.

9 *Contemporary Art of Africa, the Caribbean and Liverpool* is a case in point, featuring works by Ronald Moody, who left Jamaica at the age of 23 to spend the rest of his life in Paris and London.

10 These included Paul Clarkson, Nina Edge, Leonora Walker, Karl Eversley, Dionne Sparks, Jack Wilkie, Gerald Beserekumo and Daniel Manyika. Locally born Tony Phillips' 1994 painting and print show, *The City*, explored Liverpool, New York and Paris.

11 Others followed: *Let the Canvas Come to Life with Dark Faces* (1990), *True Colours: Aboriginal & Torres Strait Islander Artists Raise the Flag* (1994) and Lesley Sanderson's *These Colour Run* (1995), curated with Martin Barlow of Wrexham Library Arts Centre.

12 The exhibition, conceived as *Sinnlos* by Wolfgang Temmel for Kunstlerhaus in Graz, Austria, included Liverpool artist Alison Jones.

13 Julie Sheldon, interview with Bryan Biggs, May 2016.

14 Many Liverpool-based artists with a national profile, and some also international, have exhibited at Bluecoat. These include Adrian Henri, Maurice Cockrill (who went on to become keeper at the Royal Academy), Paul Rooney, Leo Fitzmaurice, Tom Wood, Paul Morrison and Imogen Stidworthy. Others with an international profile connected to Bluecoat while staying in the city included Anish Kapoor and Ian McKeever, both on the gallery's advisory committee, and Rosalind Nashashibi, who had a studio at Bluecoat, as does Fitzmaurice currently (2020).

15 The short-lived photo realist grouping comprised John Baum, Maurice Cockrill, Adrian Henri and Sam Walsh, and followed Edward Lucie-Smith's influential role in putting the Mersey poets – Henri, Roger McGough and Brian Patten – on the map. Liverpool Artists Workshop was set up by Pete Clarke, David Campbell and Sue Campbell in a disused garage in Hope Street. Its lively public programme included speakers Griselda Pollock and Terry Atkinson.

16 Plus regional artists' shows such as *Connections*, in collaboration with Cornerhouse, Manchester and Liverpool's Open Eye Gallery, and *New Art North West* with three Manchester venues, Cornerhouse, Castlefield and Chinese Arts Centre.

17 *A Pool of Signs*, January to April 1992, was in three parts, 1: John Dilnot, Anna Douglas and Julie Myers, Clive Gillman, Janet Hodgson and Janie Andrews, David Jacques, Simon Redman; 2: Godfrey Burke, Pete Clarke, Graham Gorman, Andrea Lansley, Dave Mabb, Paul Rooney, Dionne Sparks; 3: Clifford Bevan, Dave and Sue Campbell, Roy Holt, Alison Jones, Paul Lindale, Paul Morrison, Joanna Moss.

18 The programme in Hull comprised an exhibition by Nina Edge and Juginder Lamba at Wilberforce House, an exhibition by Edwina Fitzpatrick, Sunil Gupta, South Atlantic Souvenirs and Trouble at Ferens Art Gallery, and in Scunthorpe a performance by Verbal Images; at Arnolfini in Bristol, an exhibition by Carole Drake, Edwina Fitzpatrick, Sunil Gupta, Shaheen Merali, Keith Piper, Donald Rodney, South Atlantic Souvenirs and Trouble and Veena Stephenson, with live art from Bandele Iyapo.

19 Bryan Biggs, introduction to *Trophies of Empire*, Bluecoat and Liverpool John Moores University School of Design and Visual Art in collaboration with Arnolfini, and Hull Time Based Arts, 1994, p. 5. The publication was a reflection on the project and contained documentation of the commissions and a keynote essay, 'Sweet Oblivion', by Gilane Tawadros.

20 Text by South Atlantic Souvenirs (Steve Hardstaff and Rick Walker) and Trouble (David Crow) from the booklet that accompanied *The Trophy Cabinet*.

21 Juginder Lamba, *Trophies of Empire* publication, p. 54.

22 Quoted from Visual Stress publicity for the event.

23 *The Place is Here* (Nottingham Contemporary, 2017) and *Get Up, Stand Up Now: Generations of Black Creative Pioneers* (Somerset House, London, 2019) being two recent examples.

24 In addition to Mohini Chandra's work at Bluecoat, there were *Independent Thoughts* commissions at The Drum in Birmingham, Light House in Wolverhampton, Herbert Museum and Art Gallery in Coventry, Middlesbrough Art Gallery, the University of Bradford, Oldham Art Gallery, Leeds Metropolitan University, Nottingham Castle Museum and Art Gallery.

25 The *Independent Practices* symposium was staged at Birmingham University in 1998. *Independent Practices: Representation, Location and History in Contemporary Visual Art*, eds Bryan Biggs, Angela Dimitrikaki, Juginder Lamba, Bluecoat, cair/ Liverpool John Moores University and Saffron Books/Eastern Art Publishing, 2000.

26 Bryan Biggs, 'Radical Art City?', in John Belchem and Bryan Biggs, eds, *Liverpool: City of Radicals*, Liverpool: Liverpool University Press, 2011, p. 62.

27 Paul Clarkson, Juginder Lamba and Daniel Manyika.

28 Walid Sadek, *Karaoke*, Liverpool: cair/Liverpool John Moores University and Bluecoat Gallery, 1998, p. 13.

29 Robert Clark, 'New Art Merseyside' exhibition review, *The Guardian*, 25 April 1989.

Chapter 6

Bechsteins and Beyond: Music at the Bluecoat, 1907–2017

Roger Hill

The Silence

In 1906 they took the music out of the Bluecoat. When the Blue Coat school departed, its Henry Willis organ was removed from the chapel and transported to the new building in Wavertree. Willis organs are no small matter in the world of music. They grace such august premises as the Royal Albert Hall, St Paul's Cathedral and Liverpool's St George's Hall, and one – the largest in the world – would be installed in the newly begun Anglican Cathedral on St James's Mount in Liverpool. At Bluecoat, the silence must have been deafening. In the following year, Sandon Studios Society moved in, bringing with them the sounds of conversation, of meetings, gatherings, sociability and eventually, and inevitably given the diversity of their interests and activities, music. Fifty years later it would be possible to identify the makers of the Bluecoat's music, the people who commissioned it, and the organisers who managed the spaces and the performance programmes, but in the early years of the twentieth century the contributions of many such figures went unrecorded. At this point in our survey of the leading lights of the building's music history we can catch only a fleeting sense of the characters involved, and the sounds they produced.

Figure 62. Pop Mechanica gig at St George's Hall, part of *Perestroika in the Avant-Garde*, a season from Leningrad's underground arts scene, 1989. Photo: Mark McNulty.

Grand Pianos

There was, early on, rippling through the Queen Anne rooms and corridors, Debussy. Thanks to the historical account of Stainton de B. Taylor, which draws heavily on R. F. Bisson's colourful history of the Sandon,[1] we can see and hear, emerging out of the shadows of history, some of the key figures of the period, including Frank Bertrand Harrison Saunders who gave recitals on the Bechstein piano in the building's music room before the First World War. In the early years of the Sandon it is pianists who leave the strongest trace. The most successful of the recitalists was Stephen Wearing, whose name appears in the history of Bluecoat music over four decades as the definitive concert accompanist, although his career took him far and wide from the city of his birth. We learn from Taylor of the flamboyant Leigh Henry, a Sandon pianist whose adventures over the years involved internment, due to his pacifism, during the First World War, working as musical director at the School of Drama run by the great theatre innovator Gordon Craig in Florence, and devising a ritual for the Liverpool Positivists, performed at its Church of Humanity in Upper Parliament Street. W. S. MacCunn, the enduring chronicler of

Figure 63. The Sandon music room, 1980s.

the Bluecoat's first half-century and Bluecoat Society of Arts' long-serving secretary, was also the nephew of eminent Scottish composer Hamish MacCunn, and from his account, as well as Bisson's, we can learn about the early activities of the Sandon.[2] A Music Group was established in 1922 and musicians took their place alongside the painters, sculptors, architects and writers in making a net contribution to the culture of the renamed Liberty Buildings.

Soon after the Music Group was set up the Society found an outlet for its performing artists in the Sandon cabarets. The first was held in 1922 and from contemporary accounts and memoirs we can detect a distinctive Liverpool manifestation of 1920s chic. The 'satirically topical entertainment'[3] included musical contributions from MacCunn, Norman Peterkin and Arnold Clibborn. One musical artefact which has survived from the period is a handwritten score of 'The Sandon Roast Beef Carol' with words by A. K. Holland and music by Norman Suckling, a piece of original composition last performed in 1929. The social gaiety of the cabarets would be largely lost to us without the recollections of George Melly, whose parents, good solid Liverpool social liberals, performed in a number of yearly events in the 1930s.[4] Melly notes that the songs were specially written for the occasion, often by Alfred Francis, a local businessman in the bakery and catering business, who may be credited with the introduction of jazz to the Bluecoat. Francis's self-penned numbers were reminiscent of Noel Coward and Cole Porter and included 'Don't Play Jazz on the Bechstein Grand'. Melly was often taken to the Sandon but was too young to attend the cabarets, which often contained material of a mildly risqué nature. He has, however, left us descriptions of individual sections, which he saw when they were re-presented from 1933 to 1935 as part of public reviews at the Royal Court and Empire theatres, organised to raise money for charity. The cabarets were essentially private occasions which offered a yearly opportunity for Bluecoat artists and musicians to work together and indulge in some elaborate and semi-professional in-jokes. No doubt in the 1930s they also offered some diversion from a darker local and national mood.

Occasionally Distinguished

When the future of the venue was secured in 1927 with the establishment of Bluecoat Society of Arts it was renamed Bluecoat Chambers, and the former chapel on the first floor was turned into a concert hall. Thereafter, and until the 1960s, the public music making there was predominantly classical in repertoire, and consisted of recitals, opera productions and orchestral concerts, drawing on local and invited talent. An opera production that brought together a number of distinctive talents was of Gustav Holst's *Savitri* and *At The Boar's Head* in 1926, with the composer himself attending. The conductors were Malcolm Sargent and Dr J. E. Wallace, a musical polymath, church organist, director of many choirs and vocal groups, including the chorus of the (from 1957, Royal) Liverpool Philharmonic Orchestra (RLPO), and a formidable piano accompanist. With the addition in 1928 of a proscenium stage and backstage dressing rooms, the concert hall became the venue for a series of Sunday concerts and medium-scale opera productions throughout the 1920s and 1930s. The *Liverpool Daily Post* reported that 'It is elegantly decorated and of unconventional shape. The seating accommodation is roughly 400, and the acoustic properties are excellent.'[5] The smaller Sandon music room on the ground floor of the building was also used extensively for chamber concerts.

The Bluecoat at this time functioned as a social club for musicians. From its earliest days, the Sandon had included musicians working professionally as teachers from individual studios in the building. Many led a second existence as composers, and sometimes ventured into the fields of light music and theatre music, as well as contributing to the cabarets. Even in this early period of its development as a

Figure 64. Liverpool Mozart Orchestra rehearsing in the Sandon music room, with conductor John Carewe, 1965.

centre for music, the Bluecoat enjoyed a double reputation, as a venue for alternative programming and as the bearer of the classical tradition. With a broadly artistic membership, the Society had the additional advantage of a relatively cheap dining room in the centre of the city, which attracted a number of eminent musical visitors to the building. In the 1930s these included Béla Bartók and Igor Stravinsky, whose attendance in 1934 for a recital of his work at Rushworth Hall on Islington coincided with the public announcement of Edward Elgar's death, the Russian composer asking fellow diners to observe a minute's silence. Since Adrian Boult endorsed the fundraising appeal in 1929 a number of eminent conductors have also supported the venue, with visits and sometimes in performance. These include Zubin Mehta, who in 1958 conducted the Liverpool Mozart Orchestra, the aforementioned Sargent and Sir Thomas Beecham. The Bluecoat can also claim to have played a part in the musical education of one eminent contemporary, Simon Rattle, who attended The Music Box, a music club for young people run by Ray Mulholland in the building, and later played percussion with the Merseyside Youth Orchestra before beginning his successful career as a conductor, which saw him as assistant conductor of the RLPO for three years from 1977.

During the interwar years, the Bluecoat's music making offered an alternative to the concerts at the Philharmonic Hall, with a more informal and occasionally experimental programme of events, favouring the contemporary alongside the established classical repertoire, and local talent alongside nationally and sometimes internationally renowned artists. Concert-goers could expect to enjoy a range of composers, from Bach to Vaughan Williams, local composer Norman Suckling to Arthur Honegger. Unlike the Philharmonic, however, for much of the time the Bluecoat's programme was occasional, but one regular concert series began when the Liverpool Music Guild was set up in 1935 to provide professional chamber music concerts. Its programme took place in the concert hall and Sandon music room and the musical range was wide, with contemporary composers well represented. The programme featured the music of many rising stars of the English musical renaissance such as William Walton, Thomas Pitfield and Edmund Rubbra, and, as the decade moved on, many works by European modernists.

The guild was sufficiently eminent in the wider world to merit an early broadcast on the BBC, a Liverpool Regional Northern Concert broadcast from the Sandon music room in 1937. It featured another strong musical character who emerged in these early years, pianist Douglas Miller, accompanying Walter Hatton on cello. Born in 1888, he was a pupil of Frank Bertrand, a Leschetizky-trained artist.[6] In 1906 he began four years' study in Berlin with Leopold Godowsky, but returned to Liverpool, from where he developed a distinguished career as piano soloist, accompanist and composer. As a schoolboy in Liverpool, Rattle studied piano with Miller, and an early photograph shows the young pianist at the piano in the Sandon music room.

Out of the Ruins

In 1939, when war broke out, adventurous and innovative concerts were interrupted and, although attempts were made to revive them in wartime, the severe damage to the building during the Liverpool Blitz, including the destruction of the concert hall, put an end to concert-going until it was partially restored immediately after the war. From 1946 onwards it was possible to programme recitals in the Sandon music room on the ground floor, and the first, which must have been an emotional occasion as building repair work was still going on, featured Dorothy Reid singing Mahler with Dr Wallace accompanying. It was not until 1951 that the concert hall reopened, with three concerts to mark the occasion, the first featuring Beethoven and Schubert. The *Manchester Guardian* wrote warmly of the refurbished building: 'It contains a magnificently proportioned concert hall … [it] is as harmonious to the eye as are its

Figure 65. The newly restored concert hall, following wartime bomb damage, early 1950s.

airs to the ear.'[7] Given the Bluecoat's financial situation, it was inevitable that the hall (Fig. 65) was also available for hire.

At this mid-point of the Bluecoat's history as a centre for the arts we can identify some characteristic features of its operation. Finances had dominated this period, dictating cautious but inventive programming. It would not be until the 1960s that public subsidy would allow for a busy, generous and regular offering of concerts. While audiences for private concerts had occasionally been large, the Bluecoat cohort was mainly from the discerning few rather than the many, and 'amateur' could mean passionately music-loving or simply indulgently amateurish. So much had been *sui generis*, a series of often brilliantly improvised individual occasions sustained by a 'family' of extremely talented local artists and their friends, with an ethos which, if it did not represent the wider locality, embodied something of the city's ripe individualism. Already the Bluecoat's role in the city had been defined – it was where audiences went to experience unusual and adventurous programmes of often unfamiliar music. And through it all, like a richly coloured thread, could be heard the sound of the Bechstein.

A major turning point for music at the Bluecoat came in the late 1950s. At this juncture, as an arts venue already fifty years old, it began to direct its energies towards reflecting the full cultural diversity of the wider musical world. Although the death in 1958 of musical enthusiast and Bluecoat Society of Arts secretary W. S. MacCunn seemed to herald the end of an era, elements of the old Bluecoat lingered on and were refreshed by a re-energised Music Group and individuals such as Fritz Spiegl. Money from Liverpool Corporation and the newly established Arts Council had helped to diminish the building's debts, but funds awarded by the Calouste Gulbenkian Foundation in 1957 were to be dedicated to 'encouragement of the Arts'. So began the sequence of publicly funded performing arts events which would form the backbone of the programme of a contemporary arts centre under the auspices of Bluecoat Arts Forum, formed in 1961. The Gulbenkian money funded a series of themed festivals, each held over a fortnight, using mainly local forces in a variety of ensembles to explore 'all the arts in a chosen period of history in relation to their social background'.[8] In 1958 the theme was 'The Augustan Age', in 1959 'Victorian High Noon' and in 1960 'The Turn of The Century'. These first outcomes of the renewed programming reflected the Bluecoat's capacity for creating remarkable events and occasions rather than simply programming concerts. It was a distinctive tendency deriving from its tradition of 'amateur' music making that was very much to the fore in this period.

Fritz Spiegl took a leading role in producing the three themed festivals. He had played at the third of the reopening concerts in 1951 and, as the principal flautist with the RLPO, would use his classical connections to introduce concerts with the Liverpool Mozart Orchestra and the Liverpool Music Group into the venue's calendar. He was the musical joker in the pack, whose ad hoc creation of fantastic and off-beat musical occasions brought him the greatest attention during the 1960s and 1970s, and for several decades his events seemed to characterise the Bluecoat's cultural role in the city by combining the whimsical and classical in an almost eccentric fashion. Spiegl was of Austro-Hungarian parentage but thoroughly English in upbringing, and eventually an enthusiastically self-adopted Scouser, publishing the popular *Lern Yerself Scouse* books. He brought to the Bluecoat programme a fascination with language, a fanciful, sometimes surreal and satirical strand of humour, and a facility with composition, moving easily between popular and classical idioms – he composed the theme music to the television series *Z-Cars* – and his journalism and broadcasting.

Spiegl was involved in other themed events in the early 1960s, such as the *Sandwich Serenade* (1961), a 'Music While You Eat' lunchtime concert of wind music by Haydn and Mozart performed by members of the RLPO. According to the local press the audience 'might have been larger',[9] but the event itself was a comparative novelty for the city. He also helped produce two further festivals that continued the new tradition – *Bluecoat 63*, another annual celebration funded by the Gulbenkian grant and the city council, and the 1964 celebration of Shakespeare's 400th anniversary. In 1967, with Bridget Fry, he organised an extravaganza entitled *A Musical Chamber of Horrors* to celebrate the Sandon's 60th year in the building, and brought together bass-baritone John Shirley Quirk, Liverpool City Police Band, the Renaissance Music Group and the Cecelia Choir, supported by various keyboardists on piano, harpsichord and clavichord. Fritz is remembered as being sociable, opinionated, pedantic and the possessor of a lively mind, many of which qualities he contributed to the Bluecoat's musical life in these years. He also printed many leaflets for concerts at the venue through his Scouse Press, using a range of colourful recycled papers.

Another Classical

In these pages, John Belchem has already noted the criticism aimed at the Bluecoat by the early 1960s for continually 'harking back to the past and its lack of self-confidence for the experimental',[10] but the Sandon continued through the decade to hold chamber recitals with programmes that were, by the standards of the day, adventurous. The Sandon Ensemble, under David Connolly, brought together pieces from the core classical repertoire with baroque and early music, and compositions from contemporary British composers such as Gordon Crosse, Don Banks and Alan

Rawsthorne, often with the composers present. This culminated in the Group's relationship with Elisabeth Lutyens, a concert of whose music in 1963 was followed later that year by a world premiere of her new work, *Music For Wind*. Talks and demonstrations of 'modern music' and 'experimental music' were also programmed. Although the music was an intelligent combination of old and new, a note in the Society's minutes suggests that it considered the music making rather than the programming to be what distinguished its activities:

> the Sandon is an intimate society and ... the concerts given by its own members are the heart of the Music Group's activities. There are many concert promoting societies (we do not want to emulate them) but very few of them could produce from their own members players to match either the skill or the enthusiasm of the Sandon Music Group.[11]

What is less prominently recorded is that Sandon concerts were financially haphazard. Records show that the first Lutyens concert made a loss of £36, and when in 1964 the Society presented a Peter Maxwell Davies concert, at which the composer performed and took questions, the cash received was £10 5s 6d. In some cases this was the result of low attendance, but the Society was far from running as a business during this period.

The Sound of Vinyl

In 1965, at a moment when music at the venue was looking beyond the traditional limits of parochialism to a tentative interest in the future, the Sandon produced a vinyl recording, *The Sandon Sound* (Fig. 66).[12] A large part of this is taken up with a montage of sounds from the Sandon's daily life, including the voice of sculptor and studio occupant Herbert Tyson Smith. In the light of today's experimentalism this could be seen as the disc's most radical aspect, but three original compositions represent the diversity of the music being made at the Bluecoat during this period of transition. One composition, a rare recording made when he was 77, is by Douglas Miller, playing a work in his conventionally late classical style, one of two nocturnes that he composed in memory of his son Nicholas, who had died in 1958. *Elegy* by Eldon Walker, who continued to compose modernistic chamber pieces for at least another decade, is, by contrast, an extended exercise in musical modernism for voice, flute, horn and cello, which betrays the influence of Lutyens. The piece by Thomas Wess is a curiously angular improvisation for clavichord which confirms that he, too, was a Lutyens enthusiast. Wess also made clavichords, and was an active and regularly broadcast advocate of period keyboard instruments, including the

Figure 66. *Sandon Sound* LP, 1965. The cartoon is by Sandon member Edgar Grosvenor and features artist Roderick Bisson as a chimpanzee.

Figure 67. Liverpool Lieder Circle LP, 1970.

harpsichord. He was versatile, contributing more conventional keyboards to a 1965 celebration of John McCabe's music and a 1966 concert of Alan Rawsthorne's music. A snapshot of the Society in the mid-1960s, *The Sandon Sound* recording is a very clear indication that original composition was alive and well in the building, even as it represents the transition from amateur to professional, and from traditional to experimental as the Bluecoat moved into its second half-century.

'Lieding' the Way

If any personality imprinted itself on the musical life of the Bluecoat at this point it was surely Celia Van Mullem. She had been appointed joint secretary of Bluecoat Society of Arts in 1960, and brought to the role a strong predilection for music, especially classical. With her encouragement, the Bluecoat became Liverpool's home of German song. Eminent lieder singers were invited to perform and in 1968 the Liverpool Lieder Circle was established. Its recitals, often with Stephen Wearing as accompanist, were programmed in the venue alongside other classical song and choral music. Van Mullem was herself a singer – her first reviewed appearance at the Bluecoat was in 1958 – and she continued to participate in vocal concerts throughout the 1960s and 1970s. Apart from her singing, she showed her versatility in modern concert pieces such as Walton's *Façade* and in Bill Harpe's production of Stravinsky's *The Soldier's Tale* in 1964.

Throughout, Van Mullem was a ubiquitous presence both in the Bluecoat and on the city's wider music scene. A news photograph of the period shows her at the building's gates, trim and capable, her skirt demurely below the knee. Her work required her to attend to both the financial and musical aspects of Bluecoat Society of Arts. In 1976 she was interviewed for BBC North West about the arts centre's 'uncertain future' at a time when she was also using her influence to bring the eminent tenor Peter Pears to give a recital there. Apart from administrative duties, fronting the many appeals for funds during the period, she gathered around her a number of musical associates, often to be found at her house for dinner. The *Daily Post* described the occasions: 'the smaller, informal kind for a few friends, usually musicians as well. When Stephen Wearing, the pianist, is one of the guests, the party is likely to be congregated round the piano singing Lieder into the early hours of the morning.'[13]

Van Mullem also appeared in *Off Beat*, a BBC2 television programme in 1965, in the unlikely company of, among others, the poet Ivor Cutler. It was a programme whose musical content betrayed Spiegl's anarchic imprint and therefore represented that curious musical amalgam of high and popular art that had always been a speciality of the Bluecoat. The 'high' was still represented by lieder. *Daily Post* music critic Neil Barkla, a supporter of the Circle, was moved to ask in 1970:

> Can lieder be segregated from other forms of song and continue to attract a specialized audience of devotees? Has not the use of the terms 'Inner' and 'Outer' circle merely exaggerated the old and fatal fallacy that lieder is something mysterious and esoteric, available only to a rare company of initiates?[14]

Liverpool Echo arts critic Joe Riley recalled an encounter at Radio City between American composer Aaron Copland, in the city for a concert of his music at the Philharmonic, and lieder singer Peter Pears, who was due to perform at the Bluecoat that night, when Benjamin Britten, who had performed solo in his own Pianoforte Concerto at the venue in 1939, was also present. The Circle's later Bluecoat recitals, notwithstanding visits by eminent singers such as Pears and Isobel Baillie, were, by report, less charismatic affairs, and lieder's time in the venue's curiously contradictory mix seemed to reach a natural end. It is strange to think that by the time the Lieder Circle wound up its affairs in 1981 the wider music scene had experienced several rites of passage, including psychedelia, heavy rock, punk and post-punk. Having exerted a powerful influence on the musical profile of the organisation, Van Mullem's time at the Bluecoat came to an end in 1979. She had retired as Bluecoat Society of Arts administrator the year before but had stayed on as musical director for a year, and as late as 1987 was performing with the Liverpool Mozart Orchestra.

One musical legacy of Van Mullem's time at the Bluecoat resulted from her encouragement of early music which, thanks to figures such as Franz Bruggen and David Munrow, who both performed there in the early 1970s, was beginning to offer a new perspective on the classical repertoire. For some time after her departure, in part due to the support of the Early Music Network, the venue was able to programme such ensembles as the Consort of Musicke, the Hilliard Ensemble and Musica Antiqua. This strand eventually ceased when early music was subsumed, with its period instruments and authentic tunings, into the wider repertoire, a development championed by, among others, Simon Rattle.

The Hub of the New

By the mid-1960s, with Van Mullem's time increasingly dedicated to wider funding campaigns, the Bluecoat's need to derive more income from its spaces saw the Society devolving the work of commercial programming to a new specialist artistic administrator, reporting to Bluecoat Arts Forum. With the arrival of Wendy Harpe in this role came the first full cultural shock of direct engagement with the contemporary and popular arts. Democracy, popularisation and experimentation were now on the cultural agenda. Like a significant number of other leading lights, Harpe was not a native Liverpudlian. Her partner Bill Harpe had come to the city to organise, as artistic director, the opening events for the new Metropolitan Cathedral in 1967, and Wendy took on the role of programming events at the Bluecoat. She had previously organised poetry readings at the venue and assisted Bill as administrator when he ran the 1965 Commonwealth Arts Festival in Cardiff, and her first job was to raise the money for her salary, successfully persuading the city council to make a grant to the Bluecoat, which also made possible a wide-ranging programme of arts activity. By June 1966 the *Liverpool Echo* could report an 'ambitious programme' of poetry, modern dance, experimental film, youth drama, serenade concerts, poetry readings, jazz and visual art.[15]

Harpe was supported by the Arts Forum committee, and music was championed particularly by Peter Moores and Peter Rockliff, with local patrons such as James Rushworth, whose family music business had supported the venue for many decades,[16] supplementing the Forum's resources with in-kind help, for example, piano tuning and printing. Harpe, however, made all the programming choices, the music comprising a heady mix of poetry, jazz and contemporary folk. One of her signature events was a far-from-conventional *son et lumière* event produced in 1967 by multimedia artist Mark Boyle, and the same year the Bluecoat echoed to the sounds of glass instruments played by Anna Lockwood, who would later perform a significant role in New York's electronic music scene.[17]

The 'Swinging Sixties' witnessed Liverpool becoming a focus for the new flowering of pop culture, an apparent respite from the port's declining economic fortunes. The 'Liverpool Poets' – Adrian Henri, Roger McGough and Brian Patten – were becoming more representative of the city's culture than its orchestras and theatres, and Liverpool groups were dominating the pop charts. Now, the new found its way into the Bluecoat. Pete Brown, London beat poet and lyricist for blues rock band Cream, could be heard in concert with bassist Danny Thompson and guitarist John McLaughlin, who would become prominent on the UK and international folk and jazz scenes respectively; and, as a further example of the integration of poetry and music that had started with Michael Horovitz's New Departures UK tours earlier in the decade, rock/poetry outfit Liverpool Scene, fronted by Henri, also performed. Not all of this cultural expansion was to the Arts Forum committee's taste, but the programme thrived and paid its way, thanks to ongoing, if modest, city council support. Traditionalists such as Van Mullem were quietly outraged, especially when she discovered that copies of *International Times*, the leading voice of Britain's counterculture and underground music scene, were on sale at the venue.

At this time the Bluecoat was a hub for music, its tenants including many musical organisations, most of them amateur, with some expectations of being able to use the building's spaces for performance. The Bluecoat's long association with jazz was also consolidated during this period. The Merseysippi Jazz Band, at the forefront of Liverpool's home-grown trad jazz scene since 1949, had performed at the venue for the BBC's Jazz Club in 1952,[18] and when, in 1956, Louis Armstrong played the Liverpool Stadium, jazz had begun to find a reasonably secure place in the local music spectrum. By the 1960s a wide range of jazz was being reflected in the city, and from that decade on the Bluecoat hosted many concerts from the national touring jazz circuit, with concerts by, among others, Tubby Hayes, Stan Tracey, Mike Westbrook, Graham Collier, John Surman and Ronnie Scott, and eventually many eminent British jazz experimentalists. Harpe's 1969 Arts Forum report, however, noted that the number of jazz enthusiasts on Merseyside was 'too small and too poor to make jazz a viable proposition unless heavily subsidized'.[19] Although subsidy did materialise, over the following decades it was rarely sufficient – and audiences too unpredictable – to be able to maintain a consistent programme, despite some seasons of impeccable programming and visits by international names.

In 1972 Don Van Vliet, otherwise known as Captain Beefheart and a jazzman in spirit if not in style, played at the Liverpool Stadium, his visit coinciding with an exhibition of his paintings – though sadly not a gig – at the Bluecoat. At this time, the progressive spirit of the 1960s, now emancipated from the demands of chart pop, took up brief residence in the building, not least with a Zoom Cortex concert in 1972 featuring local music collective Death Kit. The band had been current on the Liverpool scene for a while, but in the early 1970s made a brief but intensely provocative series of live incursions in various local venues, including the Bluecoat. From a recording of a live BBC Radio Merseyside performance we can recognise their free-form, jazz-influenced rock and poetry as very much of their time and their city, and in tune with the venue's emerging musical ethos.

Jazz would re-emerge in the 1980s, encouraged by regional promoters Jazz North West's arrival in the building and the enthusiasm of successive Bluecoat live programming staff such as Dinesh Allirajah. That decade, and into the 1990s, featured some of the most compelling names in UK jazz, including Chris McGregor, Keith Tippett and Julie Tippetts, Lol Coxhill, Andy Shephard and Cleveland Watkiss, and international stars such as Anthony Braxton, Paul Bley, Steve Lacey and John Zorn. Another US visitor was David Murray, for a Contemporary Music Network (CMN) commission in 1996, a collaboration with the then relatively unknown Mancunian poet Lemn Sissay, which was rehearsed and premiered at the venue before touring nationally. This was followed in 1997 by another CMN collaboration, Butch Morris, the originator of an improvisatory conducting method known as 'conduction', who worked with leading UK free jazz improvisers to premiere their work at the Bluecoat. In this period, when the number of Merseyside jazz venues was declining, the Bluecoat became a major focus for those who liked their jazz on the adventurous side. Audiences were always select and often quite limited, but the flame was kept alight for challenging music in, arguably, the venue with the longest tradition of sonic experimentation. At the more popular end of the jazz spectrum, by the 1980s that junior patron of the Bluecoat, George Melly, had grown up to become a popular jazzman, writer and entertainer, and he revisited the venue to play with his band John Chilton's Feetwarmers. Becoming official patron of the Bluecoat Friends in 1985, he declared that his life had been enriched by his attendances at the Sandon. A surrealist art collector and expert, he also returned in 1981 and 1984 to give two illustrated talks, illuminating the mysteries of René Magritte and Max Ernst.

Just as jazz, rock and poetry constituted a key part of the UK's 1960s and 1970s counterculture, so too did folk music, which also found a home at the Bluecoat, albeit of a more traditional variety than the psychedelic folk template laid down by the likes of the Incredible String Band. The venue had hosted a Liverpool Folk Festival in October 1964, co-organised by the English Folk Dance and Song Society (which had an office in the building) and featuring an array of local artists such as Andy Kenner, the Black Diamonds Folk Group and the Liverpool Ceilidh Band, the event documented on an LP the following year. Liverpool folk stalwarts Jacqui and Bridie have performed at the venue and The Spinners played for a Bluecoat fundraiser in the mid-1970s. Up to the early 2000s the Bluecoat would provide a concert-sized venue for many leading folk artists, including Dick Gaughan, Bert Jansch, June Tabor, Martin Simpson, The Boys of the Lough and Niamh Parsons.

Behind the doors of individual studios, music making continued, most of it by pianists, among them the composer and musical director of Liverpool Playhouse, Ronald Settle, who made a remarkable discovery in his studio. He had been a pupil of a Russian pianist, and when clearing out his cupboard he found an original manuscript by Tchaikovsky, which must have passed through a number of hands before it reached the Bluecoat.[20] Outwardly the Bluecoat had become the very model of a contemporary arts centre, producing its own exhibitions and receiving a substantial amount of subsidised performance including music across different genres. It was a business model, and just about worked, but could it adapt to changing times? Could it lead the taste of the city, rather than just reflecting it?

'A Global Village Hall'

Many of the Bluecoat staff's leading lights have had a significant impact on its evolution as a creative space for music, none more so than the short but intensive period of Jayne Casey's tenure as director of performing arts. This may turn out to be the zenith of musical programming at the venue, not just because she brought remarkable capabilities to the job, but because the historical moment was ripe for diversity. The venue's programme was sufficiently funded and the cultural zeitgeist was aligned so as to allow integration of art forms, which was becoming the arts centre's most dependable and distinctive calling card. From 1987 to 1990 Casey was able to sustain a performance programme that included, in some cases for the first time, the post-punk sounds of Liverpool's expanding rock scene, jazz, alternative cabaret, experimental theatre, 'world music', folk and the emergent sounds of urban black music, while creating alongside this a number of large signature events of regional and national significance.

By the mid-1980s Casey had built up a formidable reputation locally as singer with seminal band Big in Japan, which also included Holly Johnson, Bill Drummond and Ian Broudie, and later with Pink Military Stand Alone and Pink Industry. She was a close associate of Roger Eagle, whose management of Eric's club had ended in 1980, and it was, she relates, as Big in Japan walked through the city centre one night after a gig at the legendary Mathew Street venue, that they paused by the Bluecoat gates and she vowed that 'One day that building will be mine.'[21] It was the domestic elegance of the building that created both a vision of it as a place of residence for wandering genius, and a sense of alienation from the culture that it seemed to represent. When Casey did later take up a position there she was well primed to take risks and create adventurous events. She told journalist Craig Ferguson, 'An arts centre should be working with a creative nucleus of a city and should be accessible to everyone at the same time – presenting things that are enjoyable to the normal person in the street.'[22] In the summer of 1988 she announced the Bluecoat as 'The Place To Be'.[23]

Although the performing arts budget was far from negligible, the key to generating larger funds for ambitious projects was to open the Bluecoat up to contemporary rock and pop. Drawing upon her own connections, Casey put on concerts by local heroes Ian McCullough, Shack, The Walking Seeds, Thomas Lang and also by post-pop icon Martin Stephenson. The median age of music fans attending Bluecoat events dropped considerably and its demographic widened to include the Liverpool black community, attracted by top urban pop acts such as Soul II Soul, The Cookie Crew and Salt'N'Pepa. Consequently, income generated from these sellout gigs, and a season ticket scheme, was able to supplement the budget for more experimental programming.

The music that began to bridge the gap between classical and rock music was 'minimalism', and the Bluecoat had already dipped its toe into these new waters, but not without some resistance from audiences. Fewer than twenty turned up for the Philip Glass Ensemble's performance of *Music in Twelve Parts* in 1975, while a performance of Terry Riley's work by the Kronos Quartet in 1988 was, for local critic Rex Bawden, 'unutterably tedious'.[24] The Michael Nyman Band performed at the venue in 1982 and renowned minimalist Steve Reich paid a visit in February 1986 to hear his *Four Organs* performed as part of a 'Steve Reich Day' organised under the Royal Liverpool Philharmonic Orchestra banner through the CMN by local composer and Bluecoat board member James Wishart. The performance, as Andrew Burn recalls, 'nearly fell to pieces when one of the players lost his place'.[25] The impetus for this work had come from Casey's predecessor as music and dance director, James Beirne, himself a composer, who brought to the venue a mix of highly regarded Indian music, early music through the EMN, and jazz and contemporary music through the CMN (often in collaboration with Jazz North West), including John Surman, Loose Tubes, Derek Bailey with Han Bennink, and other international stars such as Carla Bley, Jan Garbarek on his first UK tour, Anthony Davis's Episteme and Peter Brotzmann.

Casey planned for a number of larger, more complex events, each of which has come to represent a special vision – of the Bluecoat as a 'global village hall'. The concert by veteran American jazz experimentalist Sun Ra and his Cosmic Love

Figure 68. Sun Ra performing with his Arkestra at Bluecoat, 1990.

Arkestra in the concert hall in 1990 (Fig. 68) is well remembered. His appearance was as much the result of opportunism as determined policy. A UK booking for the band left the promoters, Blast First, for whom Sun Ra was in the UK recording an album, with a heavy accommodation bill and Casey was offered a week-long residency for the cost of the band's upkeep. She seized the opportunity to bring a musical legend to Liverpool, programming both a concert and contacts for the band with the local black music community.

The concert hall during this period, and until the building's closure in 2005, was barely fit for purpose – one commentator on the night of the concert recalled 'floorboard creaks, wheezy electrics and rattling windows better suited to a church jumble sale than a concert by eighteen intergalactic jazz troubadours'[26] – but every effort had been made with the setting, and this fusion of the timelessly old and ever-presently new was what the Bluecoat had always been about. When Sun Ra made his slow appearance from backstage and sat down at the Bechstein piano the packed audience was in no doubt that this would be a rare experience. From hushed piano solos to driving full-band funk, the show did not disappoint.[27]

Even more ambitious and internationalist was *Pop Mechanica – Perestroika in the Avant-Garde* (Fig. 62). In 1989 there was a moment to be seized. Russian President Mikhail Gorbachev's policy of perestroika had led to the collapse of the Soviet Union and cultural contact between the Soviet East and the West had opened up. American President Ronald Reagan was reported to have challenged the Russian authorities by making it a test of the opening up of cultural borders that a Russian band would play in Liverpool.[28] This actually happened that year through the collaborative efforts of the Bluecoat, the city council and the local ARK records, and the band was Pop Mechanica, a disparate group of Leningrad musicians led by piano virtuoso Sergei Kuryokhin. The programme involved a solo recital at the Bluecoat by Kuryokhin, preceded by an immense concert in St George's Hall featuring the band, a host of local musicians, live artists and fashion displays. Among the 150-strong personnel that night was an Irish marching band, a Greek bouzouki player, African drummers, the brass section of the Liverpool Philharmonic, an opera singer, a pony and a goat. The massed guitarists included members of local bands Echo & The Bunnymen, It's Immaterial, The Christians, Pink Industry and The Lawnmower, directed by Kuryokhin, who at one point also played the hall's Willis organ. The line-up recalled the curious assemblage of musical characters who, more than twenty years before, had presented *The Musical Chamber of Horrors*, a representation of an earlier version of the Bluecoat 'family'. The critics were impressed: 'two hours of musical madness and mayhem … whether it was a musical event may be debatable. But an event of some kind, it certainly was.'[29] The *Guardian* reported a 'divine madness', 'a great musical circus anchored to a large element of rock', 'a reclamation of the Dionysian tradition of Ancient Greece'.[30] Above all, it was an event that arguably could only have originated in the Bluecoat of this particular Liverpool era, a grand postmodern bricolage of everything that could be performed in the name of the city.

It was a time when the whole world seemed to be opening up to itself. Just as Wendy Harpe had opened up the Bluecoat to the cultural cross-currents of the 1960s, Casey's vision of a 'global village hall' had initiated a new period in the venue's history, when music from around the world could be encountered in central Liverpool. The Bluecoat had previously provided a space for what was termed 'world music': in 1974, for example, it had programmed *A Young People's Guide to Percussion*, in which African tribal drumming took a prominent place. Later it had showcased performances by local African dance and drum company Delado, set up in the wake of the 1981 'Toxteth riots'; but, suddenly, it seemed that world music was a major element in the programme. During Casey's time, many African artists played at the venue, including guitarists Ali Farka Touré from Mali and S. E. Rogie from Sierra Leone, South African saxophonist Dudu Pukwana, Congolese singer Papa Wemba and the Zimbabwean John Chibadura with his band The Tembo Brothers.

In 1990 Casey left the Bluecoat to run the emergent Merseyside Festival of Comedy, leaving behind a world music legacy that endured in the building over the next two decades. Indian music had found a home there, and in 1993 tabla virtuoso Talvin Singh gave a concert, while Nitin Sawhney performed in the garden, both concerts organised as part of the Bluecoat's ongoing relationship with Indian arts festival MILAP (now known as Milapfest). There was no sense that world music was ghettoised in the programme – Singh, for instance, was already notable for cross-over collaborations with pop and rock musicians. Bluecoat's achievement during the 1990s was to become Merseyside's centre for contemporary global music, providing a platform for eminent international artists in a city that had been, for more than 150 years, the UK's gateway to the world through commerce and cultural exchange. Other home-grown artists reflecting an increasingly confident British multiculturalism staged memorable nights at the Bluecoat, with the likes of dub poet Benjamin Zephania's band and, also from Birmingham, jazz veteran Andy Hamilton, and the ska-infused Jazz Jamaica featuring legendary trombonist Rico.

The venue also encouraged various world music-inflected local initiatives such as the multicultural choir Sense of Sound. The Africa Oyé festival, the largest celebration of African music in the UK, began in Liverpool in the 1990s with a number of concerts, several of them at the Bluecoat, including free courtyard events. After an Arabic musical celebration in 1998, at which the music of oud player Adel

Salameh was featured, the arts centre initiated the country's first Arabic Arts Festival in 2002 in collaboration with Liverpool Yemeni Arabic Club. This resurgence of public awareness of post-colonial and diaspora culture in the city culminated, more than a quarter-century after the disturbances in Toxteth, in the opening of the International Slavery Museum as part of National Museums Liverpool in 2007. A proper historical context for the various musics being created and programmed locally was finally put in place.

Casey returned briefly in 1996 to produce a front courtyard spectacle for Bluecoat's Euro 96 programme, made in response to the European football championships taking place in the city. The event, not surprisingly, featured dance, music, baton twirlers, a fashion display and a male stripper. Casey had been succeeded as performing arts director by Chris Layhe, bassist in Liverpool band The Icicle Works, who continued to programme adventurously, booking folk and jazz from the touring circuit, and securing such pop eminences as Tori Amos and Labi Siffre for the venue, as well as showcasing a range of other musical genres, including cajun. With Casey's departure, however, a historical moment passed and with it some of the momentum of music at the Bluecoat. It had been a moment to tap into a number of undercurrents in the city's culture, the ideas of the avant-garde, of the city as self-styled 'centre of the creative universe', Liverpool's long-submerged history of black music, its ability to integrate and adapt world forms to local social patterns. It had also been a period when popular music had moved beyond punk and new wave to embrace hip-hop and club-based dance music, and there was a discernible sense in Liverpool that, culturally, and maybe economically, the city's time was coming again.

With a general upsurge in the number of rock music venues in Liverpool, the Bluecoat's role as a home for rock and post-rock declined quickly. Perhaps it had never needed that role, nor was particularly suited to it as a building. Its spaces were not geared technically to rock gigs. During the period between Death Kit in 1972 and the closure for rebuilding in 2005, Liverpool music had moved away from its art school origins – notwithstanding the pre-punk flourishing of Deaf School who formed in the art department of Liverpool Polytechnic – and, through a number of peaks and troughs, had established itself as the home of relatively derivative pop and rock, more celebrated at home than in the wider world. In the music business, individual originality, always the city's distinctive feature, was being submerged in increasingly industrial production processes. An experimental and adventurous musical fringe continued to exist locally, and while that scene was finding a more secure place in Liverpool's cultural 'offer', the Bluecoat had other things to attend to.

The Music of Sound

By the 1990s a new kind of musician had emerged, the 'sound artist'.
Experimentation in sound production dated back to the 1960s, and by the end of that
decade Bluecoat Arts Forum was commissioning electronic music concerts. Several
of them were promoted by the Liverpool Philharmonic as part of its *Musica Viva*
series, and Bill Harpe of the Blackie played a key role in directing the programme,
as did Rod Murray, sculptor and lecturer at the College of Art. Often presented at
other venues such as Liverpool University's Mountford Hall, one concert took place
at the Bluecoat in 1969, featuring Italian ensemble MEV. Its sonic ambitions were
certainly something new to that space: 'The group, which consists of 9 performers/
composers, work with tapes and complex electronics in combination with traditional
instruments and features of the environment in which the performers are situated.
Sounds may originate both inside and outside the performing-listening space and
may move freely within and around it.'[31]

Electro-acoustic composers such as Denis Smalley and Trevor Wishart continued
thereafter to perform at the Bluecoat. In the 1990s, however, the new genre of
sound art arrived in central Liverpool. The advent of club DJing and new computer
technologies in studio production had encouraged musicians to work solo and with
only a sound mixer (or, later, a laptop) to mediate their creations to an audience. The
Bluecoat came relatively late to this development, and it was perhaps characteristic
of its slightly oblique approach to modernity that the sound artist who most
regularly came to inhabit the venue's spaces was Philip Jeck, an exponent of hi-lo-
tech, the re-creative use of vinyl. He moved to Liverpool in 1995 with his partner,
the dance artist Mary Prestidge, who was taking up a teaching post at the Liverpool
Institute for Performing Arts (LIPA), but his first appearance at the Bluecoat had
been in 1985, performing with dancer Laurie Booth, 'lying on the floor with some
record-players while Laurie pirouetted around me'.[32] In 1993 Jeck had produced the
epic *Vinyl Requiem* in London with visual artist Lol Sargent, a one-off performance
using 180 record players, nine slide projectors and two movie projectors. The musical
modus operandi was layered sound, and the effect was of great sonic waves of music.
There was nothing overtly avant-garde about Jeck's music, but the record players and
the vinyl played on them have become his signature technology, gracing most of his
sound-work at the Bluecoat.

On his arrival in the city Jeck submitted a proposal for *Live from the Vinyl
Junkyard*, a set of Bluecoat commissions predicating the music of the future by
deconstructing the music of the past. If his Bluecoat installation was more modest
in scale than *Vinyl Requiem* it was no less expressionistic. *Off the Record* was

Figure 69. Philip Jeck, *Off the Record*, installation in the gallery for the *Live from the Vinyl Junkyard* commissions, 1996.

installed in the main gallery (Fig. 69) and used 80 record players, programmed with lo-tech bravura via timers and dislocated grooves, to generate from the vinyl a continuous soundscape evoking all popular music and none in particular. *Live from the Vinyl Junkyard* was a cumulative demonstration of what the Bluecoat could do with music in a gallery context on the brink of the new century. Its conjunction of past and future sound in the artistic present was in the great tradition of all those earlier Sandon-themed concerts and the unity-in-diversity of *Perestroika in the Avant-Garde.*

At the heart of Jeck's sound-manipulation is improvisation, which has a long tradition at the venue, from jazz artists such as Derek Bailey to improviser Eugene Chadbourne, who played there in 1999. In the 1990s local improvisers' collective Frakture began a sustained relationship with the Bluecoat and started their Frakture Fest series in 2002. These performers had taken inspiration from a decades-long strand of jazz, which itself embodied in-the-moment performance impulses. Jeck's background in improvisation was less classic – art and pop, rather than jazz, had formed his technique – drawing inspiration from British avant-garde pioneer Cornelius Cardew, Christian Marclay's sound experiments, the New York hip-hop of Grandmaster Flash and studio mixer Walter Gibbons.

As the 2000s arrived Jeck could often be encountered in the Bluecoat behind a set of turntables and sound-mixer, producing music in collaboration with dancers (Prestidge's piece, *Maryland*), other musicians (Derek Bailey and Otomo Yoshihide) and poets (Rebecca Sharp). He also featured in performance with Janek Schaefer during the latter's exhibition of sound works at the Bluecoat in 2009–10. For all that, and perhaps due to his relationship with the world of art, Jeck's work exists adjacent to, rather than within, the mainstream electronic music scene. He is an eminent instance of a world-respected musical artist who has developed a long and productive relationship with the Bluecoat as his home venue. 'It's a bit like family', he says. 'I don't think of it as a musical relationship – it is all one.'

Word Up

Poetry was another art form that integrated with music over this period. In the punk and post-punk era it had found its place alongside bands and sound systems. A new kind of performer began to appear in arts centre programmes. Linton Kwesi Johnson performed at the Bluecoat in 1997, and, well before that, Liverpool had generated its own echelon of black spoken word artists such as Levi Tafari and Eugene Lange. No one better embodied both the production and performance of poetry at the venue than Dinesh Allirajah, who was seconded from Liverpool City Council to

Figure 70. Dinesh Allirajah, poet, writer and programmer of 'provocative performance' at Bluecoat.

programme literature in 1996, returning as events programmer from 2002 to 2004. Allirajah was a feted and respected poet, teacher and prime mover in establishing a place for literature and arts education in both the local and national cultural offer. He was, moreover, a powerful performer, and recordings of his sessions with local improvisers demonstrate his remarkable sense of the integration between spoken word and music. He captured the atmosphere of the Sun Ra concert in one of his stories.[33] With his encouragement, the Bluecoat became a home for various strands of provocative performance.

The Music of Art

The visual arts had always been predominant in the Bluecoat's programming, but the creative interaction between the performing arts, especially music, and gallery exhibitions had become a consistent element in the building's cultural character. In 1964 the gallery had hosted a one-man posthumous exhibition of paintings by Stuart Sutcliffe, the 'fifth Beatle'; in 1990 paintings by John Hyatt, vocalist of the post-punk Three Johns; and in 1993 jazz drawings by Mal Dean.[34] Other music-inflected visual art projects included a celebration in 1997 of the 30th anniversary of the cover art for the Beatles' *Sgt. Pepper* album and a display of Merseyside rock family trees by Pete Frame. By the 1990s much visual art was drawing upon popular culture for its content, and music was claiming its place in the spaces formerly and exclusively occupied by visual art. This relationship was brokered at the Bluecoat in a number of gallery projects in this period, one of which brought into the venue's extended family another city incomer, Alan Dunn, who contributed, and has continued to contribute, to Bluecoat visual arts projects while pursuing a parallel career as a sound artist.

Dunn's growing involvement represented a new strand of musical expression in the building. Like Harpe and Jeck before him, Dunn arrived in Liverpool with a partner, visual artist Brigitte Jurack, who had come to work in the city. What Dunn most admired when he first encountered the Bluecoat in 1994 was its 'work ethic', something that is certainly true of his multifarious contributions to the city's art scene. As a freelance artist, he was encouraged to find work in a variety of community settings during a period when 'socially engaged practice' was beginning to set the agenda for art projects. He quickly had discussions with the Bluecoat's artistic director, which led to his being appointed the venue's official Euro 96 football artist-in-residence (see Fig. 41), painting advertising hoardings in the courtyard and presenting *The Vinyl Whistle*, an exhibition of football-themed record sleeves. Dunn's work – embracing large-scale public displays in the form of billboards and video works, compilations of found sound, and the production of live art events – found a home in the heterogeneous cultural mix of the pre-millennial Bluecoat. In 1997 he returned to work on the *Live from the Vinyl Junkyard* project, for which he curated a picture disc, *Take the Mic Away*, and in 1998 to exhibit in *Glitter*, a Christmas exhibition on a pop theme.

By the early 2000s Dunn was working at FACT (Foundation for Art and Creative Technology), but he returned to the Bluecoat for various commissions including – in 2006 in the run-up to Liverpool's year as Capital of Culture – curating *Good Diversions* as part of the *City in Transition* project. In these live art commissions, performance group Foreign Investment drove several buskers around the city centre in a horse-drawn carriage. For Dunn, the Bluecoat 'gave me confidence to pursue an exploration of the spaces between curating, community art, sound art, visual art, music, billboards, lecturing, etc. Almost everybody I met in Liverpool stemmed from the Bluecoat, the spirit of generosity and links to post-punk practitioners, academics, historians and community artists.'[35]

In the 1980s, as the last quarter of the Bluecoat's arts century opened, it was clear that musical developments were accelerating and that the venue needed to be even more responsive to changes than it had ever been. A more diverse range of outsiders had been welcomed into the Bluecoat 'family', and it was more likely than in its early years, when a coterie spirit had prevailed, to be abreast of, or occasionally ahead of, the new and contemporary. Meanwhile the Bechstein had been sold and vinyl and turntables had arrived. Music had infiltrated the galleries, and spilled into the exterior spaces. And yet the playful, sometimes whimsical, often defiantly eccentric individualism had survived all of the changes and continued to intrigue and attract a widening audience. The old and the new now not merely coexisted in the Bluecoat, they positively cohabited, and in so doing promised a future for the city.

Setting the Tone

The role of developing music in the Bluecoat had always involved curation, partnerships, fundraising and management and, as we have seen, not everybody who carried out this work was a practising musician. They were inevitably, however, all music lovers. The person who has set the tone for nearly forty years of Bluecoat music joined the staff as an administrative assistant and has continued to be a practising visual artist, but, as the self-confessed punk fan who regularly attended Eric's club, Bryan Biggs has had a presiding influence on Bluecoat music, which helped to make other recent developments possible. Following a long period running the gallery, then as overall director of the arts centre, he took on the role of artistic director in 2006, when the organisation appointed its first chief executive. He steered the Bluecoat into its 300th year and its century plus as a centre for the arts in Liverpool. In many subtle ways, he has cleared the path for distinctive projects and musical alliances.

Like so many others in the Bluecoat 'family', Biggs arrived in the city from elsewhere, to study at the Art School, and when he graduated in 1975 his tutor recommended he apply for a job at the Bluecoat. The rest is, for this key period of the organisation's development, history. He has set the tone for events, seeing the building as the 'home of unusual music', while admitting that his influence on music has often been indirect, advising other staff. He has encouraged music's cross-over with other art forms, not least by ensuring that several gallery exhibitions were accompanied by live music events. Cultural diversity in the programme has always been a priority for him, so he has welcomed a number of festivals, including several with a strong music focus, such as Indian arts festival MILAP and Liverpool Arab Arts Festival, to use the various spaces for their own programming. Without his continuing personal appreciation of musical quality in the building, a delight in the sheer variety of sounds produced and presented, it is unlikely that the music programming of this period would have succeeded as it has.

Among Biggs's other achievements in ensuring that music continued to permeate the programme are those occasions when he has led interview and Q&A sessions with music journalists and chroniclers about their latest publications. In 2003 Paul Du Noyer introduced his *Wondrous Place* book on Liverpool music, while Barney

Hoskyns has discoursed on Tom Waits and Rob Chapman on Syd Barrett. Biggs has also explored – through curating exhibitions and live art commissions, writing for a range of publications, and lectures – the interaction between popular music and contemporary art. Thanks to his encouragement of the regular record fairs, the Bluecoat has become the home of unusual records. Even more significantly perhaps, he helped open the door to bring the city's legendary record shop Probe Records to occupy premises at the front of the building. All this has served to reinforce the significance of music as more than just a live experience at the Bluecoat.

Meanwhile the venue has had the benefit of Biggs's DJing, an always provocative array of sounds from his unfeasibly diverse vinyl collection. As someone who has an unbroken four-decade overview of events in the building, he can, of course, cite a number of personal musical highlights. Top of the list is *Acid Brass*, one of the most ambitious of the *Mixing It* commissions, when Jeremy Deller worked with the Williams Fairey Brass Band to create a concert in which the band played a selection of classic acid house anthems, a concert which, like *Perestroika*, took place off-site, at LIPA. Biggs also cherishes memories of Sun Ra, Philip Jeck's record player installation, Nitin Sawhney's concert in the garden, and *Whirled Music*, when Max Eastley, Steve Beresford, David Toop and Paul Burwell whirled instruments and objects tied to lengths of elastic and string to startling – and dangerous – effect, the audience sitting behind a safety net and the performers wearing protective wicker masks.

Since the Bluecoat's refurbishment and redevelopment in 2005–08, music has continued to feature as part of its programme, though in recent years less consistently. The new performance space has seen performances in as wide a range of musical genres as ever – jazz from a returning Mike Westbrook, beatboxing from Beardyman, acerbic rock from local band Clinic, and electronic sound art from Liverpool collective Deep Hedonia – but the whole building has at times been animated by music. Terry Riley's minimalist classic *In C* was performed throughout the galleries and performance spaces by a large a.P.A.t.T. ensemble led by composer Jon Hering, and the venue has been home to local grassroots music festival *Above the Beaten Track*, programmed by the enterprising Mellowtone. Initially, in 2008, dedicated music programming was the responsibility of a specialist programmer, Richard Kingdom, but, as the building reached its 300th year and its 110th year as a centre for the arts, live music programming has for the first time in fifty years been without a dedicated curatorial voice, the result of severe cuts in funding, its presence reliant largely on working in partnership and generating project funds, as for the successful Pierre Henry *Liverpool Mass* event staged at the Metropolitan Cathedral in 2017.

Music at the Bluecoat has been many things to many people in the last hundred years: cultural, experimental, a bridge between old and new, classical and fanciful and between art forms, playful individualism intersecting with social engagement, gatherings both private and public, haphazard and focused, timeless but contemporary, harmonious and discordant, eccentric and sometimes wilfully esoteric, inclusive and exclusive, retrospective and futuristic. It is again in transition, poised to spring anew as it always seems to have done, and it seems almost impertinent to anticipate its next manifestation.

The Silence

Despite the huge diversity of music that Bluecoat members and staff have produced and programmed over more than ten decades, it is tempting to speculate that the building itself has played a part in the creation of that sound landscape. Its character has certainly impinged on musical events. As Bryan Biggs has suggested, it has not always been the easiest place to turn into a performance venue, and yet Philip Jeck speaks affectionately of the resonances in the former concert hall, with its curved wall where once the Willis organ was installed. For Wendy Harpe, the concert hall was a 'beautiful, beautiful' space, and Jayne Casey has suggested, with a sense of its ever-present history, that it might in some way be musically haunted. Sounds from the past and the history of Liverpool have surely crept into its fabric, along with the sounds – and sometimes music – from nearby Church Street, with its legion of buskers. In its turn, the building has, for many decades, infused music into the wider city. If there is a musical spirit inherent in the place, it may have been most audible in the brief silence between keyboards, between the departure of the Willis organ and the arrival of the artists with their pianos.

Notes

1   Stainton de B. Taylor, *Two Centuries of Music in Liverpool*, Liverpool: Rockliff Brothers, 1976; R. F. Bisson, *The Sandon Studios Society and the Arts*, Liverpool: Parry Books, published on behalf of the Sandon Studios Society, 1965.

2   W. S. MacCunn, *Bluecoat Chambers: The Origins and Development of an Art Centre*, Liverpool: Liverpool University Press, 1956.

3   Taylor, *Two Centuries of Music*, p. 66.

4   George Melly, *Scouse Mouse, or I never got over it*, London: Weidenfeld and Nicolson, 1984.

5   'A new concert hall', *Liverpool Daily Post*, 27 September 1938.

6   In the nineteenth century, Theodor Leschetizky's private piano studio in Vienna was highly regarded, attracting students from all over the world.

7   'Preserving a cultural link with the past', *Manchester Guardian*, 25 November 1952.

8   'Arts celebration', *Manchester Guardian*, 19 March 1958.

9   'A munch with music has an appetising start', *Liverpool Daily Post*, 17 May 1961.

10 See Chapter 2.

11 Treasurer's Report at the Sandon Music Group's Annual General Meeting, 1963.

12   As part of the Sandon's 60th birthday, this private-pressing LP was produced in a very limited edition by Sandon member and Bluecoat-based architect George Hall.

13   'Informal and relaxed', *Liverpool Daily Post*, 15 October 1969.

14   'Lesser-known songs of Schubert', *Liverpool Daily Post*, 19 May 1970.

15   'Forum now has arts administrator', *Liverpool Echo*, 5 June 1966.

16   See Nicholas David Wong, 'The Rushworths of Liverpool: A Family Music Business. Commerce, Culture and the City', PhD thesis, University of Liverpool, 2016, pp. 190–93, https://livrepository.liverpool. ac.uk/3000433/1/200021607_March2016.pdf, accessed 4 January 2020.

17   Lighting was by Harvey Matusow and sound by Ron Geesin, with glass supplied by Pilkingtons and other glass manufacturers.

18   Broadcast 26 January.

19   *Bluecoat Arts Forum Artistic Administrator's Report 1968/69*, Liverpool Record Office, 367 BLU/18/16.

20   As told to the author by Joe Riley, former *Liverpool Echo* arts editor.

21   Conversation with the author, 2016.

22   Jayne Casey, interview with Craig Ferguson, 'Pink turns to blue', unidentified and undated 1988 publication, from Bluecoat press archive.

23   Quoted in feature by Craig Ferguson, 'Summer hot-spot', unidentified and undated 1988 publication, from Bluecoat press archive.

24   Rex Bawden review, *Daily Post*, 21 March 1988.

25   Andrew Burn, from a conversation with the author.

26   Dinesh Allirajah, 'A Different Sky', in *Scent: The Collected Works of Dinesh Allirajah*, Manchester: Comma Press, 2016, p. 57, first published in Maria Crosssan and Eleanor Rees, eds, *The Book of Liverpool*, Manchester: Comma Press, 2007.

27   See *Bido Lito* podcast, Jayne Casey in conversation with Bryan Biggs, which includes the Sun Ra event: https://www.podomatic. com/podcasts/bidolito/episodes/2018-11-30T04_57_26-08_00

28   As publicity for the Pop Mechanica gig, their first in the UK, the *Liverpool Echo* produced a supplement featuring as its headline the quote from Reagan.

29   Phillip Key, *Daily Post*, 31 January 1989.

30   Bill Harpe, *The Guardian*, 1 February 1989.

31   http://archive.theblack-e.co.uk/archive/ category/music/electronic/content/musica-electronic-viva-8-9th-oct-1969, accessed 4 January 2020.

32   Interview with the author, 2016.

33   See note 25.

34   *Mal Dean 1941–1974: An Exhibition of Cartoons, Illustrations, Drawings & Paintings*. On the opening night, Dean's collaborator Pete Brown performed in a gig that also featured Dick Heckstall-Smith and Mervyn Afrika.

35   Interview with the author, 2016.

Chapter 7

A Creative Community

Bryan Biggs

n the 1988 film *The Tichborne Claimant*, a horse-drawn carriage turns up outside Bluecoat; its passengers disembark and process to the front doors, which open to reveal a sumptuous interior full of guests in period costume. In an episode of Liverpool TV soap *Brookside* in 1998, the camera follows a young couple through David Jacques's exhibition in the gallery and into the garden, where they have an almighty row. As teenage tearaway David McCallum speeds down School Lane in a stolen laundry van towards the end of Basil Dearden's *Violent Playground* (1958), the arts centre can be glimpsed in the background. Blink and you miss it. Film location is one of several different functions that Bluecoat has fulfilled and, for many people, their memories of or associations with the building are related, not necessarily to the arts, but to some other activity. This chapter takes an oblique look at the life of Bluecoat beyond the public arts programmes that are interrogated elsewhere in this book, to uncover a patchwork of activities that have taken place over the past century or so. A hint of these are given in artist Nils Norman's enigmatic words that greet the visitor at the College Lane entrance, painted on to the brickwork: *hiccup, ferment, leap, chorus, knot, potter, craft, change.*[1]

This journey through Bluecoat's labyrinthine spaces and history attempts to chart an alternative account to complement the official story, portraying a shifting 'creative community' that is integral to the narrative of an umbrella institution whose many tenants, regular hirers and occasional users, and its hosting of unexpected events,

Figure 71. Ceramicist Julia Carter Preston in her studio overlooking the Bluecoat garden. Photo: Sean Halligan.

distinguish it from other arts centres. A myriad of activities has arguably enriched the centre, helping to break down barriers to access for audiences oblivious or resistant to the arts, and opening up possibilities for the cross-fertilisation of creative disciplines. Attempts to harness such a multifaceted, even wayward, offer into a coherent brand have been a perennial challenge, but it is perhaps this promiscuity that gives the building its identity. And unlike a single-offer arts venue, the identity of such a wide-ranging facility is more likely to be contested: witness the passion with which some visitors claim Bluecoat as primarily a gallery, others a café and place to meet, or somewhere to browse for books, an independent record shop, or a retail outlet for quality crafts. For the arts centre staff and those with businesses based in the building, Bluecoat is a place of work.

People's sense of ownership of a particular facet of Bluecoat is most acute when things change – the cinema closes, the garden is re-landscaped, the café reopens under new management, a new performance space is created, the gallery is relocated. This chapter looks at some of those developments and also reveals organisations, individuals and initiatives that have found a home in the building, sometimes only fleetingly. It discusses external partners worked with, as well as how different spaces have functioned over time, and argues that little in the School Lane premises, apart from elements of the historic architecture, is fixed. The aim is also to present Bluecoat as much more than just a centre for the arts and, echoing earlier chapters, for it to be considered as a dynamic complex of relationships, sometimes contradictory, that contributes to the claim for a wider, more inclusive definition of the culture of the place. Like its early arts programmes, records of all that has gone on since the charity school vacated Bluecoat are patchy, and the following survey does not pretend to be comprehensive. Drawing on the arts centre's press archive, annual reports of Bluecoat Society of Arts – the landlord since 1927 – *Gore's* (and, from 1924, *Kelly's*) *Directory of Liverpool* and other sources, it does, however, try to piece together some of the overlooked or little-known strands that are woven into the fabric of the building's history.

***

After three centuries, 'Bluecoat' is still used to refer to the oldest building in Liverpool city centre, despite the many variations on this name, as ownership changed and its role shifted from charity school to arts centre. This chronology of names runs from 'Blue Coat Hospital' (also referred to as 'the Charity School') in 1717, to 'Bluecoat Society of Arts' in 1927, then oscillating between 'Bluecoat Arts Centre', 'The Bluecoat' and 'Bluecoat', reduced further to the colloquial 'Bluey'. For many, 'Bluecoat Gallery' was used as a catchall for the arts venue and you still hear references to 'Bluecoat Chambers', the official address adopted in 1927, while no one alive remembers 'Liberty Buildings', the short-lived rechristening by the building's second owner, William Lever, in 1909, a name that Roderick Bisson, chronicler of the Sandon Studios Society, considered 'absurd' and RIBA (the Royal Institute of British Architects) thought 'ruthlessly destroys the association with the past'.[2] The arts centre mailbag has brought some interesting corruptions of the address – 'Glucose Heart Centre' and 'Blue Clay Gallery' – while tenants of the building, such as publishers Bluecoat Press and book and art suppliers Bluecoat Books/Bluecoat Arts, took the name with them when they left. All the while the Blue Coat school has continued in a separate building several miles away.

The confusion of names is not perhaps surprising, given the plethora of activities encountered in the building at different times since the school's departure in 1906. Before the artists moved in the following year, the earliest tenants appear to have been the Palestine Committee, presumably a local group in support of Jewish nation-building in Palestine in the period before the Balfour Declaration. When the Sandon

Figure 72. Rehearsal for a puppet show by Sandon Studios Society chairman, Philip Radcliffe Evans (right), with Olga Radcliffe Evans and Alan Oversby, 1950s. Image courtesy of Mark Radcliffe Evans.

Studios Society rented space at Bluecoat, they occupied rooms in the west wing, gradually encroaching on other parts of the building. The life – artistic and social – of this independent art school-cum-club is described in Chapters 2 and 3, and artists' studios were central to its occupancy, these tenants engaged in painting, wood carving, enamelling, millinery, model making and teaching music and singing. But, even then, there were commercial tenants renting rooms, such as Baxendale & Co., listed as wholesale ironmongers and then sanitary engineers. There was a printing company, an accountant, an auctioneer, an umbrella repairer, a house furnisher, photographers, starch manufacturers, a show card maker, an advertising contractor and forwarding agents. A resident housekeeper, Annie Jones ('Joney'), was employed by the Sandon for over two decades, her duties doubtless including keeping an eye on their all-night parties when, on one occasion, the front courtyard was decorated with plants and lanterns and a temporary swimming pool set up in the garden, the revellers going to great lengths to fashion ornate costumes on an exotic theme in which to dance to the new tango craze, before collapsing outdoors on to temporary beds made of trusses of hay.[3]

Architecture was established as a significant part of the Bluecoat community when Charles Reilly moved his school there from the university's Waterhouse Victoria Building in 1909, transforming the previous school chapel upstairs into a drawing studio and the downstairs into an exhibition space, redecorating the building and installing window boxes and potted shrubs in the courtyard. He set up his Department of Civic Design, the world's first planning school, above the Sandon rooms.[4] There were architectural exhibitions and conferences on civic design and town planning, further embedding architecture in the venue. This was consolidated as a succession of practices set up offices in the building, including Reilly himself and his successor as Roscoe Professor in Architecture at the university, Lionel Budden; the noted town planner Patrick Abercrombie; Stanley Adshead; Shepheard & Bower, which led the building's 1927 and post-war restorations; and Campbell & Honeyburne. This architectural presence continued right through the century. Another Liverpool architect, Harold Hinchcliffe Davies – whose 'drive and energy', according to Roderik Bisson, 'stimulated the most hectic and venturesome period of the [Sandon] Society's existence'[5] – employed sculptor Edward Carter Preston to design the decorative glass on The Clock, on London Road. Other prominent Liverpool architects, Francis Xavier Velarde, Herbert Thearle and Bernard Miller, were also Sandon members who commissioned Bluecoat craftsmen and artists for their schemes. In 1930 the Sandon hosted a visit by Clough Williams Ellis, to whom Herbert Tyson Smith had supplied sculptural and building material for his fantasy architecture project at Portmeirion in North Wales. Post-war, Liverpool

Architectural Society, which had first been established in the building in 1927, had its club rooms at Bluecoat and took over the old Sandon dining club; there were regular talks on architecture by the likes of Reyner Banham and Nikolaus Pevsner (in 1960); and architectural practices continued as a strong presence from the 1950s onwards, with the likes of Hall, O'Donahue & Wilson, Kingham Knight and Audrey Walker.

There was a noticeable increase in cultural societies resident in the building once Bluecoat Society of Arts was established as landlords, their presence realising a key strand of its 1927 constitution, to build a critical mass of like-minded organisations in the arts centre. In 1928 such tenants were both professional and amateur and included Liverpool Philharmonic Society, Liverpool Playgoers' Club, Liverpool Amateur Photographic Association (staying until the mid-1970s) and, of course, the Sandon. A record of other tenants during the late 1920s and 1930s makes for an eclectic mix: US news agency the *Christian Science Monitor*, a paper merchants and wholesale stationers, Liverpool Women Citizens' Association Council, Liverpool Union of Girls' Clubs, Liverpool Youth Movement for Peace, and Robert Gladstone, honorary secretary of the Record Society of Lancashire & Cheshire, who had been there since 1922. When the building's future was rendered uncertain in 1925 by the death of its owner Lord Leverhulme, the ground floor's central block had been let to the Voss Motor Car company as a car showroom. The new tenant said,

> Our intention is simply to transfer our Church-street premises to the Blue Coat School, because we found people had an aversion from inspecting cars so near to the public gaze. Apart from our name on the front, the front of the building will remain as now exactly. There will be no vandalism. We shall have room for 30 cars, but all the work will be done from the rear.[6]

A wide door was created to enable vehicles to enter the space from the garden, where presumably entry from College Lane was possible via the yard at the end of Tyson Smith's studio. When Bluecoat Society of Arts took over two years later, the new owners appear to have had no qualms about letting cars park in the front courtyard, giving permission to guests at functions at the nearby gentlemen's club, the Athenaeum.

As well as considering prospective tenants, the Society met monthly to decide on outside hires: meetings of the Liverpool Practical Psychology Club and the Christadelphian Church were accepted, while a badminton club was rejected and an arts and crafts exhibition organised by the League for the Restoration of Liberty by Distribution of Property was considered 'undesirable'.[7] Exhibitions were by no means all of contemporary art. In 1932 there was a display by the Liverpool-based

Ship Model Society, with over 200 items and 'daily demonstrations of putting the ship in the bottle'.[8] Bluecoat was becoming a centre for a wide range of events and would continue to develop as a conveniently located focus for the city's cultural and social life, through trade exhibitions, antiques and craft fairs, public lectures, meetings by all manner of societies, dances, cabarets, puppet shows and Hogmanay parties, many of these social events organised by the Sandon (see Fig. 72). Later, the concert hall and other rooms would be let out for exams in accounting and music, and trade fairs, including one in 1963 by MKE – Modern Kitchen Equipment (Fig. 73) – where one could 'inspect a wide range of light and heavy duty catering equipment'.[9] In 1957 a large exhibition, *Catholic Liverpool*, was organised for the 750th anniversary of the city's charter, documenting the religion's enduring presence over this period in 'the most Catholic part of England'.[10] Exhibits ranged from a fourteenth-century crucifix dug up at Gillmoss to Lutyens's 1930 designs for the Metropolitan Cathedral (a scheme which, at a projected cost of £27 million, had to be abandoned). Today, outside lettings continue to provide an important source of income for Bluecoat, including a successful business in weddings, with the building now licensed to conduct ceremonies.

Figure 73. Modern Kitchen Equipment (MKE) trade fair in the concert hall, 1963. Image courtesy of Michael Swerdlow.

The applied arts and craft skills that Sandon artists such as Tyson Smith and Carter Preston represented were evident elsewhere in the building. Cabinet maker William Burden, a Sandon founder member, was a tenant for over thirty years, occupying the space of the current Bluecoat Display Centre. In the 1920s he was one of several Sandon artists to contribute to making a new booth, designed by George Harris, for a popular Liverpool institution, Professor Codman's Punch & Judy show, which graced the podium of St George's Hall and was in dire need of repair. In the years after the Second World War, many Bluecoat studios were occupied by craft makers, with ceramicist Julia Carter Preston (Fig. 71), silversmith Stan Hill and artists apprenticed to Tyson Smith's sculpture studio such as James McLaughlin (Fig. 74) having long tenures in the building. It was natural, therefore, that a contemporary craft gallery should open in the single-storey building overlooking the garden in 1959. Bluecoat Display Centre was established by Robert Gardner-Medwin, Professor of Architecture at the University of Liverpool, to 'encourage good design and workmanship in everything made for the furnishing and embellishment of buildings and to make known the work of distinguished artists, industrial designers and craftsmen – particularly those who work within the Merseyside region'.[11] It was one of the first such craft centres – for both exhibition and retail – and has maintained a continuous programme of high-quality work by designer-makers that has earned it a national, and indeed international, reputation, with many leading artists working across the crafts spectrum exhibiting. A capital refurbishment led by architect Maggie Pickles in 1998 greatly enhanced the space and was accompanied by commissioned artworks including an elegant window shutter on College Lane designed by Definitive (Gareth Roberts and Helen Brown).[12] Today, an associated educational programme brings the Display Centre's work to a wider audience, while memorable events such as Andrew Logan's jewellery performance in the garden in 1994 during the arts centre's *Summer in the City* have brought its adventurous contemporary crafts centre stage.

Individual makers working on public commissions have occupied studios, such as ceramicist Alun Jones. Studios keeping alive more traditional crafts have included Sylvia Gregory and a group of women weavers in the 1950s/1960s (Fig. 75), the Amalgamated Institute of Antiquarian Crafts in the 1970s and Chinese kite maker Da Bei Feng in the 1980s, through to silversmiths Bob and Joan Porter – the former can be seen on television on Grand National Day engraving the winning horse's name on to the trophy – and more contemporary designers in studios today, such as jeweller Anthony Wong and textile artist Nawal Gebreel. Across the decades there have been horologists and a picture restorer, Harriet Owen Hughes, and musical instrument makers, from harpsichord maker Thomas Wess to Michael Phoenix Violins.

Music, as Chapter 6 demonstrates, has been integral to Bluecoat from the beginning. At times it has been as significant as visual art, a hub for many amateur societies, rehearsals, lessons, concerts and festivals. The Liverpool Mozart Orchestra grew from this concentration of music, playing its inaugural chamber concert at the venue in 1951 and becoming a fixture, with a combined repertoire of classical and contemporary, gaining an increasing reputation through its musicianship and the conducting of John Carewe (Fig. 64). Other groups included the Liverpool Baroque Ensemble. The English Folk Song & Dance Society held dances in the central hall from 1927, and in 1952 established its north-west headquarters in the building. Liverpool Youth Music Committee arrived in 1968, organising an annual schools' music festival that took over the whole building. Bluecoat was home to music teachers from as early as 1910, a tradition that continued for many years with popular tutors such as Geoffrey Walls, Kathleen Duncalf and Ronald Settle, and more contemporary tuition such as the trumpet classes provided by blues musician Alan Peters. Merseyside Arts promoted its new music series *2002 Tomorrow's Music* in the concert hall in 1974/75, and Jazz North West was based in the building in the 1980s/1990s, collaborating with the arts centre on high-profile gigs. Club promoters Medication organised their iconic student dance nights from a Bluecoat office in the early 2000s. While music currently plays a less prominent role in the arts centre, the new intake of tenants in 2008 saw female choir and singing agency Sense of Sound – with Jennifer John, Saphena Aziz and Perri Alleyne-Hughes also running their own individual projects – and artist Alan Jones creating electronic beats from his studio.

Bluecoat is also a place to consume recorded music, with a regular record fair, established in 1975, still going – one of the longest-running fairs in the country. In its heyday the fair occupied the whole of the concert hall, its organiser Trevor Hughes, who also promoted comic fairs at Bluecoat from 1974, making these events into real occasions, with visits by special guests, such as British psychedelic

Figure 75. Weavers' studio at Bluecoat, late 1950s/early 1960s.

legends Arthur Brown (of The Crazy World) and Twink (Pink Fairies and The Pretty Things) and figures from the Merseybeat era during an annual 'Beatleday'. Liverpool independent record shop Probe Records, trading from the retail unit created by the 2008 development (from what had been the yard for the café on the west wing ground floor), was preceded by Blue Bird Records, which sold house/dance music in the 1990s from a shop that, like Probe, opened directly on to School Lane. This unit, in the east wing, has seen a succession of retail tenants, from The Bag Shop (selling the wares of leather craftsman, Mr Soloch) to the School Lane Barber Shop. Today it is a hairdresser, yet in 1927 an application from the Hairdressing Academy to open a shop at Bluecoat had been rejected.

Books have a long history in the building. Liverpool City Council ran its Central Lending Library on the ground floor when the building reopened after the war, while antiquarian bookseller Alan Wilson had a space, and the long-established book fairs continue every month. Bluecoat Books was situated next to the old gallery in a cramped space that led to the café and garden. Operated by Paul McCue, who also ran an art materials shop off the front courtyard, the heaving shelves of mainly remaindered books, many of them sourced in the US, were a popular attraction for academics, general readers and children – specially catered for by the installation of a colourful wooden car they could sit in. Both the book shop and art shop moved to Hanover Street when the building closed for redevelopment. Bryan and Alwyn Kernaghan have kept the book tradition going with their shop occupying the site of the Sandon dining and reception rooms, offering a wide selection of volumes, with an emphasis on the rare and collectible. The publisher of local interest books, Bluecoat Press, grew from another building tenant, Light Impressions, which started as a commercial photographer and publisher. Olwen McLoughlin opened Editions, a shop specialising in editioned artists' prints and greeting cards, as well as a picture-framing service. Now in Cook Street, the shop was located in Bluecoat's front courtyard, one of several tenants to move into this part of the arts centre when it adopted a more commercial approach to its physical assets in the 1980s. Letting the public-facing rooms in the front courtyard to retailers echoed the College Lane-facing Display Centre at the rear of the building. Tenants have included independent retailers, such as local history shop The Liverpool Connection, and outlets for young designers, florists and gift ranges not to be found on the high street. While some of these commercial tenants, including a lingerie shop, have seemed somewhat inappropriate for a contemporary arts centre, most have been deemed broadly cultural.

While the opening up of the front courtyard helped enliven it and attracted visitors from nearby Church Street, the labyrinthine nature of the building meant that some activities remained invisible. Tucked away at the rear and reached by a circuitous route, Merseyside Film Institute (MFI) was, however, far from obscure, with 2,000 members in its heyday in the late 1940s. Established in 1933, its 'most valuable and pioneering work'[13] was welcomed by Bluecoat the following year and, though temporarily housed off-site for seven years following wartime bomb damage (and its activities suspended for a year), it remained the oldest such organisation in the UK, predating the British Film Institute, and was one of the largest. It was regarded as an art house cinema long before these became a feature of many cities and towns. It also presented films in the Philharmonic Hall, but its cramped theatre at Bluecoat became its real focus and, with an accompanying Vietnamese, then Thai, food offer in the 1980s, it was hugely popular. It offered Merseysiders an eclectic and staggering range of films, old and new, a consistent programme of the latest in independent, European, American and world cinema and classics, as well as guest talks by directors such as Terence Davies and Mike Leigh, and others, facilitated by the Goethe-Institüt, from the new German cinema. For many regulars, it provided a vital education in cinema history. MFI closed in 1993 in its sixtieth year, the result of a combination of competition from commercial cinema operations in the city, notably the 051, an increasing availability of films on video, the arrival on British TV of Channel 4, which screened the sort of programme to be found in independent cinemas such as MFI, and an inability to upgrade its projection equipment. There had been a scheme in the late 1970s, worked up with the BFI, to build a film centre in the south-west wing, but this never materialised.

The MFI spaces were taken over by Merseyside Moviola. Though not operating a regular programme of film screenings, the new tenant ensured that the 'kinematographic' arts mentioned in Bluecoat's deed of constitution continued – though of a very different kind – in the building. Moviola had rented a small office in the arts centre in 1988, from which to plan its first *Video Positive* festival of video art and moving image installation the following year, and, over the next decade, it grew to become the UK's leading agency for commissioning and presenting this area of art practice. Under the visionary direction of Eddie Berg, supported by a board that included locally based academics at the leading edge of discourse around new media and the possibilities of the emerging digital world,[14] Moviola positioned itself – at a time when Liverpool was yet to pull itself out of the economic doldrums – as 'part of the future of the city rather than its troubled past or present'.[15] The organisation, which became FACT (the Foundation for Art and Creative Technology) in 1997, collaborated with Bluecoat on many exhibitions (see Chapter 5) before moving to a new building in 2003. Film production company and community resource Mersey Film & Video was also based in the building.

Alongside arts organisations, the regional offices of several national funding, educational and cultural bodies contributed to making Bluecoat an important hub from the 1970s onwards. These included the British Council, which, alongside the Merseyside Conference for Overseas Students, had an international remit, though it was, like another, more incongruous tenant, Northern Counties Athletic Association, not involved in Bluecoat's artistic life. The Arts Council's devolved responsibilities at the end of the 1960s involved locating its Merseyside Arts Association (MAA) office in the building, where the new organisation also ran an art shop in the front courtyard, dispensing information and tickets. By the late 1980s, with an increasing professionalisation of the arts that would crystallise the following decade into the 'cultural industries' sector, arts industry specialists arrived on the scene and, when MAA moved to Duke Street, Bluecoat provided a natural home for this new breed: arts marketing consortium TEAM, arts recruitment agency Artrain and arts management consultancy Practical Arts, with subsequent iterations as Positive Solutions, Euclid and L&R Leisure.

Tenants since 1960, the north-west branch of the Workers' Educational Association occupied most of the first floor of the north-east wing, while some of its practical art classes were run in rooms in the building. Bluecoat Society of Arts organised its own programme of lectures about art for schools as early as 1960 and children's art weeks and various classes continued as a regular feature. As outlined in Chapter 4, through a pilot 'Bluecoatconnect' programme, participation became a central strand of the arts centre's work in the late 1990s. Educational activities at Bluecoat, however, date back to 1907, when the Sandon artists ran life drawing classes, continuing even after the Society ceased to function as an art school. The practice of drawing from life was taken seriously: in 1921, for instance, easels were repaired, a special lamp acquired to light the model, copies of drawings by the great masters adorned the walls, and the stove was moved to a more suitable position. There was even a curator of the life room and a model steward.[16] The situation had clearly changed after the war, according to the contrasting impression given in a painting of the life room by Donald Lynch[17] and also by a contemporary photograph, both showing a spartan and shabby space (see Fig 29).

Printmaking can also be traced to the early Sandon days, the large press still in use today in Bluecoat's etching studio being reputedly used by Augustus John, though evidence for this is scant.[18] Jean Grant's long relationship with the Bluecoat started, she recalls, in 1962 when she and another artist, Fanchon Frölich, used the press before the facility was formalised into the print studio, and when they had to bring their own materials, tools and even acid baths.[19] Many local artists, amateur and professional, have since developed their skills in the studio, located on the top floor of the north-east wing, under the tuition of artists including George Drought, Simon Roodhouse, Meg Robbins, Graham Williams, Bev Hayes, Emma Gregory, Hannah Fray and, most recently, Fran Disley. Printmaking was expanded after 2008 with the addition of a screen-printing studio – used not just to make fine art editions but for posters, tote bags and T-shirts – and the arrival, as tenants, of letterpress specialists Juniper Press, since departed. Other classes and workshops have been run externally – from drumming, belly dancing and improvised music to more 'lifestyle' classes such as slimming and yoga. Tenants have offered all manner of tuition including elocution lessons, starting with a teacher in 1924, through to Ernest Hopner in the 1980s. Bluecoat has proved itself a venue well suited for rehearsals too, used by a range of performers, from late 1950s/early 1960s female pop chart act The

Vernons Girls to national touring companies performing in the city such as Welsh National Opera and the Royal Ballet in the 1970s and 1980s. The space is today used weekly by a range of organisations such as the homeless community choir The Choir With no Name, and the innovative young people's theatre company 20 Stories High.

A 1952 list of Bluecoat tenants includes Liverpool Corporation's Arts Committee, five cultural societies, three firms of architects, other tenants 'occupied with various aspect of art' and 17 painters and sculptors and a number of craftsmen.[20] Long before artists colonising redundant buildings became a feature of Britain's post-industrial cities (in Liverpool, this started with Bridewell Studios in 1976), Bluecoat's spaces were turned into studios for artists. Theirs has been a century-long presence in the building but, apart from the Sandon and other informal groupings holding occasional exhibitions, they have not manifested themselves as a cohesive 'Bluecoat artists' group. The cohort reflected in a *Lancashire Life* feature in the 1960s included a diverse mix: public sculptor George Thomas, easel painter Eve Thompsett, architectural model-maker William Bateman, St George's Hall organist Caleb Jarvis and surrealist painter George Jardine.[21] Despite later competition from other, cheaper studio groups, Bluecoat continued to attract emerging artists exploring new approaches to painting, such as Clement McAleer, Mark Skinner and Laird Downie, and in 1987 the arts centre coordinated a city-wide open studios weekend. 'Sunday painters' and those impervious to the latest developments in conceptual, video or other new trends could still be accommodated, either as tenants, like the long-standing Liver Sketching Club or, unofficially, on the railings on a Saturday.

Many tenancies have been short-lived, and delving into the archive reveals cultural organisations that have left little trace, including, in the 1980s, Africa Arts Collective and performing arts cooperative Oduduwa, listed in 1985, the same year that Friends of the Earth had an office in the arts centre. Some tenants became partner organisations of Bluecoat, delivering programmes and festivals that enabled the arts centre to significantly expand beyond what it was able to present on its own, and to reach new audiences. This way of working had its origins in Bluecoat Arts Forum, one of whose functions was to draw together many different societies in the building and beyond, and this helped Bluecoat take on a pivotal role as a festival venue for the city. From hosting Festival of Britain events in 1951 and its own themed festivals in the late 1950s/early 1960s to events such as *Summer in the City* and Euro 96 in the 1990s, the venue, with its admirable range of spaces and central location, has been well placed to host this type of concentrated, often multi-art-form celebration.

Liverpool experienced an explosion of festivals in the 1990s and many focused on Bluecoat: Africa Oyé used both indoor and outdoor spaces from 1992 to 1998, with musicians such as Justin Vali (Madagascar), Bajourou (Mali), Chico Ramos (Belize) and the dance/drumming group Wagogo (Tanzania) (Fig. 77). Indian arts specialist MILAP started its promotions at the venue and collaborated with Bluecoat on many dance, visual art and music events, including commissions, as its annual festival developed. Liverpool Arab Arts Festival – LAAF, originally Liverpool Arabic Arts Festival (Fig. 78) – emerged through a partnership, *Nadey al Bluecoat*, between Bluecoat and local Yemeni cultural organisation Nadey Al Cul. Initiated following a concert by Palestinian oud player Adel Salameh in 1998, its first event, an 'Arab Weekender', took place the following year. The festival continued to grow in scale and stature, becoming the UK's most significant celebration of arts from the Arab world and its diaspora, sustained by the commitment of Bluecoat's programmers Dinesh Allirajah, Clare Owens and Ngozi Ikoku, who directed it, with input from external curators, as it became independent from Bluecoat (though it is still organised from its base there). Another fixture on the Liverpool cultural calendar with offices at the arts centre since 2008 is Deaf and disability arts festival DaDaFest, whose collaboration with Bluecoat goes back further to the organisation from which it grew, North West Disability Arts Forum. Before that, the arts centre had worked with the Disablement Resource Unit's Arts Integration Merseyside team in the mid-1980s on gallery workshops. Other disability arts tenants, past and present, include Fittings Multimedia and Common Ground Sign Dance Theatre, resident before the capital development that would result in improved physical access in the building. This increased accessibility made the building more suitable as a hub for larger city-wide festivals such as the Liverpool Biennial – providing an ideal point for orientation for the artworks sited across the city – and launches and major gatherings such as the popular LightNight, as well as for discrete festivals such as Timesis' physical theatre festival Physical Fest.

Merseyside Civic Society's *Artists in Townscape* exhibition was hosted at Bluecoat in 1974 and the society has returned on many occasions, most recently for its participative 'State of the City' discussion and workshop days, a focus for future thinking about Liverpool. As a discursive space in the centre of Liverpool, the arts centre has a long tradition, stretching back to debates about Post-Impressionism in 1911. A lecture theatre was created in 1928, when the central ground floor core (the present reception and espresso) was divided up, the new space flanked by the offices of the Liverpool Architectural Society and Liverpool Philharmonic Society. There were many public talks here, and in 1953 the English Speaking Board moved in as tenants, while, over half a century on, a Philosophy in Pubs group started using the new facilities for regular discussions in 2008 in the bistro.

Figure 77. Tanzanian dance and drumming group Wagogo in the garden, part of the 1996 Africa Oyé festival. Photo: Colin Serjent.

Figure 78. Liverpool Arab Arts Festival family day in the front courtyard, 2003. Photo: Sean Halligan.

Since Charles Reilly and the Sandon recognised the importance of having a social space at the heart of the building, there have been a succession of, initially private, places for food and drink at Bluecoat. The Sandon's dining club (Fig. 17) hosted a dinner for Russian ballerina Anna Pavlova in 1912, and others followed for Sir Thomas Beecham, Sir Edwin Lutyens and others. Many eminent visitors – in Liverpool to perform at a music or theatre venue – were brought to dine, and several signed the visitors' book. Started in 1922, this document (Fig. 22), now in Liverpool Record Office, reads like a cultural who's who of the interwar years and beyond, and includes the signatures of George Bernard Shaw, Sybil Thorndike, Gustav Holst, Osbert Sitwell, Igor Stravinsky, Béla Bartók, George Balanchine, Margot Fonteyn, Eric Coates, Kathleen Ferrier, Michael Tippett, Stanley Spencer, Laurence Olivier, Peter Pears, Joan Littlewood and many others. Another café, the Blue Bird, is recorded in 1927 but appears to have been short-lived, and the Sandon dining room continued into the 1960s, the space remaining a members' club when the Liverpool Architectural Society took it over. Sandon members dug out a basement to create an intimate (and, with no means of escape, ultimately condemned) subterranean bar, whose Lanson champagne and Guinness was a popular treat. After a failed attempt as 'Blundells' restaurant, a catering offer for the public finally opened, initially located in a cramped space just inside the main entrance (later occupied by the bookshop), then in 1989 as a café bar in the old Sandon premises, run by the Everyman Bistro, which made it a popular success right up until the building closed for its refurbishment in 2005.

On the final page of his account of the Sandon Studios Society, Roderick Bisson notes that 'from early years, the artistic ventures and even sometimes the Annual General Meetings, were accompanied by entertainment',[22] and the society clearly liked to party. Before the First World War, they made the venue Liverpool's fashionable social hub through fashion shows and cabarets, suppers and parties. For one of these, Sandon musician Arnold Clibborn composed a tango, 'The Sandono', which was danced to by Audrey Kearns who, according to Bisson, 'set the pace in fashion and modernity, wearing the very latest from Bacon's of Bold Street'.[23] Sandon parties for children continued until well into the 1950s[24] and as the building opened up much more to the public in subsequent decades, it proved a popular choice for a wide range of social activities and partygoing. In the 1980s one of the artistic tenants, Arthur Black, staged a series of elaborate and meticulously planned fancy dress parties on themes such as a Ruritanian state ball, Latin America, Dickens and the Russian Revolution, reviving the spirit of the Sandon but with an acute sense of escapist irony, born out of the grim economic reality that then engulfed the city.

The garden has proved especially attractive for such parties, this hidden gem witnessing many special occasions, as well as physical changes over the building's long history, as outlined in Chapter 1. Alterations to this 'commodious yard'[25] have often been accompanied by controversy. In 1974 a 'plant-in' helped silence criticism of the previously relatively barren landscape and, alongside the planting, the arrival of benches – some donated in memory of past Bluecoat users, others purchased with Tourist Board support – made the garden a more conducive place to meet, or for quiet contemplation, a tranquil space in the heart of a busy city centre. Its maintenance has been dependent on volunteers, an essential ingredient of the arts centre throughout its history and across the organisation, from its board of directors to those who invigilate the gallery or steward events. Brenda Evans devoted many years, from the 1970s until the building closed in 2005, to tending the garden, assisted by other volunteers, including some of her colleagues from Friends of the Earth, and adding to the diversity of the planting, enriching the garden's magical quality in the process. Despite it being a best-kept secret for many years, the garden has also been an active space, hosting sculpture exhibitions, art workshops, live art and dance interventions, poetry readings and music performances from summer concerts to festival gigs by Liverpool Arab Arts Festival, MILAP, Above the Beaten Track, LightNight, and one-off gigs by the likes of Hank Wangford, It's Immaterial and many others. When it reopened in 2008 following a wholesale re-landscaping, the garden had lost much of its charm, and the new look divided opinion. While its appeal as Liverpool's 'secret garden' had undoubtedly diminished, it was more visible from the building's main core and physically more accessible, and greater numbers of people were now able to discover and enjoy it, particularly as a place to take food and drink from the new espresso, an oasis in the increasing hubbub of the encroaching Liverpool One development.

Artist Alec Finlay's bird boxes, high up in the trees in the garden as well as in those at the front of the building, were commissioned to mark Bluecoat's reopening in 2008. Brightly painted in reference to the exotic birds depicted on postage stamps from around the world, the boxes are used by families of blue tits, and also remain as a symbol of migration and of Bluecoat as a place of homecoming at the centre of a welcoming Liverpool. And, for the visitor today, surrounded by sounds from the working studios that enclose the garden and art glimpsed through the windows of the gallery and Display Centre, the experience is little different from before the development, when sounds from singing lessons, piano practice, a rehearsal in the concert hall or a noisy video installation in the gallery would waft into the garden, the life of the arts centre seeping into its public spaces, inviting the world to listen. When the building was almost entirely emptied in 2005, an eerie silence descended before the contractors moved in to prepare for the capital development scheme. In that lull, the Bluecoat was, for one night only, subjected to psychic investigation by the popular television programme *Most Haunted*. While nothing supernatural materialised, some ghosts had been laid to rest, and over the coming months construction work would prepare the building for the arrival of a new creative community.

Notes

1   Artist Nils Norman was commissioned to enliven this entrance in 2011.

2   R. F. Bisson, *The Sandon Studios Society and the Arts*, Liverpool: Parry Books, published on behalf of the Sandon Studios Society, 1965, p. 154; and *Journal of the Royal Institute of British Architects*, 17, 1910, p. 694.

3   C. H. Reilly, *Scaffolding in the Sky: A Semi-architectural Autobiography*, London: George Routledge & Sons, 1938, p. 136.

4   For an account of the Architecture School's time at Bluecoat, see Reilly, *Scaffolding in the Sky*, pp. 130–36.

5   Bisson, *The Sandon Studios Society*, p. 164.

6   Mr Voss, quoted in 'Art and commerce: no need for anxiety about old Blue Coat School', *Liverpool Echo*, 25 July 1925. The showroom could house 30 cars.

7   *Bluecoat Society of Arts minutes books, 1927–29*, p. 67, Liverpool Record Office, reference 367 BLU/1/1.

8   *Catalogue of the 1st Annual Exhibition & Magazine of the Ship Model Society*, 3–8 October 1932.

9   Invitation card to the event, courtesy of Michael Swerdlow.

10   Catalogue for exhibition *Catholic Liverpool 1207–1957*, held at Bluecoat, 30 September–13 October 1957, p. 10.

11   Founding mission, reproduced in *Bluecoat Society of Arts Chairman's Report, Balance Sheet and Revenue Account, 1961*.

12   For the shutter, Kevin Carroll crafted the metal element and Louis Thompson the blown glass.

13   *Bluecoat Society of Arts: Annual report for the year ended 31 March 1934*, p. 5.

14   Board members included Roy Stringer (chair) from pioneering digital tech company Amaze and media studies academic Sean Cubitt, then teaching at Liverpool John Moores University.

15   Lewis Biggs, in Angelica Cipullo and Karen Newman, eds, *We are the Real-time Experiment*, Liverpool: FACT, 2009, p. 14.

16   *Sandon Studios Society Painters, Sculptors & Designers Group minutes*, 15 January 1921.

17   Lynch's account on the back of his undated watercolour, *Sandon Rule 4, to Provide Artists for Models*, collection Victoria Gallery and Museum, University of Liverpool, describes the scene and is an extract from a letter from Lynch to C. Vaillant, 27 July 1957: 'It was a meagrely attended "life class" in the old life room. The model was lazy, the night cold, the four of us not very interested – I got on top of a step ladder at the back and drew the scene. Steve (William Stevenson) I think was drawing the head – the rest tells its own story.' A later inscription by Herbert Tyson Smith, also depicted in the painting, reads: 'The model is married with two children.'

18   In a conversation with the author, artist Jean Grant recalled this claim by Sandon member Gerry Grindley; however, it is doubtful as, according to Bisson (*The Sandon Studios Society*, p. 190), the press's arrival dates from after John's involvement in the Sandon.

19   Email from Jean Grant, 15 July 2019.

20   *Bluecoat Society of Arts 1952 Annual Report*, p. 5.

21   'For art's sake', *Lancashire Life*, 13.12, December 1965, pp. 48–51.

22   Bisson, *The Sandon Studios Society*, p. 211.

23   Bisson, *The Sandon Studios Society*, p. 96.

24   Richard Hill, whose father, Stan, was a Sandon member and Bluecoat tenant, recalls the Christmas party, some time around 1953–55.

25   The garden area was thus described in James Wallace, *A General and Descriptive History of the Ancient and Present State of the Town of Liverpool*, Liverpool: R. Phillips, 1975; *The Picture of Liverpool, or a Stranger's Guide*, 1805.

Chapter 8

Academics-in-Residence

Panayiota Vassilopoulou and Paul Jones

The programme for the celebration of Bluecoat's 300th birthday had been in the making for several years, and part of the preparation involved reflecting on its history with a view not only to uncover its identity in relation to the past, but also, and more importantly, to construct or transform the arts centre's identity for the future. This included a process of self-knowledge and self-realisation – an opportunity to celebrate achievements and learn from the past, but also to question established norms and shape new directions for the future.

Philosopher-in-Residence: Panayiota Vassilopoulou, 2013–15

It was in this context that the Academic-in-Residence programme developed between Bluecoat and the Philosophy Department of the University of Liverpool, and was introduced with an inaugural lecture in November 2013.[1] Artist residencies in cultural institutions have a long history and, indeed, have been a much-valued practice at Bluecoat. Visual artists, musicians, dancers, curators and poets from the UK and internationally held residencies that provided opportunities for the residents to develop professionally and personally, but also for Bluecoat, local artists and audiences to be exposed to new ideas and cultures. However, this was the first time in the UK, and perhaps internationally, that a philosopher was appointed and

Figure 79. Vincent Woropay sculpture in the front courtyard during his exhibition *Distant Thunder* with Andy Goldsworthy, 1988.

that the residency, rather than involving one individual or a group of individuals as is common practice, was framed as a cross-institutional collaboration between a cultural and an academic institution.

The residency thus provided a new framework for embedding academic research into the workings of the host organisation and its publics, and conversely, for co-developing with the resident researcher new research and artistic projects. Prior to the residency there was some presence of philosophy at Bluecoat, with the community group Philosophy in Pubs regularly meeting there, and some philosophical questions and themes had been explored through curatorial practice and invited speakers. Similarly, the Department of Philosophy had been particularly active in pursuing collaborative projects with Bluecoat and other cultural partners, including collaborations with Liverpool Biennial. But what the residency uniquely offered was an opportunity to foreground philosophy both as an academic discipline and as a form of socially engaged practice in which research is not simply disseminated but is closely co-developed with publics that it directly concerns. Thus conceived, philosophy at Bluecoat was practised during the residency as a continuous process of dialogue, reflection and evaluation that opened up new directions for research and social practice in direct response to the challenges that individuals and institutions face in our rapidly changing cultural landscape.

One dimension of this has to do with changes in the kind of art we encounter: the artistic production of our times is characterised by a diversity of objects, projects or situations that audiences find increasingly challenging to understand or relate to, either because it is too removed from ordinary experience (for example, very abstract contemporary art) or because it is too close to it (for example, by being represented in everyday objects or embedded in everyday activities or practices). The last few decades in particular have also witnessed a clear shift from the artistic object to the creative process which, accelerated by technology and social media, has issued new forms of socially connected and collaborative creative processes: *we are all artists now*. The 'democratisation' of art, as it is commonly perceived, challenges both the theoretical and practical aspects of the creation and reception of art. Distinctions between different artistic genres and between what is and is not art are blurred, if not altogether obliterated. Moreover, previously held norms of authorship, artistic genius, status, autonomy and, above all, value are put into question, and so is the role of cultural institutions (including arts centres, galleries, festivals and museums), which endeavour to actively engage their publics in the co-interpretation and co-creation of art. In view of these developments, as well as the severe public funding cuts for the arts and humanities sector in recent years in the UK and elsewhere, both cultural and academic institutions are called to justify the value of their creative and research activity in terms of the contribution it makes to society, thus increasingly shifting the question from '*Why* is it good (in itself)?' to '*What* is it good *for*?' Negotiating between intrinsic and instrumental values, as between the numerous other tensions that characterise our culture, is not easy, especially if the aim of *understanding* is not merely one of justification but also one of change. And change, at all levels – personal, institutional, societal – is always triggered by questions, rather than answers.

It was precisely a shared keen interest in pursuing questions – that is, in cultivating a philosophical culture – that motivated the introduction of the Bluecoat residency. Art spaces could be conceived as sites of discourse and, for example, Charles Taliaferro's recent discussion (published a year after the residency finished) argues for the promotion of a 'Philosophical Culture Museum Model' in order to further develop this conception and explore its potential.[2] Bluecoat, of course, is not just a museum or gallery; as an arts centre it is a polymorphic organism – it is the building, galleries, performance and lecture spaces, artists' studios, shops and garden, as well as its people, staff and publics – and so describing it as a site of discourse, especially if the notion of discourse is understood as related to the active and sustained pursuit of lines of enquiry, is all the more fitting.

However, the communities that shape Bluecoat and the art world more generally – communities of artists, curators, theorists and audiences – each employ different kinds of discourse, often facing considerable difficulties in communicating the aims and outcomes of their theories or practices. Moreover, while traditionally these different discourses were structured in well-defined hierarchies, in the context of the democratisation of art these are continuously challenged: the entire process between the creation and reception of art is broadly conceived as a discourse in which all participants are treated as equal, both with regard to status and the quality of their contribution. But does this conception establish democratic freedom or merely assume it? We may be in danger of reaching the point that Claire Bishop has identified in connection to some contemporary participatory art: 'In a world where everyone can air their views to everyone we are faced not with mass empowerment but with an endless stream of egos levelled to banality.'[3]

In a world where political, economic, social and educational inequalities are anything but diminishing, how can we ensure that every contribution to this common discourse is, at least in principle, of equal value? It is becoming increasingly clear that in order to foster a collaborative, reflective dialogue between diverse communities of art, academia and the public, more inclusive but also more empowering forms of communication are needed. The gap needs to be bridged between the authority or expert and the public: participants need to be provided with the conceptual tools and the amount of contextual knowledge necessary for an appropriate use of these tools if they are to fully engage in and benefit from this kind of discourse. And this educational responsibility falls equally between cultural and academic institutions, which need to reflect on and re-evaluate their practices. Academic disciplines, particularly philosophy, could make a significant contribution here through reflective and critical analysis of the relevant aesthetic, ethical, political and social dimensions. But such involvement with the 'real world', as it were, would need also to motivate a revision of philosophy's own history, theories and methodologies. The effectiveness or value of such endeavour is anything but given: it depends on the co-development of new lines of enquiry that challenge disciplinary boundaries, as well as traditional distinctions between theory and practice. The philosopher-in-residence initiative was thus an experiment, quite successful in this respect, to develop new conceptual and cross-institutional models of collaboration, enabling its participants – institutions as well as individuals – to question effectively and accordingly to (re-)interpret collaboratively our history, values and future aims.

The residency's activities took place over a period of two years and developed in two interrelated directions: public-facing events and institutional-focused interventions. The public programme included two main strands of activity that particularly mark its originality: a 12-week course on aesthetics, and a series of philosophy workshops, corresponding to the main exhibitions that took place during the residency: *The Negligent Eye* and *James McNeill Whistler* (Liverpool Biennial) in 2014; and *Listening, Xavier Ribas: Nitrate, Tricia Porter: Liverpool Photographs 1972–74* and *Resource* in 2015.

Aesthetics is a formal part of the undergraduate and postgraduate curriculum of the Philosophy Department and it was the first time that a course of this kind was delivered off campus, at Bluecoat, offered not only to students but also to the public. In a sense, the history of modern aesthetics as a philosophical discipline is coextensive with Bluecoat's. The building, initially an educational institution, was constructed just five years after the publication of Addison's seminal essay 'On the pleasures of imagination' (1712); Baumgarten published his *Aesthetica*, in which he coined the term 'aesthetics', in 1750; Hume published his essay 'Of the Standard of Taste' in 1757; and Kant's *Critique of the Power of Judgement*, which established modern aesthetics as the philosophy of beauty and art, was published in 1790. Bluecoat was thus a particularly appropriate host for a set of lectures that followed the development of aesthetics from Enlightenment to post-modernism, since this development is materially and functionally inscribed in the building itself and its various transformations through its 300 years. Moreover, since the aim of the course was not simply to familiarise the audience with aesthetics from an historical point of view but rather to engage participants in research and the co-interpretation of art, the lectures were largely informed by my own past and ongoing research in aesthetics and creativity. This introduced a particular perspective from which to examine works of art, some of which were shown at Bluecoat during the residency, or had been shown in the past. Works of art were not treated simply as illustrative examples of various theoretical views (as traditional classroom lectures tend to do), but as rich sources of meaning, the concrete experience of which motivated reflective responses that could lead to different interpretations, different perspectives to approach them from. The lectures were highly interactive, inviting the participation of the audience in the assessment of the various theoretical views and art examined; they provided first-hand experience of how a piece of research is developed, and gave participants the opportunity to directly contribute to its development.

The dynamic of the space, Bluecoat's performance theatre surrounded by the art on display in the galleries, as well as the diversity of the audience – students, artists, museum professionals, educationalists, of all ages – resulted in a systematically high level and quality of debate around key theoretical questions and artistic practice, unprecedented in a university classroom or cultural space. And indeed, this had some immediate effects on both artistic practice and philosophical research. For example, one of the lectures was led by my research on the philosopher Plotinus and the conceptual artist Bruce Nauman, which subsequently formed the source of inspiration for *Mythos*, a performance piece created by vocal artist Steve Boyland, who attended the aesthetics course. The work premiered in Liverpool in 2014 and has since been performed in many venues around Europe. Boyland's artistic project and contributions from other members of the audience led to the (co-)development of my research in new directions, as reflected in its outputs.[4]

The sense of a community of enquiry engaged creatively in lively debate was further enhanced by the activities under the residency's second strand, the philosophy workshops. These were of two kinds, one for adults and one for children and their families, and offered participants a free forum to reflect philosophically on the ways they think and feel about given artworks and their relevance or value. The methodology deployed in the workshops, 'philosophical enquiry', was developed under *Patterns of Thought*, a project that I led with colleagues from the Philosophy Department (2010–15), in collaboration with Bluecoat and other cultural partners. It is greatly indebted to the Philosophy for Children movement, which originated with Matthew Lipman in the 1970s in the US and has seen a revival in recent years through the work of organisations such as the Society for Advancing Philosophical Enquiry and Reflection in Education (SAPERE) and the Philosophy Foundation, but was substantially modified, including making it appropriate also for adults and for supporting audiences to engage with the art that they actually see as part of their museum and gallery visits. Art engages us in many different ways, not just cognitively, and so while this kind of enquiry facilitates critical reflection, it does so in a way that involves emotion, imagination and, most importantly, promotes an ethos respectful of the dynamic of a community and the individual perspectives that coexist within it. The Bluecoat workshops did not *teach* participants art or philosophy – unlike the lectures, they did not aim at delivering any specific content – but rather provided participants with the methodological tools and space to make sense of their own experience. Experiencing, analysing and critiquing art as part of a reflective communal practice of philosophical enquiry empowered individuals to unravel their own interpretative thread, communicate it to others, defend, enrich or change it.

These two sets of activity were complemented by three keynote lectures marking the residency's milestones,[5] and contributions to other Bluecoat events including '*To Hell with Culture*: A film by Huw Wahl', an in-conversation event with the film's director about its subject, the art historian, poet, educationalist and philosopher Herbert Read, and a philosophy workshop, 'I know little of women. But I've heard dread tales' as part of a celebration of International Women's Day.

The success of the philosopher-in-residence programme was soon acknowledged by other institutions interested in supporting the initiative by incorporating philosophy more systematically into their programmes. In collaboration with colleagues and students I organised research and public engagement events at other local arts venues that included philosophy workshops and lectures with invited guest philosophers from around the UK, talking about current exhibitions and projects at different galleries,[6] thus introducing to Liverpool a diversity of philosophical perspectives and themes.

Over the two years, I co-designed and delivered about forty events at Bluecoat and other cultural institutions, almost all fully subscribed, confirming the public's strong interest and support. More than 3,000 people participated in these, and a popular 'Philosophy Day' at Bluecoat in 2014 brought together philosophical practices of East and West, ranging from talks to tea drinking sessions, yoga and artistic performances.

I was invited to contribute to Bluecoat's strategic programme development, staff-training sessions that explored ways for philosophical theory and practice to support their professional role, and the development of new collaborative research projects. The residency was instrumental in establishing new partner consortia and networks, including *Cre-AM* (2013–16), a European-funded project delivered by an international consortium of creative industries partners, who worked together to identify new ways of using technologies and tools, as well as new business models and policies to enhance creativity. The project *Situating Impact* (2017) assessed the residency's impact and the future potential of this model of research and public engagement collaboration.[7] Participant feedback on individual activities and focus groups throughout the residency provided evidence of improvements in participants' understanding, engagement and professional practice, and also highlighted how instrumental the residency had been in strengthening community bonds within and beyond Bluecoat. This feedback was documented in a short film produced in collaboration with artist film-maker Tristan Brady-Jacobs (shown at Bluecoat in 2014). Returning to Bluecoat in 2016, an international symposium, *Galleries of Inquiry*, brought together curators, artists, philosophers and arts professionals to explore how philosophy and other subjects may be deployed systematically under academic residencies for the benefit of the public, artists and art institutions. Bluecoat's Academic-in-Residence programme was subsequently supported by other University of Liverpool departments and organisations[8] and continued at Bluecoat with Paul Jones as sociologist-in-residence.

Sociologist-in-Residence: Paul Jones, 2017

How often does a completely new context open up the possibility of radically questioning what one usually takes for granted? Having worked in universities for a long time – primarily the University of Liverpool – and having studied there before that, I had not realised just how much the introduction of student fees had transformed my job, the context I worked in, and the culture of university study. Being resident at Bluecoat changed all of that, and has encouraged me to approach study, teaching and the whole endeavour of sociology differently.

I had previously delivered a public lecture at the venue in 2013 to mark the fifth anniversary of the building's renovation by Biq Architecten. Here, I met Bluecoat's artistic director Bryan Biggs and chief executive Mary Cloake, both of whom were genuine advocates for a more socially engaged approach to the institution's practice, and who saw a great deal of potential in the concept of a sociologist-in-residence. Panayiota Vassilopoulou's philosophy residency had been a real success, and the idea of continuing this type of collaboration between the University of Liverpool and Bluecoat would allow us to pursue our respective interests in making our work more public.

My residency coincided with the building's tercentenary and, against this backdrop, I shared with Bluecoat an interest in work that engages with the city, that questions the ways some things change while others stay the same. I also saw this as an opportunity to make what I usually do – teaching and researching, and talking about that – more 'public'. Les Back, who introduced my inaugural residency lecture, calls for 'sociology beyond the paywall'[9] – in other words, opening up this way of thinking as far beyond the university campus as is possible – and I wanted to explore one way of doing this (and the extent of the public's appetite for it).

Consequently, one of the central planks of my residency was to do some teaching outside of the university campus, at the arts centre, focusing on an undergraduate module, 'Cities', and opening this up to whoever wanted to come along. This would bring together undergraduate students with non-undergraduate students (for whom there would be neither entry requirements nor fees) in the same class, connecting with the same ideas from a range of urban sociologists, both classic and contemporary.

I taught this module in Bluecoat's performance space, which was virtually full every week (see Fig. 80). Following each session, the registered students returned to campus for a series of accompanying seminars,[10] while I led a discussion based on the lecture with those who wanted to stay after the session. These were lively discussions, characterised by a range of different viewpoints, drawn from variant experiences. I learned a lot from these groups and I hope that the other attendees did too.

Something very interesting happened in one of the early weeks of the course. One of the undergraduate students – smart, young, full of ideas – asked me about what I had come to think of as a successful experiment. Why, she asked, were the 'members of the public' not being charged a fee to attend, while the students were? And why did I think people that 'didn't have to come' were coming? This exchange, perfectly pleasant and courteous, took me by surprise, partly because it reflected an internalisation of the student-as-consumer, and partly – *mea culpa* – because I was a little stung that it was not completely self-evident that I, and the fascinating sociological material we covered in the lectures, was so illuminating that everyone would *want* to come. However, these questions were good starting points, at least if you run the first one the other way around: 'What is anyone paying for when they're paying for classes, a degree?' 'Why does sociology matter, and should it be made more public?'

With these questions in mind, and in addition to the 'Cities' module, I also taught a small group of MA 'Visual Methods, Visual Analysis' students at Bluecoat, and contributed to, and occasionally delivered, some more

Figure 80. The audience at one of Bluecoat sociologist-in-residence Paul Jones's talks on urban sociology, 2017. Photo: Paul Jones.

conventional public research lectures: US sociologist Doug Harper, documentary photographer Chris Leslie, and colleagues from the University of Liverpool and other academics talking about their research.[11] A highlight was a day-long symposium, *Concrete Utopias*, that connected to Bluecoat's tercentenary arts programme, and brought together sociology, architecture, literature, music and visual art practices, including presentations by artist Jessie Brennan on her work around brutalist architecture, poet Chris McCabe on concrete poetry and Mark Goodall on *musique concrète* – an enriching and thought-provoking gathering that demonstrated the value of interdisciplinary discourse. I also contributed a public lecture on digital futures of the city as part of Liverpool's *LOOK/17* photography festival.

The residency also involved a monthly public reading group, ironically called *Bad Taste*, facilitated in collaboration with doctoral researcher Laura Harris. Attracting artists, photographers, trade union activists, curators and a revolving cast of interested – and interesting – people, the group discussed art, aesthetics and cultural meanings. The proposal for Laura's research – a study of the arts centre – grew out of our collaborations detailed here and, working closely with Bluecoat, she was able to bring together sociological and philosophical enquiry with critical theory and cultural studies approaches to her PhD thesis. With a particular focus on the *In the Peaceful Dome* exhibition, her research included making a short film relating to 'art literate' labour, the behind-the-scenes work (such as is carried out by gallery technicians) that is crucial to the arts centre's functioning, but is hidden from the public.[12]

Revealing relations most often hidden was a common thread throughout the sociology residency, which sought to demystify contemporary – and historic – thinking about urban societies, including interrogating the workings of a cultural space in the heart of a city. It is very rewarding that so many people came to the public manifestations of my year with Bluecoat, a response that at times I found – and still find - overwhelming. Opening this space together has made me think differently about the university environment as a place of learning, the wider social role of an arts centre, and the practice of sociology itself. While personally rewarding, the residency really only worked as a collaborative endeavour, a collective space occupied by a diversity of people and interests, coming together to do a range of things. The space of the residency is an important reminder that anything that is social in nature can – by definition – be different.

***

How does the Academic-in-Residence programme fit within the process of Bluecoat's celebration of its history and its future development? What kind of change or value has this intervention to offer? If, as Martha Nussbaum suggests, there is currently a tendency in our institutions to produce 'generations of useful machines, rather than complete citizens who can think for themselves, criticize tradition, and understand the significance of another person's sufferings and achievements',[13] interventions like these two residencies may prove an antidote to or an act of resistance against this trend. If there was indeed a value in the residencies beyond their localised activities, this was their contribution to shaping an empowered, reflective, critical and self-critical public by collaboratively pursuing lines of enquiry that really satisfy and further the conceptual and creative interests of its members.

Notes

1   All activities under the residency were free.

2   Charles Taliaferro, 'The open museum and its
     enemies: an essay in the philosophy of museums',
     in V. Harrison, A. Berqvist and G. Kemp, eds,
     *Philosophy and Museums: Essays in the Philosophy
     of Museums*, Cambridge: Cambridge University
     Press, 2016, pp. 35–54.

3   Claire Bishop, *Artificial Hells: Participatory Art
     and Politics of Spectatorship*, London: Verso, 2012,
     p. 277.

4   Panayiota Vassilopoulou, 'Images of a moving
     self: Plotinus and Bruce Nauman', in T. Botz-
     Bornstein and G. Stamatellos, eds, *Plotinus and
     the Moving Image*, Leiden/Boston: Brill/Rodopi,
     2017, pp. 187–209.

5   'Leaving Traces: Reflecting on the Value of Art'
     launched the residency; 'Philosophy and Leisure'
     on completion of the first year; 'Truth and Lies
     about the Work of Art' at its conclusion.

6   At Tate Liverpool, FACT (Foundation for Art
     and Creative Technology), Open Eye Gallery
     and National Museums Liverpool, under the
     Philosophy in the Gallery series, funded by the
     British Society of Aesthetics.

7   Delivered in collaboration with Professor Elena
     Antonacopoulou, University of Liverpool, and
     the post-doctoral researcher engaged in the
     project, Huw Fearnall-Williams, and supported
     by Arts and Humanities Research Council's
     Cultural Engagement Fund.

8   For example, my residencies with Bury Arts
     Museum (2017) and the NHS Research and
     Development team, North West (2018–20),
     together with colleagues Michael Hauskeller
     and Rachael Wiseman on *Thinking Matters*; and
     Pauline Rowe, poet-in-residence, Open Eye
     Gallery.

9   Back makes this argument here: www.academic-
     diary.co.uk, accessed 4 January 2020.

10   Delivered by my colleague, Maike Potschulat.

11   These included Kirsteen Paton, Terence Heng,
     Michael Mair, Barnabus Calder, Ronnie Hughes,
     Jude Robinson, Camilla Lewis, Florian Urban
     and Jo Hudson.

12   Laura Harris's film was publicly screened at
     Bluecoat and elsewhere and is available at
     https://m.youtube.com/watch?v=7PwLjQN-
     VHc, accessed 4 January 2020.

13   Martha Nussbaum, *Not for Profit: Why
     Democracy Needs the Humanities*, Princeton, NJ:
     Princeton University Press, 2010, p. 2.

Chapter 9

A Reflection on Bluecoat's Tercentenary

Bryan Biggs

Taking the year 1717, inscribed in Latin on Bluecoat's façade, as the date of the charity school's dedication, the arts centre decided to mark the building's tercentenary in 2017, acknowledging that the school did not in fact open until 1718 and that it took a further seven years for the building to be fully completed. The 300th birthday would provide an opportunity both to celebrate Liverpool's oldest city-centre building and to interrogate its claim to be the UK's first arts centre. The challenge for 2017 was to devise a programme that would bring together these two elements and make connections between the different forces that had driven the building's development and ensured its survival – to find, perhaps, a continuum across three centuries by looking at distinct strands that continue to resonate.

This final chapter summarises the tercentenary year and some of the thinking that informed Bluecoat's programming decisions. In presenting such an overview, a picture will hopefully emerge of an arts centre enriched by a particular history, regarded not as two unrelated chapters – charity school, then contemporary arts venue – but representing a series of echoes. The year attempted to crystallise the many threads that have woven through the building over time, including philanthropy, education and learning; global trade and international connections; and architectural and artistic ambition – in order to make the argument for Bluecoat

Figure 81. Archive display in the Vide in 2017, featuring posters from 50 years of Bluecoat exhibitions and events. Photo: Brian Roberts.

as a cultural hub for Liverpool, a symbol of the city's resilience and character. The aim of the tercentenary was also 'to extend, enhance and surprise audiences through … a programme that marks out Bluecoat as an arts centre relevant to our times … [that would] significantly raise our profile locally, regionally, nationally and internationally'.[1]

The year encompassed music, literature, dance, visual art, film, performance, participation, new commissions and international work, reflecting current directions in arts practice. At the same time, substantial support from the Heritage Lottery Fund enabled Bluecoat to go deeper than had been possible before in interrogating its history, including researching the identity of the building's architect and how it was funded. Heritage – of both the building and the contemporary arts – emerged from the year to provide a significant legacy, and a central strand of ongoing activity. The heritage context also provided further stimulus for this book.

The snapshot of the year that follows attempts to emphasise the continuing vitality of the idea of the arts centre. It makes the case for arts spaces like Bluecoat having an increasingly important role in civic life as places for public discourse, independent thinking and providing pathways to creativity for audiences. It was evident that being able to draw on a 300-year history enriches these processes. The chapter also attempts to bring together the various strands discussed in this book, and make some observations, and offer some conclusions, about how the pairing of contemporary art and a historic building can flourish, providing lessons perhaps for the wider heritage sector as it seeks to bring sometimes uncomfortable histories about ownership and power into its remit, through working with contemporary artists.

***

The start of 2017 saw the final days of Keith Piper's gallery exhibition *Unearthing the Banker's Bones*, a collaboration with Iniva (Institute of International Visual Arts). Its centrepiece, which provided the exhibition's title, was one of eight works commissioned for the Arts Council Collection's 70th anniversary. Comprising three large-scale video projections, Piper's film employed a science fiction device, inviting viewers to consider the excavation and dissection of the present from an imagined future. The film's narrative of economic and social collapse drew on extracts from apocalyptic fiction by Octavia Butler and Mary Shelley to address contemporary anxieties about race and class. These themes were echoed in *Robot Bodies*, Piper's interactive digital work, first shown at Bluecoat in 1998 – updated and reprogrammed for the exhibition – in which the robot, android and cyborg were examined as metaphorical carriers of contemporary anxieties around racial difference. Alongside the *Banker's Bones* film, 'physical evidence' of ledgers belonging to the banker of the title was displayed next to replicas of human bones, these objects playing off against the film's unfolding dystopian narrative. The show was completed by a series of mixed-media works on unstretched canvas, future projected images of the present that referenced nineteenth-century history painting.

The exhibition marked a return to Bluecoat for Piper, who first exhibited in *Black Skin/Bluecoat* in 1985 at the start of his career, and celebrated his long-term relationship with the venue that included the 1992 commission project *Trophies of Empire*. The new show reflected the arts centre's commitment to working closely with an artist over many years and, at the start of a year that would see another Bluecoat alumna, Lubaina Himid, win the Turner Prize, was a strong statement about the continuing vitality and relevance of this generation of black British artists that emerged in the 1980s, many of whom had early support from the Liverpool venue. Alongside Piper's show, emerging artist Adham Faramawy's *Janus Collapse*, interrogating fluid identities in the advertising-saturated, digital present, was a continuing reflection of this early support for diverse artists.

The tercentenary programme itself was structured around 300 days, from February to November, and each day was announced with a tweeted Bluecoat fact, snippets of information that provided a snapshot of the building's history, from the minutiae of school life to significant art exhibitions. This retrospection was continued with *Public*

Figure 82. *Public View* exhibition by Bluecoat alumni, 2017: South Atlantic Souvenirs & Trouble's *Trophy Cabinet*, first shown in *Trophies of Empire*, and (behind) John Akomfrah photo-work, *The Utopian Palimpsest*. Photo: Brian Roberts.

View (Fig. 82), an exhibition featuring 106 of Bluecoat's artistic alumni that attracted over 31,000 visits for its diverse intergenerational mix of local, UK and international artists, many of whom had made early career appearances at Bluecoat, including Yoko Ono, Sonia Boyce and Jeremy Deller, and who generously donated work for a fundraising online auction later in the year. Liverpool photographer Sean Halligan presented 300 images that he had taken of Bluecoat over the previous three decades. A panel discussion, *Northern Peripheries*, with academics from the UK and Switzerland examined some of Bluecoat's curatorial strands as reflected by the exhibition in the context of wider developments in British art. As Mike Pinnington observed in his *Art Monthly* review of *Public View*:

> the breadth and diversity is such as to put some larger, better-known institutions to shame. What starts to emerge … is a clear sense that, while many leading galleries are just catching on to the idea that it pays (both creatively and otherwise) to exhibit so diverse an array of artists of different genders, sexualities and cultures, Bluecoat seems always to have been doing this.[2]

Figure 83. Siobhan Davies Dance, *material / rearranged / to / be*, in the gallery, 2017. Photo: Brian Roberts.

Figure 84. Interactive installation, *New possibilities in familiar places*, by Simon & Tom Bloor, *Abacus* exhibition, 2017. Photo: Brian Roberts.

Two solo film and installation shows in the gallery followed, by mid-career and emerging artists Larissa Sansour and Louisa Martin. The centrepiece of Sansour's *In the Future, They Ate from the Finest Porcelain*, which combined live motion and computer-generated imagery, explored the role of myth in history and national identity, making reference to her own Palestinian background. Choreographing sound and light, Louisa Martin's installation, *Proxy*, created an immersive environment that played on the body's senses. A related events programme included Liverpool artist David Jacques's short animation, *Oil is the Devil's Excrement*, and a discussion about the importance of research in the work of an artist with a long association with Bluecoat, including his major work in 2011 that drew on Robert Tressell's classic working-class novel, *The Ragged-Trousered Philanthropists*, as part of Bluecoat's year themed around the idea of Liverpool as 'City of Radicals'.[3]

As part of Siobhan Davies Dance's national tour, *material / rearranged / to / be*, the company took over the gallery for nine days in July, radically transforming it and visitors' experience of the space with video and sculptural interventions and the dancers' compelling performances, which also attracted attention from passers-by outside through the College Lane windows. Although dance interventions in the gallery had taken place before, this was the first time the whole of the space had been given over to contemporary dance and was a reminder of a continuing interdisciplinary strand of programming at the arts centre. It was accompanied by film documentation of early work by Bluecoat residents Liverpool Improvisation Collective (LIC), whose *INHABIT* project continued to develop new audiences, as well as their own practice, and was the main dance focus across the year. This programme included a visit by Australian choreographer Russell Dumas, and *POOL*, created by LIC artist Mary Prestidge and musician Philip Jeck in the small garden, which had been the school's cold-water bath and was landscaped in 1928 – with shrubs donated by Mrs Frank Hornby, wife of the inventor of Meccano – by Sandon artists Herbert Tyson Smith and his son Geoffrey, who tended it over the next four decades.[4]

The central presence of children to the building's history was evoked in the summer exhibition *Abacus*, curated especially for children, which invited interaction with the works. It featured new commissions designed with play as their focus: Liverpool artist Emily Speed created a giant environment of small-scale sets while Simon & Tom Bloor's colourful, room-sized chalkboard proved irresistible to doodlers of all ages (Fig. 84). An associated events programme included Huw Wahl's film *Everything Lives*, a meditation on the life of his father Ken Turner, a pioneer of young-people-focused community arts in the 1960s and 1970s, and Paula Hampson's multimedia dance performance *WONDER*, exploring creative learning inspired by her young son.

In 2009 Bluecoat celebrated the life and work of Wirral-born writer Malcolm Lowry (1909–57) whose *Under the Volcano* (1947) is often cited among the most significant novels of the twentieth century. Set in Mexico as the world headed towards war, the book is structured around a single day – the Day of the Dead – in the life of an alcoholic ex-British consul and is a richly layered meditation on the human condition and a portrayal of self-destruction. Bluecoat staged a major exhibition featuring artists from different points on Lowry's compass – Merseyside, Isle of Man, Mexico, Canada – including paintings by his contemporary, Edward Burra, a new video by Paul Rooney and other new and historic works and ephemera. An associated programme included a song cycle by poet Ian McMillan and composer Luke Carver Goss, film screenings, dance and poetry events, a Day of the Dead community participation event, a psychogeographical coach and walking tour of Lowry's Wirral, and the publication of a book of essays.[5] Each year since then, a group of Lowry enthusiasts, the Firminists (named after *Under the Volcano*'s protagonist), have worked with Bluecoat to research and celebrate the writer and reconnect him to Merseyside through an annual 'Lowry Lounge' event.[6] Although Lowry considered Liverpool to be 'that terrible city whose main street is the ocean',[7] Merseyside is vividly recalled in his writing, and these annual gatherings demonstrate his continuing influence on writers and other artists. Staged in 2017 on the 70th anniversary of the publication of *Under the Volcano*, the eighth Lounge was Bluecoat's most ambitious to date, comprising an international conference with Liverpool John Moores University that involved leading Lowry scholars from North America, Europe and New Zealand. Though Lowry never returned home, his childhood haunts inform his writing, not least in his 'lost' novel, *In Ballast to the White Sea*,[8] set largely in Wirral, Liverpool and Preston, and this was a central focus of the conference. It was accompanied by a richly layered multimedia performance, *The Lighthouse invites the Storm*, commissioned from Alan Dunn, Martin Heslop and Jeff Young, and staged at Bluecoat and Mariners Park retired seafarers' home in Wallasey, whose residents participated in the project. Two years after this event and the conference, and after a decade of advocacy by the Firminists, Wirral Council honoured the writer in 2019 with a blue plaque – 'like a giant piece of punctuation in a landscape that Malcolm Lowry knew so well'[9] – in his birthplace of New Brighton. Bluecoat proposed the plaque's wording and selected its location, on the sea wall looking out to the Mersey estuary, a resonant site for a writer whose voyages took him across the oceans, and one that relates to the arts centre's own maritime origins.

Across 2017 there was more literature: Sean Borodale was artist and writer-in-residence, developing several projects and a public performance comprising an installation of prints in the performance space and live improvisation of the texts by vocal artists Steve Boyland and Saphena Aziz. Children's author Leila Rasheed and other writers discussed *Megaphone*, a new development scheme for Black, Asian and Minority Ethnic writers aimed at those interested in the publishing industry. Carol Mavor talked about her new book *Aurelia: Art and Literature through the Mouth of the Fairy Tale*. There were poetry readings with Liverpool John Moores University Writers' Workshop, and Deborah Mulhearn continued her Liverpool literature walks. Five poets were commissioned by French art historian Catherine Marcangeli to respond to *The Mersey Sound* poetry anthology to mark its 50th anniversary, the event previewed by BBC Radio 4's *Front Row*, broadcast live from Bluecoat and including two of the original Liverpool poets, Brian Patten and Roger McGough, and two new generation poets, Andrew McMillan and Lizzie Nunnery. *Tonight at Noon: New Writing*, the reading of the commissioned poems at Bluecoat, also featured Paul Farley, Eleanor Rees and Deryn Rees-Jones, and was supported by Liverpool City Council as part of its '50 Summers of Love' programme, marking fifty years since The Beatles released *Sgt. Pepper*. Bluecoat also contributed to this with a talk at Hard Day's Night hotel on the continuing plagiarism of the LP's iconic cover, and an early morning activity themed around the song 'Good Morning Good Morning', with live Indian music in the courtyard and a *Sgt. Pepper*-themed DJ set. Witnessing this, Seán Street responded with a poem that also referenced the day's political news:[10]

Morning Raga at the Bluecoat

Akash Parekh – Sitar, Kousic Sen – Tabla, Bryan Biggs – turntables. Sgt. Pepper Celebration, Liverpool, 7.30 a.m., the morning after the UK General Election, 9 June, 2017

A hung parliament of blackbirds,
  and Lucy was there in the sky
with rhinestones the morning
  an unslept in
night tried to say good morning
good morning,
  then died leaving Friday
  and her unborn
sisters here to fend for themselves,
fixing a hole.

I came to domesticate this place
  for a while, this voice of a time
that's speaking to a place
  from the time in
which it was first imaged
to what's left
  of any certainty,
  change over change
insinuating a future,
fixing a hole.

Sitar, tabla and gull, Liver birds
  singing, the Georgian stone
listening, chickens home
  to roost. Sunlight
still undecided emerged
devoid of

an attention span.
  So what this place
means remains a site of contest
just as always.

Although chaos is now near complete
  and what I am in relation
to all that surrounds me
  open again,
I walk off through confusions
of showers
  consoled by a silver
  music, with my
day in this life recalibrated
and a hole fixed.

For now at least I'm moving away
  between glass buildings still shouting
one another down in
  temporary
precincts across old pathways,
still trying
  to be my own city
  to the tune of
She's Leaving Home, wherever that
may be right now.

Another 50th anniversary, that of Liverpool's Metropolitan Cathedral, was also marked by Bluecoat with a performance there of Pierre Henry's *Liverpool Mass*. This electronic Mass had been commissioned for the cathedral's opening in 1967 but, not completed in time, was only partially performed. Working with film academic Mark Goodall, who had suggested the idea, and involving over two years of planning, fundraising and negotiations in Paris with the French composer and in Liverpool with the cathedral, staging the Mass in its original entirety was one of the most ambitious music events in the arts centre's history. It related back to Bluecoat's late 1960s experimentation under Wendy Harpe and Bluecoat Arts Forum's support for Bill Harpe, who coordinated Henry's Liverpool project in 1967, to deliver experimental music in the city. In 2017, with a new sound design involving 40 loudspeakers arranged around the cathedral's circular space, the *musique concrète* work was performed by Henry's collaborator Thierry Balasse, creating a memorable soundscape that resonated with its dramatic setting. *Liverpool Mass* received wide acclaim, with national radio and other media coverage and an audience of almost 900. Pop celebrity and Henry fan Jarvis Cocker introduced the concert (Fig. 85), which also included a new commission from Paris-based electronic composers Vincent Epplay & Samon Takahashi. Prior to the concert, a symposium, *Concrete Utopias*, was presented at Bluecoat in collaboration with the University of Liverpool's sociology and architecture departments and Mark Goodall, looking at three cultural strands that coalesced in the 1960s: *musique concrète*, concrete poetry and brutalist architecture. This was followed by a walking tour of Liverpool's brutalist buildings, led by Liverpool Modernist Society, ending at the local shrine to concrete architecture, the futuristic cathedral itself.

In November, forty-five years after Don Van Vliet, better known as Captain Beefheart, staged his first ever exhibition of paintings at Bluecoat (Fig. 86), the arts centre worked with independent curator Kyle Percy and poet Chris McCabe on a

Figure 85. Jarvis Cocker introducing Pierre Henry's *Liverpool Mass*, presented by Bluecoat at the Metropolitan Cathedral, 2017. Photo: Brian Roberts.

packed weekend celebrating the cult US rock musician as 'total artist'. Presenting Beefheart in a fresh light, it interrogated and re-evaluated his entire oeuvre, exploring how music, art, poetry and performance overlapped and fed off each other. It also focused on his relationship to Liverpool, where he performed several times between 1972 and 1980. Preceded by a live performance at Liverpool Philharmonic's Music Room by his reformed band, The Magic Band, the interdisciplinary programme involved poets, musicians, artists, curators, fans and experts, and featured a reading by thirteen commissioned poets made in response to each of Beefheart's albums. The poems also featured in a 'zine, *Click Clack*, along with illustrations from Bluecoat's resident inclusive arts group, Blue Room. There was a day-long symposium with contributions from, among others, Beefheart's biographer Mike Barnes and painter Graham Crowley. Versions of his music were played by local duo Old Farts at Play, and a gig at District featured eight Beefheart-influenced local bands, with US guitarist Gary Lucas as headliner, who concluded, 'Liverpool has to be the epicentre of Captain Beefheart consciousness.'[11] A psychogeographical walk uncovered the city's psychedelic and alternative music history. A week-long workshop, *Ice Cream for Crow*, organised by John Hyatt and based on Beefheart's unfettered approach to art, involved art students from six universities in northern England and Dublin, and culminated in an off-site exhibition at Make in the north docks, followed by a live gig. On New Brighton beach, Alan Dunn recreated an iconic 1968 Beefheart performance at Cannes, resulting in a short film, while another video responding to his work was created by Blue Room, who also produced visual artwork, exhibited as part of an archival display relating to Beefheart's 1972 Bluecoat exhibition, and another film by Lucy Cullen who curated that show when she was Bluecoat's gallery director. Other music events in 2017 included 1980s' post-punk band The Three Johns performing shortly after the opening of *Public View*, which included work by the band's singer, John Hyatt; an in-conversation evening about independence in the music industry with Rough Trade record shop/label founder Geoff Travis, hosted by local music publication *Bido Lito*; and a performance by Liverpool new music exponents Immix Ensemble.

The year's final gallery exhibition, *In the Peaceful Dome*, was conceived as a conversation across time. Arranged thematically, it comprised a rich collection of artworks and historical material relating to Bluecoat's heritage as charity school and arts centre. The model for the exhibition was *Democratic Promenade*, curated by Bluecoat in 2011. This exhibition had reflected on a century of radicalism in Liverpool, taking three manifestations from 1911 – the general transport strike that paralysed the city, bringing it 'near to revolution',[12] the opening of the controversial Liver Building at the Pier Head, and the Post-Impressionist exhibition at Bluecoat – from which to try and locate the radical in the present, with reference to different historical moments that

Figure 86. Captain Beefheart outside Bluecoat during his first exhibition of paintings, 1972. Photo: Don Valentine.

continued to resonate. In *In the Peaceful Dome*, Bluecoat's connections – to global trade, philanthropy, transatlantic slavery, and developments in contemporary and applied arts, literature and performance – were explored through new commissions that included a wallpaper designed by Grantchester Pottery and works previously presented at Bluecoat by Janet Hodgson, Susan Fitch and Geraldine Pilgrim that engaged with the school history (see Figs. 58, 59, 11, 12). Loans included a substantial body of largely unseen early modernist paintings by artists associated with Bluecoat such as Edward Carter Preston (from Liverpool Hope University) and Roderick Bisson, and – from the Whitworth in Manchester – Jacob Epstein's *Genesis*, this monumental sculpture of a pregnant woman returning eighty-six years after first being shown amid controversy at Bluecoat in 1931 (see Chapter 3). Generating significant income for the building then, the work's imminent return was used as a successful crowdfunder for the exhibition. Presented prominently, facing College Lane's busy thoroughfare through the windows of the gallery, *Genesis*'s serene presence still elicited debate about representation of the female body and Western appropriations of African art, and contributed to further discussion about art's relationship to war and gender provoked by other works in the same space (Fig. 87): Carter Preston's designs for war medals and sculptures from the first half of the twentieth century and Jo Stockham's mixed-media feminist works, first shown at Bluecoat in 1990.[13]

Figure 87. *In the Peaceful Dome* exhibition, 2017: Jacob Epstein's *Genesis* (1929–31, collection The Whitworth, University of Manchester), and works behind by Jo Stockham, including (left) *Canon, model 3* (1989-2017) and *Empire Made* (1989).

Exhibiting artist Philip Courtenay ran a series of open workshops, *A Cargo of Questions*, as part of his gallery installation *RE:LODE*. Revisiting his *LODE* project of twenty-five years earlier – a 'relational aesthetics' project *avant la lettre* that was an innovative collaboration with local youth arts group Yellow House to interrogate their place in the world at a time of increasing globalisation – he explored themes of national identity and connections between the UK and the rest of the world, particularly Europe, at a time of national uncertainty over Brexit. The trade routes that Blundell and other eighteenth-century merchants who supported the charity school exploited were evoked in this work, as Courtenay presented film footage of stopping-off points he had visited on a global journey, a 'lode line' that passed through the east coast port of Hull and then circumnavigationally back to Liverpool, juxtaposed with Google maps and current information on geopolitical fault lines in Europe, Central Asia, the Far East and Latin America. The charity school's growth, enabled in part by funds derived from the slave trade, was referenced in the exhibition in archival material relating to prominent benefactors, while contemporary artists Grace Ndiritu, Paul Clarkson and Uriel Orlow explored the legacies of the trade and colonial and imperial expansion through video and painting. Several themes from *In the Peaceful Dome* – its title taken from an abolitionist poem by William Roscoe[14] – were further explored in a contextual programme that included talks on Roscoe's importance as the 'father of

Liverpool culture' by Walker Art Gallery curator Xanthe Brooke, and by Paul O'Keeffe on the impact on Liverpool art of the seminal Post-Impressionist exhibitions staged at Bluecoat in 1911 and 1913.

These echoes across time, the stirrings of global capital found in Liverpool's foundational mercantile maritime years that resonate today, were heard in the *Peaceful Dome* exhibition through mixing artworks and documents from a 300-year span, the school history thus brought into dialogue with new art. Almost incidentally, other links were revealed that connected the school's history to the practice of art. For instance, in the corner of a popular print of the school's St George's Day Parade in 1843[15] (Fig. 7), included in the exhibition, an advert for a picture framer, 'Lacey's Repository of Arts, 100 Bold St.', was unexpectedly spotted. Blundell himself was discovered to be a competent painter of ships, a selection of these being reproduced for *Peaceful Dome*. Research also revealed that drawing was introduced into the school in 1813 to equip pupils with a 'highly useful knowledge of design',[16] and an art exhibition was staged in the building in 1843 that was open to the public.[17] An old boy of the school, Samuel Austin, became a well-known watercolourist, 'celebrated as a perspective delineator'.[18] Another 'Old Blue', Richard Ansdell, also became an accomplished artist and a Royal Academician, and gifted to the school a painting of the governors in gratitude for his education. His best-known composition is *The Hunted Slaves* (1861), which today hangs in the International Slavery Museum at Liverpool's Albert Dock, close to where slave ships departed from.

This theme was further explored as the year drew to a close with experimental vocalist and movement artist Elaine Mitchener's powerful *Sweet Tooth* performance (Fig. 88), a collaboration with three other musicians developed over a lengthy period of research into the connections between sugar, the slave trade and her own British/Jamaican heritage. With funding from Arts Council England and the Performing Rights Society Foundation, this commission was a Bluecoat collaboration with the Stuart Hall Foundation and the International Slavery Museum (ISM), and the performance was recorded live and later broadcast on BBC Radio 3. *Sweet Tooth* introduced a weekend programme, *Bluecoat 300: Charity, Philanthropy and the Black Atlantic*, that addressed the significance of the transatlantic slave trade to the development of the Blue Coat school in the eighteenth century. A symposium, organised in collaboration with ISM and five north-west universities,[19] took place at the Dr Martin Luther King Jr building at Albert Dock, and involved international speakers, with a keynote by Catherine Hall and a discussion with Elaine Mitchener about her *Sweet Tooth* project. It was followed by a participation day at Bluecoat involving films, talks, a display and a walking tour of city-centre sites connected with the slave trade, led by local historian Laurence Westgaph. Bluecoat hosted another symposium, *To Draw The Line: Partitions, Dissonance, Art – A Case for South Asia*, which addressed another historical trauma, the partition seventy years before that accompanied India's independence, and artists' interrogation of it. Organised by *Third Text* journal, its participants included two Bluecoat alumni: Naiza Khan, who premiered a new performance/film piece, almost thirty years after first exhibiting at Bluecoat, and Mohini Chandra (see Chapter 5).

Several events drew on Bluecoat's historical relationships with other cultural organisations in its building. *Merseyside Film Institute: The Director's Cut*, a day reflecting on the UK's first film club, based at Bluecoat for many years, provided an opportunity for people involved, as organisers and audience, to reminisce about the MFI, and for a younger audience to consider the future of independent cinema in Liverpool city region. As well as an archival display of original film posters and other ephemera, there were two screenings: *Don Quixote* (dir. G. W. Pabst), the first film that MFI showed in 1933, and its most frequently screened film, Werner Herzog's *Aguirre, Wrath of God*. The Deaf and disability arts organisation DaDaFest organised a weekend of performances and a symposium, *Disability: Past, Present and Possibilities*, which included discussion of Bluecoat's role in supporting disability arts at the venue. A conversation event with Liverpool Arab Arts Festival chair Taher Qassim, charting the development of the popular festival, which began as a Bluecoat initiative, also emphasised the venue's critical role in building this organisation, which like DaDaFest is still based in the building. Five prominent Liverpool artists (their work shown concurrently at Birkenhead's Williamson Art Gallery) who exhibited regularly at

Figure 88. Elaine Mitchener, *Sweet Tooth* performance at Bluecoat, 2017, with (left) Jason Yarde and (right) Sylvia Hallett. Photo: Brian Roberts.

Bluecoat in the 1960s–1980s were the subject of a panel discussion, *Going Backwards*, that included writer and critic Edward Lucie-Smith. The event considered how Adrian Henri, Maurice Cockrill and other artists created a distinctive Liverpool art, comparing this with the city's current scene, dominated by artist-led spaces.

In addition to Bluecoat's existing partnerships with the University of Liverpool, a new one was established with its School of Architecture. This led to the results of a student project to redesign Bluecoat's arts wing being displayed in the Vide; an animation envisaging a ruined Bluecoat in a post-anthropocene future by one of the students, Edmund Tan, was later included in *Peaceful Dome*. Following a previous philosophy residency with the university's Panayiota Vassilopoulou, the arts centre appointed Paul Jones as Bluecoat sociologist-in-residence for the year, a world-first in the arts (see Chapter 8). His inaugural lecture, introduced by social anthropologist Les Back, was followed by weekly talks on urban sociology, symposia and other events looking at recent changes to Liverpool's urban fabric. Open to the public as well as students, these proved popular, helping position Bluecoat in a more civic role and opening up conversations about the arts centre's engagement with the city. A final lecture, *Punctum*, reflected on the residency year and was introduced by sociologist and *Guardian* writer Lynsey Hanley. Discursive events associated with the residency included *Cities of the Future*, in which Fei Chen looked at the evolution of cities, with a focus on China's rapid urban expansion, while *Guardian* columnist George Monbiot introduced his pertinent new book *Out of the Wreckage: A New Politics for an Age of Crisis* in an in-conversation arranged in partnership with the university, where the event was held.

Central to the tercentenary was My Bluecoat, a year-round heritage archive and participation project funded by the Heritage Lottery Fund that told the building's story through displays, building tours, a schools' programme, a new website, a free booklet and many events. Two dedicated staff were appointed, assisted by a team of volunteers. People shared their Bluecoat stories, and over twenty of these were turned into engaging short films by Soup Collective. These oral histories were by a range of people connected to Bluecoat, from ex-Sandon Studios Society members to artist tenants, Blue Room members and contemporary dancers, and were included on the My Bluecoat website and shown continuously on a large 300-year timeline in the Vide that became a visual heritage focus. Here, on the back wall stretching the full height of the space, a poster display from Bluecoat exhibitions and events proved especially popular (Fig. 81), along with a changing archive display that brought to life the building's layered history, charting the arts' century-long presence at the heart of the building. Across the year there were seven further exhibitions in the Vide's upper levels themed around architecture, the school, participation, film, music, and Bluecoat and slavery. For National Heritage Open Days, the 300th birthday was officially marked with a cake and singing in the garden, a week-long programme of installations and performances, and a talk by TV celebrity and Georgian architecture expert Dan Cruickshank, who spoke with authority on the context of the charity school's origins.

For the My Bluecoat website over 20,000 items were digitised, documents including Blue Coat school founder Bryan Blundell's account of the school's early years; minute books of meetings of the school, the Sandon and Bluecoat Society of Arts; catalogues from the 1911 Post-Impressionist exhibition and others staged by the Walker at Bluecoat during the Second World War; season brochures from the early 1980s to the present; slides of gallery and garden exhibitions from the same period; and many posters, photographs, exhibition invitation cards and visitors' books. Packs for primary schools, developed in collaboration with a local school, comprised downloadable resources covering different aspects of the heritage story, and family activities that year had a heritage focus.

Volunteers were vital to the success of My Bluecoat, one group for instance scanning material at Liverpool Record Office which, together with the Blue Coat school, was a project partner, with material being pooled from their respective archival holdings. Reconnecting to the educational establishment that had founded the building, and bringing together records from different sources, enabled the compilation of a more comprehensive Bluecoat narrative spanning three centuries. In this, some connections were made during 2017 between the historical facts of the charity school and our own time, for instance the still unfolding legacies of colonialism. The investment of architectural value at key moments in the building's history that ensured its resilience and survival was articulated. Though no longer a school, the presence of children as integral to the life of the building was celebrated. And a continuum of local entrepreneurialism could be detected, evident in the religious philanthropy that created the school in the eighteenth century, in the audacity to make the building a centre for progressive culture at the start of the twentieth century, and in an inclusive ethos – of both art forms and audiences – that has characterised much of the period since Bluecoat's formation as an arts centre.

All of this points to the building's ongoing civic presence: even as a school, when it was essentially closed off to the public, it remained a visible and enduring symbol of Liverpool's philanthropic endeavour. Bluecoat's formalisation as a constituted arts centre in 1927 declared a pioneering intent for the city, even if it took some years for its doors to be fully open to all. And at a time of dwindling public resources today, the venue – as the discursive emphasis of its 2017 programme demonstrates – has confirmed its capacity as an independent space for new ideas and conversation, the 'democratic promenade' perhaps that Walter Dixon Scott discerned in Liverpool over a century ago.[20] Despite their own funding pressures, arts venues are arguably now well placed to perform this vital function and to meet the seemingly increasing necessity and appetite for public debate. The tercentenary provided a challenge to summon up Bluecoat's history without recourse to sentiment, nor shying away from uncomfortable narratives. In re-presenting its heritage in dialogue with the present, through exhibitions, events and other means, and by making it available to artists to explore, reinterpret and create new work around, the building's past was given new vitality and relevance, and audiences, judging by their feedback on the year, discovered ways in which this history enriched their experience of the contemporary.

Notes

1   Bluecoat internal vision document, 2016.

2   Mike Pinnington, review of *Public View*, *Art Monthly*, 405, April 2017, pp. 30–31.

3   'City of Radicals' was a city-wide Bluecoat-initiated programme for 2011 that included the *Democratic Promenade* exhibition featuring Jacques and other artists.

4   See R. F. Bisson, *The Sandon Studios Society and the Arts*, Liverpool: Parry Books, published on behalf of the Sandon Studios Society, 1965, pp. 160–61.

5   Bryan Biggs and Helen Tookey, eds, *Malcolm Lowry: From the Mersey to the World*, Liverpool: Liverpool University Press, 2009.

6   The idea for the Firminists was conceived by Yorkshire-based film academic and music enthusiast Mark Goodall, and was broadened to encompass Merseyside Lowry fans Bryan Biggs, Ailsa Cox, Colin Dilnot, Robert Sheppard and Helen Tookey.

7   Malcolm Lowry, 'The Forest Path to the Spring', in *Hear Us O Lord from Heaven Thy Dwelling Place & Lunar Caustic*, London: Picador, 1991, p. 226.

8   Malcolm Lowry, *In Ballast to the White Sea: A Scholarly Edition*, ed. Patrick A. McCarthy, annotations by Chris Ackerley, Ottawa: University of Ottawa Press, 2014.

9   Ian McMillan, quoted in Bluecoat press release for the unveiling of the plaque, June 2019.

10 The poem appeared as 'a poem for Europe' in *The New European*, 3 August 2017.

11 Gary Lucas, comment to audience at the Beefheart gig, 11 November 2017.

12 See Eric Taplin, *Near to Revolution: The Liverpool General Transport Strike*, Liverpool: Bluecoat Press, 1994.

13 Stockham exhibited with Sophie Horton, Val Murray and Louise Scullion in *New Sculpture* (1990) and with Darrell Viner in *Working in the Dark* (1997) and curated *The Negligent Eye* (2014).

14 William Roscoe (1753–1831), 'Mount Pleasant: a descriptive poem', 1777, in which the charity school is described as a 'peaceful dome'.

15 *Recollections of the Blue-Coat Hospital, Liverpool, St. George's Day, 1843*, an 1850 lithograph. The print was after a painting by Henry Travis at the Blue Coat school and shows the school band leading pupils through the gates, watched by teachers, school governors and the public.

16 John R. Hughes, 'A sketch of the Origin and Early History of the Liverpool Blue Coat Hospital', lecture delivered 5 May 1859, *Transcriptions of the Historic Society of Lancashire and Cheshire*, XI (1858–59), 1859, pp. 62–65. On the recommendation of the school treasurer Matthew Gregson, a drawing master was appointed and, though this was short-lived, Hughes reports that drawing later returned to the curriculum.

17 'Exhibition Free – Bluecoat Hospital', advert in *The Liverpool Mail*, 29 July 1843. Travis's St George's Day parade painting, referred to in this chapter, was included, alongside portraits of the governors and trustees, probably by Ansdell.

18 Hughes, 'A sketch of the Origin and Early History of the Liverpool Blue Coat Hospital', p. 65.

19 Liverpool John Moores University, University of Liverpool, Edge Hill University, Liverpool Hope University and University of Central Lancashire.

20 Walter Dixon Scott, *Liverpool*, London: A. and C. Black, 1907. He describes the city's half-mile raft, the landing stage, as a 'democratic promenade' (p. 39).

Bluecoat Timeline

Key dates and selected events in the development of the school and the arts centre.

1708 • Blue Coat Hospital, a school for orphans, founded at St Peter's church by Revd Robert Styth and master mariner Bryan Blundell.

1715 • Old Dock completed. Blundell's ship *The Mulberry* is first to enter.

1716 • Foundation stone laid for new, larger boarding school.

1717 • Building dedicated, with Latin inscription frieze, and is in use the next year.

1725 • Construction completed at cost of £2,288. Built by mason Edward Litherland and engineer Thomas Steers, both responsible for Liverpool's Old Dock.

1732 • Liverpool's first workhouse built by Blue Coat on land leased by the Liverpool Corporation.

1756 • Blundell dies and is succeeded as treasurer by his son Richard, then in 1760 by youngest son Jonathan.

1763 • School buys adjacent land and builds a manufactory for making stockings.

1771 • Factory turned into warehouse for rent after benefactors protest at pupils' exploitation. In 1778, however, children still employed spinning cotton and later pin making.

1777 • William Roscoe's poem 'Mount Pleasant' published, referring to Bluecoat as 'the peaceful dome'.

1783 • Trustees agree to end child labour in the school and all manufacturing ceases.

1796 • Graffiti from this year can still be seen carved into a front courtyard cornerstone.

1800 • 107 pupils run away after attending the Liverpool fair.

1807 • Britain abolishes the slave trade, whose profits supported the school's growth, but slavery continued legally in British colonies until abolition in the early 1830s.

1812 • School adopts Dr Bell's 'Madras system', in which older pupils teach younger ones.

1820s • Curved elevation added to central block and wings at back of building extended.

1838 • Blue Coat Brotherly Society set up for old boys of the school; one for girl pupils follows in 1857.

1874 • Willis pipe organ installed in the school chapel upstairs.

1881 • Single storey building along College Lane built, enclosing the rear yard.

1906 • School vacates the building, moving to new premises in Wavertree.

1907 • Sandon Terrace Studios (later Sandon Studios Society), a breakaway art group from the university, moves in.

1908 • Painting by French Impressionist Claude Monet included in exhibition staged by the Sandon, whose honorary members include Augustus John and Charles Rennie Mackintosh.

1909 • Liverpool University's School of Architecture moves in, including the world's first department of civic design, staying until 1918. Its professor, Charles Reilly, persuades William Lever (later Lord Leverhulme) to rent the building.

1911 • Post-Impressionist exhibition includes work by Picasso, Matisse, Van Gogh and Cézanne, alongside Sandon artists. The Liver Building opens and Liverpool is brought to a standstill by General Transport Strike.

1913 • Lever buys Bluecoat, which he renames Liberty Buildings to reflect his victory in a libel action, but plans to invest in it as an arts centre do not materialise.

1914 • Contemporary Art Society's purchases for the nation are exhibited, including paintings by Gwen John, Duncan Grant and Walter Sickert. Lancashire Society of Arts proposal for the building unrealised. Outbreak of the First World War, in which several Sandon artists die.

1922 • St Peter's church, which established Bluecoat in 1708, demolished and replaced by Woolworths, a relocation of the company's first UK store in Church Street.

1925 • Leverhulme dies, leaving no provision for Bluecoat in his will. Part of building let as car showroom.

1926 • Two plane trees planted in courtyard to complement two already on the pavement outside. Campaign to buy the building, led by Fanny Calder, after it is put on the market.

1927 • Aided by an anonymous last-minute donor, building bought. Bluecoat Society of Arts founded, the UK's first arts centre. Herbert Tyson Smith's sculpture studio established.

1928 • Restoration work provides a concert hall, opened the following year, and studios for artists, architects, craftspeople, photographers and cultural organisations.

1929 • Annual exhibition includes work by Henry Moore and other artists at the forefront of modern art, curated by Sandon artist and medallist Edward Carter Preston.

1931 • Jacob Epstein's sculpture *Genesis* displayed. Nearly 50,000 visitors view Britain's most controversial sculpture, generating funds for the building.

1934 • Russian composer Igor Stravinsky, dining at Bluecoat, asks fellow diners to stand and honour 'England's greatest composer', Sir Edward Elgar, who had just died.

1937 • Proposal that Liverpool Council for Social Services take over Bluecoat rejected.

1939 • Bluecoat becomes Liverpool's main art gallery as the Corporation stages exhibitions there while the Walker is requisitioned by the Ministry of Food. Programmes continue till 1951.

1941 • Building suffers extensive damage during the May Blitz when Liverpool experiences heavy bombing. Fire guts the concert hall and east wings.

1946 • Unrealised plan to drive an inner ring road through part of Bluecoat. An earlier plan by Liverpool Corporation to take over the arts centre as an art gallery also rejected.

1948 • Merseyside Film Institute Society installs new cinema. This popular film club, established in 1933, continues adventurous film programming until the 1990s.

1951 • Bluecoat reopens after reconstruction, aided by War Damages Commission and Arts Council of Great Britain, with concert series. Festival of Britain events directed in the venue.

1952 • Building receives Grade I listing for its architectural and historical significance. Caretaker's flat built overlooking the south quadrangle (later the garden).

1955 • Liverpool Corporation opens a library on the ground floor.

1957 • Calouste Gulbenkian Foundation funding secured for three annual arts celebrations. The reopened Walker Art Gallery stages first John Moores Painting Prize exhibition.

1958 • Leading UK contemporary craft gallery Bluecoat Display Centre established.

1961 • Bluecoat Arts Forum set up to bring together the building's cultural societies and artists, take on Merseyside-wide role to promote the arts, and develop arts programmes.

1963 • *Bluecoat 63* festival demonstrates building's suitability as a popular venue for visual, performing and literary arts.

1967 • Yoko Ono performs. John Willett's *Art in a City* published. Beatles' *Sgt. Pepper* and *The Mersey Sound* poetry book released. Metropolitan Cathedral of Christ the King opens.

1968 • Arthur Dooley leads protest on Bluecoat railings about local artists being priced out of the gallery. Liverpool Lieder Circle set up, adding to Bluecoat's classical music activity.

1969 • Bluecoat's mortgage from 1927 finally repaid.

1972 • Californian rock musician Captain Beefheart's first exhibition of paintings at venue.

1977 • Queen Elizabeth's silver jubilee is also Bluecoat Society's golden jubilee. Ceramic plaque installed at College Lane entrance, designed by tenant Julia Carter Preston.

1981 • Touring exhibition *Women's Images of Men* comes to Bluecoat in a year marked by disturbances in Liverpool 8, dubbed the 'Toxteth riots'.

1982 • Cindy Sherman and Keith Haring among New York artists in *Urban Kisses*, on tour from London's ICA. Retractable seating installed, improving facilities for performances.

1983 • George Melly becomes Bluecoat Friends' patron, reconnecting to the venue that introduced him to bohemia, as recounted in his autobiography *Scouse Mouse.*

1985 • *Black Skin/Bluecoat* exhibition marks start of long engagement with artists addressing race and diversity. Militant-controlled city council passes an illegal budget.

1987 • Bluecoat's first cultural exchange programme with Liverpool's twin city of Cologne, revived in 2000 as *Eight Days a Week*.

1988 • Merseyside Moviola (later Foundation for Art and Creative Technology [FACT]) becomes tenant, organising *Video Positive* festivals. Visual Stress 'cleanses' Bluecoat of its slave history with multimedia intervention. Tate of the North opens.

1989 • Underground Leningrad artists' first UK visit: Popular Mechanics' gig at St George's Hall and a Bluecoat exhibition. Berlin Wall falls.

1990 • US jazz legend Sun Ra and Arkestra perform, provoking 'wildest and keenest audience response' of their UK tour. Lily Savage (Paul O'Grady) comperes alternative Merseyside Festival of Comedy Queen event.

1992 • Artists' commission project *Trophies of Empire* responds to colonial legacies in Liverpool, Bristol and Hull in the year of the Columbus quincentenary.

1994 • Artist Ann Whitehurst's *On the Map: Placing Disability* critiques Liverpool's and Bluecoat's disabling environments through a life-sized board game in the gallery.

1996 • Alan Dunn is football artist-in-residence during Liverpool's hosting of the Euro 96 championships, in a programme including a fashion show, *Tackle*.

1997 • Jeremy Deller's *Acid Brass* premiered at LIPA – house anthems played by a brass band. Other artists' commissions interrogate independence fifty years after India's partition.

1998 • Ramps installed at entrance and in garden. Collaboration begins with local Yemeni community, leading in 2002 to Liverpool Arab Arts Festival, the UK's first such event.

1999 • Bluecoat participates in first Liverpool Biennial and is involved in all subsequent editions. *Bluecoatconnect* collaboration programme established for people with learning disabilities. This develops into inclusive arts project Blue Room in 2008.

2002 • Bluecoat curates first *Liverpool Live* programme for the Biennial. Events include Chinese artists Mad for Real's soy sauce and tomato ketchup fight in courtyard.

2004 • Liverpool designated UNESCO World Heritage Site, which includes Bluecoat.

2005 • Building closes for capital refurbishment. Participation programme continues off site.

2006 • TV show *Most Haunted* films in empty building. For the Biennial, Humberto Velez's *The Welcoming* at Albert Dock welcomes Afghan asylum seekers.

2007 • Five-year *ART Valley* programme established in partnership, taking art and artists into communities across the city.

2008 • Building reopens in Liverpool's European Capital of Culture year with new arts wing, restored historic fabric and access improvements, designed by architects Biq Architecten. Yoko Ono returns. New tenants include Deaf and disability arts festival DaDaFest.

2009 • Screen printing added to printmaking offer. Angie Hiesl + Roland Kaiser's *TWINS* performance off-site. Malcolm Lowry centenary marked with major festival.

2010 • *Bluecoat Bed-In* actions 'for a better world' staged over 62 consecutive days.

2011 • *Democratic Promenade* exhibition, part of 'City of Radicals' year, looking at radical Liverpool. *Honky Tonk* exhibition explores Liverpool's Country and Western connections.

2013 • *The Universal Addressability of Dumb Things*, curated by Mark Leckey, a Hayward Touring collaboration made possible since the gallery was enlarged.

2015 • Anne Harild's courtyard installation *We Approach* created with Blue Room and Out of the Blue after-school art clubs. Bisakha Sarker's dance installation commission in the Vide.

2016 • *Bloomberg New Contemporaries* returns after thirty years. Keith Piper's *Unearthing the Banker's Bones* commission with Iniva for Arts Council Collection's 70th anniversary.

2017 • Building celebrates 300th anniversary with year of special exhibitions and events including Pierre Henry's *Liverpool Mass* performed at Metropolitan Cathedral.

2018 • Archive website, My Bluecoat, launched. International residency programme starts.

2019 • Over 650,000 visits to the building recorded.

Further Reading

Biggs, Bryan, 'Liverpool Art City?', in John Belchem and Bryan Biggs, eds, *Liverpool City of Radicals*, Liverpool: Liverpool University Press, 2011.

Biggs, Bryan, and Julie Sheldon, eds, *Art in a City Revisited*, Liverpool: Liverpool University Press and Bluecoat, 2009.

Bisson, R. F., *The Sandon Studios Society and the Arts*, Liverpool: Parry Books, published on behalf of the Sandon Studios Society, 1965.

Gee, Gabriel N., *Art in the North of England, 1979–2008*, Abingdon: Routledge, 2016.

Healey, Peter, ed., *The Liverpool Blue Coat School Past & Present 1708–2008*, Liverpool: Liverpool Blue Coat School Foundation, 2008.

MacCunn, W. S., *Bluecoat Chambers: The Origins and Development of an Art Centre*, Liverpool: Liverpool University Press, 1956.

Melly, George, *Scouse Mouse*, London: Weidenfeld and Nicolson, 1984.

Taylor, Stainton de B., 'Music at the Bluecoat', in *Two Centuries of Music in Liverpool*, Liverpool: Rockliff Brothers, 1973.

Willett, John, *Art in a City*, London: Methuen, 1967; reprinted with a new introduction by Bryan Biggs, Liverpool: Liverpool University Press and Bluecoat, 2008.

Index